THEY WILL BE VICTORS

To Gloria,
Thanks & God Bless!
You have always worked hard for children

THEY WILL BE VICTORS

The Remarkable Story of One Man's Passion for Second Chances

By Robert E. Wollack, Jr.

R.E. Woll—

Corby Books
Notre Dame, Indiana

THEY WILL BE VICTORS
The Remarkable Story of
One Man's Passion for Second Chances

Copyright © 2010 by Robert E. Wollack, Jr.

All rights reserved. No part of this book may be used or reproduced in any manner whatsoever without the explicit permission of the publisher.

10 9 8 7 6 5 4 3 2 1

ISBN 978-0-9819605-9-3

Published by
Corby Books
A Division of Corby Publishing
Box 93
Notre Dame, IN 46556
(574) 784-3482
Website: corbypublishing.com

Table of Contents

Acknowledgments ix
Foreword xiii
An Introduction. xvii

PART ONE – HARD LESSONS
1 "Run, Bobby, Run" 1
2 Breaking Away 11
3 Running with the Devil 17
4 The Trial 31
5 The Milan Connection 39
6 A Price on My Head 47
7 Turning Point 55

PART TWO – STARTING OVER
8 Understanding Dreams 67
9 The Right Choice 77
10 Thinking Outside the Box 85
11 Saints, Heroes, and Role Models 95
12 Dreams of My Sons 101
13 The Brooklyn Cowboy 109
14 Taking Risks 117
15 Day of Reckoning 127

PART THREE – MAKING VICTORS
16 The Launch 137
17 War and Peace 149
18 The Gentle Giant 161
19 A New Venture – Gator Human Services 169
20 Meeting New Challenges 177
21 The Continuing Challenge for Social Justice 191
22 Giving Forward 205
23 In Another Time 207
24 Vassar House 213
25 From Victims to Victors 217
Epilogue 225
Endnotes 227
Selected Bibliography 229
Appendices 233

To Judith,
Who lived the Wolverine story with me;
To my four sons, Craig, Robert, Zack, and Matthew;

And, to Mark Glesener, who awakened me to the value of social therapy.

"Power and the sense of significance, are intertwined. One is the objective form and the other the subjective form of the same experience."

> Rollo May
> *Power and Innocence: A Search*
> *for the Sources of Violence*

"Atonement is a process that never ends. I believe that. Maybe it's a New England thing, or an Irish thing, or a Catholic thing. Maybe all of those things. But it's as it should be."

> Edward M. Kennedy
> *True Compass: A Memoir*

Author's Note

This is my story; the events recalled in this book are true to the best of my memory. All the people portrayed in this book are, or were, actual living persons. However, a few names have been changed to protect their privacy. I believe it is also important that the reader understand that this book reflects my recall and interpretation of events and no one else's. It has been my intent to record my memories as accurately as possible. Nevertheless, other witnesses to or participants in some of the events that have been recorded may see them in a different light.

Acknowledgments

Reviewing my life's journey has been fraught with emotion—it is not easy to look back on one's life and to relive early mistakes and hurts; yet, the experiences of my youth and young adulthood were formative in shaping and directing my career and commitment to help troubled youth to have a second chance. This book is the culmination of the efforts of many people, and I am indebted to each of them. Their many and varied contributions are what made this book a reality.

First, I extend my deep gratitude to my wife Judith who has lived the Wolverine Human Services story with me. She has provided me with unswerving love, loyalty, patience, and inspiration. Her late father, Clarence Fischer, was a source of wisdom and encouragement during the early years of the formation of Wolverine Human Services. I deeply cherish my four sons—Craig, Robert, Zachary, and Matthew—each in his own way has made me very proud of his accomplishments. Their love has been affirming and a source of ongoing encouragement.

Second, I am grateful for the deep and enduring friendship and loyalty of my special friends Pete Walsh and Bill Tilton. I have also been blessed with the friendship of many other loyal friends; they are too many to name, however, there are several whose names are firmly etched in my mind and heart because of their dedication to making the dream become a reality by serving as board members.

Those who served on the initial board are the following: Bill Dufek, Don Dufek, Bob Ellis, Howard Holmes, Bruce Kintz, Rick Leach, Jim Libs, Jerry Meter, Jim Minder, Jon Walgren, the Rev. Jimmy Ward, and Ron Warhurst. I am grateful for these men who had confidence in me and were willing to help me to get Wolverine established.

The current members (2009) of the board of trustees are: Bruce Kintz (Chairman), Ron Warhurst (Vice Chairman), Jerry Meter (Treasurer), Jim Libs (Secretary), Vince Brennan, James Cavicchoili, Marty Daly, Rick Leach, Sam McCargo, Ward Manuel, Karen

They Will Be Victors

Paciorek, John Wangler, and Michael Wilson. I cannot thank these people enough for their dedication to the mission of Wolverine Human Services and for their counsel and encouragement to me.

The fruition of this narrative would not have been possible without the contributions of Milton Nieuwsma who spent many hours interviewing various people for this book and helped me to record my story.

I am indebted to many individuals, whose skills and dedication were essential to the improvement of the manuscript. They have checked facts, shared anecdotes, conducted research, and contributed to editing. I want to thank in particular Bob Blumenfeld and Harold Gazan. Each read the manuscript at various stages and offered insightful feedback. Moreover, Harold worked along with me with diligence and tenacity to bring this book to fruition.

I am grateful to Charles Updike, the Assistant U. S. Attorney who treated me with respect and dignity even though he was prosecuting me. More importantly, he handled my case with objectivity and saved my life from those would just as soon have seen me rubbed out. I am indebted to him for his thoughtful Foreword to this book. He also painstakingly read an early draft of the book and made many helpful suggestions.

I attended Eastern Michigan University for my undergraduate studies. I was privileged to have Professor Don Loppnow as my first instructor in social work. He awakened me to the challenges and excitement of the social work profession. He gave me an opportunity to be his teaching assistant even though I was only an undergraduate student. I did not graduate from EMU; however, in 2006 the university granted me an honorary bachelor's degree.

I am genuinely appreciative of the mentorship and friendship of Professor John Tropman of the University of Michigan School of Social Work. He has provided valuable guidance to Wolverine Human Services as a consultant and seminar leader. He wrote the Introduction to this book for which I am grateful.

The University of Michigan has special meaning for me. My first contact with it was while I was an inmate at the Milan Prison. The

Acknowledgments

university opened up the gates of education to me, even though I was a kid from a Brooklyn working-class family. It was the University of Michigan that gave me the academic and professional tools with which to shape Wolverine Human Services.

I would be remiss if I did not express my gratitude to all the kids who allowed me to touch their lives. They also taught me a lot about the new-age delinquent. They understood the empathy I had for them that only a person who has walked in their shoes could have. They gave me their trust.

Lastly, while an undertaking of this nature involves the contributions of many, I alone am responsible for the contents of this book and any errors that may have inadvertently crept into it.

Foreword

In April 2000, Robert Wollack delivered the commencement address at his alma mater, the University of Michigan School of Social Work, on a topic about which he had become most passionate: giving delinquent teens a second chance. "We have seen aimless, parentless, abused, neglected, and delinquent kids change and go on to college, skilled trade and technical services," he told the graduates. "My goal is helping these children to be victors."

Mr. Wollack knew whereof he spoke. His life story is a tale of extraordinary personal redemption—of getting a second chance and making the most of it. As the founder of Wolverine Human Services, Inc., a Michigan non-profit organization dedicated to juvenile rehabilitation, he has been responsible for providing a second chance to thousands of young people who started out on the same troubled path he did.

When I first met Mr. Wollack, I was a thirty-one year-old Assistant U.S. Attorney in the Southern District of New York and Chief of the Narcotics Unit in that office. Mr. Wollack was a twenty-six-year-old undercover cop, a highly-decorated member of the New York Police Department's elite Tactical Patrol Force. He was married and a father.

He was also a cocaine user who aided and abetted Elvin Lee Bynum, a major East Coast distributor of narcotics whose operations stretched from Washington to Boston. Mr. Bynum was particularly adept at corrupting police officers, which led to his becoming a target of our investigation.

On Christmas Eve morning in 1970, two agents ushered Mr. Wollack into my office in the Federal Courthouse in Manhattan. He had been arrested the night before and was appearing for his arraignment. After his arrest, Mr. Wollack was offered opportunities to cooperate with the investigation of Mr. Bynum and his enterprise. He declined in part out of respect for the code that paints informants and cooperating witnesses as dishonorable people and, in part, because he believed, most likely correctly, that cooperation would make him a target for violence. I was the lead prosecutor at his trial, which resulted in a guilty verdict and a six-year sentence to the federal prison at Milan, Michigan.

It is at this point, really, that Mr. Wollack's story begins. Like any adversity, time in prison has many lessons to offer. It's hard to know why Mr. Wollack took with him the lessons that he did, but clearly they were positive and of great value. He substantially extended his formal education. In the process, he met people who recognized his native intelligence and fundamentally sound moral values. They became life-long friends and mentors. He also met and befriended people at Milan who later assisted him along the way as colleagues in his various endeavors.

Through a process he recounts with engrossing candor, Mr. Wollack becomes increasingly focused upon helping young people to avoid the mistakes that had proved so costly for him. He does not return to New York, and the powerful commitment he makes costs him his first marriage. Upon release, starting a new life in a new place, Mr. Wollack remains doggedly devoted to his new vocation. The same energy and charisma that made him successful as a young policeman are focused on the perennial problems of young people in trouble.

The growth of Wolverine Human Services, Inc., and his many awards are a powerful testament to Mr. Wollack's success. His willingness to innovate, to accept new challenges, to fight bureaucracy and political prejudice on behalf of those he was committed to helping are all part of this story.

Describing his own youth growing up in Brooklyn, Mr. Wollack speaks critically of his time in Catholic schools. Yet the seeds of his fundamental notions of right and wrong were probably planted at that time. The tension between right and wrong, good and evil, pervades his book. It appears as if, having lost a battle with the devil

Foreword

early on, Mr. Wollack was determined never to lose such a battle again with respect to himself. Equally important, he wanted the satisfaction of assisting people whose youth resembled his own in fighting similar battles.

This is a story without a happy ending (yet) only because it is not over. Robert Wollack continues to impact the lives of thousands of young people in positive ways. No doubt his own triumph over adversity provides inspiration not only to his charges but to the coworkers and staff who have helped and supported him along the way.

For reasons not clear to me, Mr. Wollack credits me with helping to turn his life around. Perhaps I said something or offered a word of encouragement that made a difference in his life, in the same way that a high school or college teacher may unwittingly direct a student along a certain path and be (to their surprise) thanked for it years later. While Mr. Wollack's conviction and subsequent prison time were clearly a turning point for him, what he has made of his life since then is his doing, not mine.

There are some factual matters as to which Mr. Wollack's recollection differs from mine and he speculates as to some legal principles that also not accord with my understanding of the law. I do not believe, however, that these differences detract from the fundamental story of a life salvaged and converted into a life of dedicated service to young people in crisis.

I hope his story will give hope to other young people whose early mistakes in life are similar to his. And may it give fresh insight to social workers, law enforcement officers, judges, legislators, and others who wage the fight on behalf America's troubled youth.

> Charles B. Updike, J.D.
> New York City, NY
> November 2009

An Introduction

THEY WILL BE VICTORS is the story of an American Odyssey. In this memoir, Robert Wollack, Jr., sketches the journey of his life from a street gang kid in New York, through Catholic school(s), into the Army Reserve (Special Forces Group), to a stint as a New York City cop; and, as a twenty-six-year-old who was corrupted by his cooperation with an East Coast drug king. He was arrested, convicted, and sentenced to Milan Prison in Michigan. While there, he had a transformative experience at an early morning mass on Christmas Day inspiring him to undertake a vigorous program of self-improvement. Capitalizing on his high native intelligence, he engaged in a rigorous program of self-education, and then attended Eastern Michigan University in Ypsilanti, and graduated from the School of Social Work at the University of Michigan at Ann Arbor. With friends he initially met in prison and with other friends, he founded Wolverine Human Services, an agency that helps young men (and recently women) who themselves have run afoul of law enforcement. He is now a very successful and respected human services executive who has been able to turn his own experiences with criminal behavior into a life of dedication to help others achieve a similar turnaround. Wolverine's motto, "Helping Children to be Victors" reflects Robert's commitment to such transformation. His choice of the Wolverine name both connects to the mascot of the University of Michigan, but more deeply embodies the tenacity required to achieve such results, both from the agency and its clients.

At one level, this gripping, engrossing story can be read as a personal journey. Personal transformation—young thug makes good and gives back to society—these are core elements of the American dream. Other books have celebrated it as well, for example, Robert Timberg's *John McCain: An American Odyssey* (Clearwater: Touchstone Books) and Ron Susskind's 1988 book *A Hope in the Unseen*:

They Will Be Victors

An American Odyssey from the Inner City to the Ivy League (New York; Bantam).

But there are other themes that place this book in a broader perspective, one of which is suggested by the title itself. Whereas this personal journey is certainly of interest to readers, a "second chance" represents something that we all crave and adds to the appeal of Mr. Wollack's tale. Indeed, America itself is a country of "second chances", one which was founded and continues to be populated by the "runaway." But perhaps "run-to" would be a better word. Everyone who came to this country was running *away* from something, and running *to* something. A second chance was that something.

A second theme is organization building. Robert Wollack built a very successful human service organization—Wolverine Human Services. He reveals, but does not discuss, how astute he was at recognizing and using talent. Some of those he was able to identify and draw into his efforts to help others were also ex-cons. Another was a Vietnam War protester, also an ex-con for protest-related activities. Another was his wife, Judy, a social worker and daughter of a social worker. The list goes on. But it becomes clear in the book that while much of Robert's success was due to his own contribution and efforts, a large part was his ability to recognize and use the talent of others. He saw the potential for contributions in them, and they in him. The organization-building literature stresses the need for a talented team again and again. The collective nature of any organizational success is something constantly emphasized in the life and work of Edwards Deming, the late quality guru, who preached a lesson that Detroit never learned. And Robert Wollack did.

There is another feature to Robert Wollack's leadership of Wolverine Human Services. It is an adherence to a key principle of successful, impactful organization expressed in the 2008 book *Forces for Good—The Six Practices of High Impact Nonprofits* (New York: Wiley) by Leslie Crutchfield and Heather Grant. These organizations both serve and advocate. That book seeks to operationalize the "Good to great" principles Jim Collins discussed in his 2005 monograph *Good*

_____ An Introduction

to Great for the Social Sector (Jim Collins, Publisher). What Crutchfield and Grant found was that impactful organizations both served and advocated for better policies. This dual emphasis—to serve and advocate—is characteristic of Robert and of Wolverine. As much as Robert is focused on direct service, he and his staff recognize as well that governments must have more socially-just policies, and must run with increased efficiency. His discussion of Harold Gazan from the (then called) Michigan Department of Social Services illustrates the impact that the "statesman-bureaucrat" can have, and how that person can be a force for good. And in some of the later chapters of the book, Robert reveals his focus on advocacy in his appeal for legislation to protect the rights of young people.

Finally, this book is also a discussion of the American stratification system, one man's extraordinary achievement raises the question about the lack of opportunity and accomplishment for so many others. Too many citizens are trapped below the glass floor, in the basement of the stratification system, unable to reach any exit. Robert's story forces us to ask at least two questions: "How can we explain that situation" and "How can we address it?" Robert would love to see many others have a "second chance." His intention is to move away from the CEO position in the near future in order to establish the Friends of Wolverine Human Services Foundation, which will provide support for a wide range of *second chance* opportunities. One can have the conviction that the same energy and Wolverine-inspired determination that pushed Robert personally and Wolverine Human Services to greatness will now be focused on taking the idea of second chances to the next level.

John Tropman, Ph. D.
Ann Arbor, MI
November 2009

PART ONE

HARD LESSONS

"Young men in the inner city. . . . are often the inhabitants of an impenetrable as well as an inescapable cultural and geographic underworld where prevailing 'codes of the street' are like coils of concertina wire."

Luke Bergmann, *Getting Ghost*

CHAPTER 1

"RUN, BOBBY, RUN"

JUNE 1958. Tommy's reflection is standing guard as I apply just the right amount of Vaseline to my jet-black boyishly thick hair.

"Bobby!" my mother shouts from the kitchen.

Tommy watches me with a look that teeters between admiration and curiosity. He's watching all the time, quietly observing my rituals, and, privately, I take a lot of pride in this—like he's looking to me to teach him, to show him how things should be done, how business should be handled.

"Bobby!" she shouts again over the din of children's voices that perpetually fill our two-bedroom flat on St. John's Place in Brooklyn's notorious Bedford-Stuyvesant neighborhood.

In the midst of all the noise, both inside and outside the apartment, I'm thinking about my meeting with the Chaplains over at Nate's Candy Store two blocks away and across from the Albany Projects. Nate's was our hangout; it was where my father and I worked together on Sundays as short-order cooks. It was also where I first observed corruption in action. As I stood behind the counter shelling out eggs and English muffins, I'd see cops coming in and getting their food for free, never even having the decency to throw Nate or me or my father a tip. These seemingly benign experiences constituted an informal education of sorts for me, and would later form the basis for what I referred to as the "Good Citizen" theory of corruption—that common citizens offering cops free goods and services paved the way for a descent into wholesale corruption. And of course, these experiences would influence the foundations of my own moral construct.

Tonight we have a job to do. Our "chapter" is only one small part of the Chaplains' network, a gang whose members number over a thousand throughout the projects. There is another large gang in the area named the Bishops, and two smaller gangs—the Corsairs Lords and an all-white Italian gang known as the Black Hawks. I smile at the irony of my being a member of the Chaplains, my mother's zealous religious fervor somehow penetrating even the most un-religious elements of my life. I wonder if, in some strange misguided way, she would take pride in the name we've chosen for our gang. But she doesn't know I'm in a gang. I'm pretty sure she doesn't even know it was my fourteenth birthday last week.

"Bobby!" my mother yells shrilly and more earnestly. "I need you to run to the butcher's before supper!" My feelings for my mother are best characterized as ambivalent. Her devotion to the local parish and the nuns of the Guardian Angel Home is at least partially driven by her overwhelming compulsion to keep up appearances. Even as a kid, I've already seen it at work. When Tommy got ringworm, she pulled us out of St. Gregory's School and hauled us to St. Matthew's, eight blocks out of the way, just to avoid embarrassment. And those kids whose voices she's screaming over—they're an ever changing mix of my siblings and the foster kids who came to our family literally off the streets.

Today my relationship with my brothers and sisters ranks among my life's greatest treasures. Tommy is a New York City firefighter whose unit was one of the responders to the Twin Towers disaster on 9/11/2001. Virginia is an RN who currently manages a large home health-care service agency in Florida, and Maryanne retired after a career as an RN. Christine became a CPA and served

"Run, Bobby, Run"

as a high level administrator in the finance department of New York City. Joanne retired after teaching twenty-seven years in the NYC Catholic School system. Rosemarie is an interpreter for the hearing impaired. And Charlie is a computer technician. Like me, they each in their own way shared and overcame the chaos, the uncertainty, and the many challenges that our neighborhood, our home and our parents presented. And we helped each other weather the storm.

But back in 1958 sibling rivalry and my rebellious nature trumped my affection. Regardless, between my brothers and sisters and me, and the countless kids she took in, my mother was able to hold herself up in the neighborhood as a good Catholic, surely destined for heaven, and bring a few extra bucks into the sparse, overpopulated tenement we called home.

"Bobby!" my mother shrieks frantically. "The butcher closes in five minutes. You gotta get down there. And I need you to make dinner so I can go to my meeting at the church at 7 o'clock." I check my hair one last time in the mirror, shove past Tommy, grab two dollar bills from my mother, and run down three flights of stairs and out the door. The minute I emerge, I hear my mother, her head and shoulders leaning out the window. "Run, Bobby, Run!" I half-heartedly jog up the sidewalk, past stagnant pools that never seem to dry up, keeping pace with a paper bag dislodged from one of the countless piles of trash that, like the puddles, are permanent fixtures in our Bed-Stuy landscape.

Carl the Butcher pays me 25 cents each for home deliveries. It's 1958, and if you're a kid in Bed-Stuy making some money, you know that every penny of it is going to pay the bills at home. So here I am with eight deliveries worth of money completing the cycle that makes up what I'd later learn is known as the economic multiplier effect. Carl keeps us in business as a family; we help keep Carl in business. But that warm feeling of recognizing something important—even if you don't know some big fancy word for it—quickly fades as I come up to the butcher shop and confront the dingy "CLOSED" sign. "Shit!" I tinker with the idea of just heading over to Nate's Candy Store, but conclude that would only make things worse—if that's possible.

Standing outside our apartment door, it occurs to me that the fear I used to feel has somehow muted to resignation. I guess uncertainty really is the main ingredient for fear – knowing makes things easier to accept. I can hear the CLOP-clop, CLOP-clop of my father's shoes on the floor as I stare at the door handle. I swallow and see my hand reach out, as if I were a distant observer, and push the door open. "Carl was already closed up by the time I got there . . . ." I hear myself say, steadily but still somewhat pathetically. My mother's face gets that uniquely mean look to it. She screams at me and then turns to my father as she has countless times before and shrieks, "Well, aren't you going to do something?" And as he has countless times before, he removes his belt from his stained, wrinkled trousers. He raises his arm, and I break for the door and run out of the apartment, my mother's voice rising to glass-shattering levels. Certainty may make things easier to accept, but it doesn't make them any easier to endure.

I bolted out onto the street and didn't bother to look up at my mother as she spewed angry reminders of what awaited me when I returned that night. If things remained true to form, my dad had already downed a shot, poured another, and cracked a beer. My mom had listed the litany of infractions committed by the kids, and at some point Dad would mete out punishment.

For all that chaos and dysfunction, I never really blamed either of my parents. I wrote off my mother's actions to mental illness, and my father's to learned behavior and basic survival instincts. And in 1958 Bed-Stuy, our home—sans the foster kids—wasn't a whole lot different from anybody else's.

For example, we had to cope with cockroaches. For the most part they were not seen except at night when the kitchen light would be turned on and then you would suddenly see them scampering and scurrying about and then quickly disappearing into the crevices; sometimes there were so many of them I thought the floor was moving. Periodically, my dad or one of us kids would spray a powerful insecticide into the crevices; we were all required to cover our noses and mouths with handkerchiefs, and the cockroaches would come pouring out onto the kitchen floor like a flood and we would stomp on them and kill them and then clean up the kitchen floor.

Because I was the oldest, it fell on me to do other chores while my mother went to parish meetings. I often did the cooking for the family. I also hung the wet laundry on a clothesline which was strung between our third floor flat and the adjacent apartment building. The clothesline was a double line strung between the two buildings with pulleys on either side. I had to lean out of the window to hang the clothes using wooden clothespins. I was initially fearful—looking down on the ground from the third floor window was a fearsome sight. Because I was a kid I had to stretch way out to securely pin the clothes on the line, and it was my ass if I let any article of clothing drop to the ground!

My dad was recruited to the workers' rights movement by the Jesuit Christian Socialists. He was elected secretary of the United Rubber Workers Union local at Kentile Floors. It seemed to me he was on strike almost as often as he was working. I felt sorry for him. His life was a series of misfortunes. The fact that he had polio as a child didn't provide any relief from my grandfather's discipline—likely where he learned the "belt" technique. And the disease left him with one leg shorter than the other, complimented by a flat foot. His need to wear corrective shoes into adulthood resulted in his trademark footsteps, resonating like a cowbell in the ears of his kids.

The connection between upbringing and parenting isn't as clear for my mom. My Grandma Costello was an odd duck—likely schizophrenic, in hindsight—who had a fear of contamination. In response, she would boil everything—even hamburgers. And she had a recurring belief that my Uncle Leo had stolen things, which made for interesting holiday conversation. I remember my Grandpa Frank being a nice enough guy. He was Frank Costello, "the newspaper reporter—not the gangster!" as he loved to remind people.

They Will Be Victors

As a reporter for the *Brooklyn Eagle*, he knew more people and more about the city than anybody else. He knew, for example, how the A train from Manhattan's west side to Bedford-Stuyvesant paved the way for blacks to leave an overcrowded Harlem, which led to the construction of the Albany Projects. He knew how the Gambino family infiltrated unions, sharked loans, and trafficked in drugs. He even knew trivial things like the address where Ralph Kramden, Jackie Gleason's character on *The Honeymooners*, lived. (It was 328 Chauncey Street, a stone's throw away, where Gleason grew up). But most important he knew the history and culture of Brooklyn, and Bed-Stuy in particular.

The gangs of the '50s were different than the gangs of today. We were equal opportunity street urchins. The blacks were moving in and the Italians and Irish were moving out. But I didn't care since they were my friends, Chaplain brothers black and white. Every once in a while someone would beat the shit out of a rival gang member, which would precipitate a rumble. I was small and slender, but damn it I could fight and I could bite. And I could smack you in the shins. Sometimes I'd play stick-ball with the Italian guys from the Black Hawks gang. But if anybody messed with the Chaplains or invaded our territory at the Albany Projects, there wasn't any question where my loyalty lay. Once in a while somebody would get hurt, but mostly we were just showing our machismo. Our activity largely centered on petty theft and vandalism, and, of course, we were always cruising for girls.

Danny Boy greets me at the door of Nate's Candy Store. He's a year older than me, and several inches taller. "Bobby, we gotta job to do tonight," he says.

Four Chaplains besides Danny Boy and me are already there. In the next few minutes three or four more drift in. Danny Boy locks the door, pulls down the window shade, and nods to Sleepy, our leader.

"Listen up you motherfuckers," Sleepy says. "We gotta job to do tonight," parroting Danny Boy's words.

As I wait for him to continue, I think about my initiation here six months ago and how embarrassed I was. They made me drop my pants so they could inspect my penis. If it was too small, I was out. If it was big enough, I was in. I was in.

"Tonight we're taking back our turf from the Bishops," Sleepy says. "We're going to meet at Brower Park and kick their asses. Motherfuckers think they can just come into our territory and jump Treetop—we got some get back comin.'"

"Bobby," he continues, "you come with me to the projects to pick up Sonny and Jinx. We'll meet the rest of you guys at Kingston between Park and Prospect with the bats and chains. Danny Boy, you're in charge of the knives and the zip gun." We all dispersed, then as we walked along Kingston Ave, a few guys would rejoin the group. By the time we got to the park, there were over eighty of us.

The Bishops came in from Brooklyn Ave. It was dark, so it was hard to tell how many of them there were—probably fewer than we had, but they were some tough thugs, and they weren't afraid of us any more than we were of them.

As we came to the center of the park, there was some hesitation, each of us sizing up the other, wondering what would set things off. Whatever it was, suddenly everyone was throwing fists or stones or bottles, swinging bats or belts, and taking guys down. I got a few solid shots in, and ended up on the ground with a gash in the back of my head from a rock thrown by an unseen adversary. As the sirens approached, we ran our separate ways some of us bloodied and hurt. It was over in just a few minutes.

Aside from these fairly infrequent gang wars, we stuck to our routine. That summer, every time we threw a garbage can out onto the street, or poked out a streetlight, or committed some petty larceny, I worried about getting caught, but nothing happened. The police never showed up at the candy store. All summer long we pulled off more petty thefts, but nothing happened.

Still, I kept worrying about getting caught. During my time at St. Matthew's I became an altar boy and continued in this role upon my return to St. Gregory's. The Mass was recited in Latin, as was the custom at the time, and a particular section—the *Confiteor*—came to resonate with me in a deep and powerful way. It was during the People's Confession portion that I had to bow down, and strike my chest three times during which I prayed, "*mea culpa, mea culpa, mea maxima culpa.*" It is during this somber, physical element of the prayer that one pleads with God for forgiveness. But what does a young boy know about grievous sins?

When I completed my seventh grade class, my mother persuaded Monsignor Sullivan to allow me back into St. Gregory's, convincing herself—and announcing to anyone within earshot—that I would become valedictorian. A year later, my eighth grade graduation was approaching and nobody was the wiser about my gang connections. The ceremony was scheduled to take place at St. Gregory's Church next to the school. The day arrived and Monsignor Sullivan presided. He called out the names of the graduates as we walked past the altar in our blue caps and gowns. Finally came the moment for the class honors to be awarded.

"And now," the Monsignor said, "we award the gold cap to the valedictorian of the Class of 1958." Everyone fell silent as he slipped his hand into an envelope and drew out a card. He studied the card for a moment and then looked up. "The student who scored the highest on the eighth grade final with a score of ninety-eight is"—and he looked at the card again—"Francis Derwin."

A burst of applause filled the room as Monsignor Sullivan called him up to the platform. Because he had gone to St. Gregory's the whole time I had been at St. Matthew's, I hardly knew the kid, but I knew he was the son of one of my mother's friends. I wondered if my mother bragged to *her* about my ninety-seven score and told *her* I was going to get the gold cap. Who else would care but my mother anyway, and she cared only because she had blabbed to everybody that I was going to get it.

At the conclusion of the ceremony the graduates stood up and recessed back down the aisle and out the front door. As I walked the half block back to our apartment with my family, I could tell that I had disappointed my mother. When we reached the sidewalk out of sight of the other graduates, she turned and slapped me in the face knocking off my blue cap. I was stunned. As the fog of shame gradually lifted, I heard her say, with controlled fury in her voice, "Don't you ever embarrass me like that again!" Nothing was ever good enough. I bit back the tears, and vowed to myself that *she* would never do *that* to *me* again.

Despite my mother's disappointment, my status as second best in my class enabled my parents to wrangle a scholarship to send me to Power Memorial High School on Manhattan's west side. The first problem was that it meant an hour-and-a-half commute each way. Every morning at 6 o'clock I would catch the Number 3 train at the Kingston Avenue station and transfer twice before getting off at 66th Street in Manhattan. Then I'd have to walk another five blocks to the school at 61st and Amsterdam.

The second and much bigger problem was that the school was run by the Irish Christian Brothers who had a reputation for tough discipline. Moreover, they paid their teachers a pittance. They were mostly Fordham University graduates who couldn't get hired in the public schools and so got hooked on the Brothers' mission to educate boys to become good Catholics. They took pains to instruct the Fordham teacher recruits in the art of sadistic discipline. The only redeeming quality of Power Memorial wouldn't emerge until a few years later when a skinny six-foot-five black freshman basketball player named Lew Alcindor (later Kareem Abdul Jabbar) led the school to three straight New York City Catholic High School championships.

I was a terrible student, not only because I hated the discipline, but also because I was more interested in making money on the side, whether it was delivering meat for Carl the Butcher, or hustling with the Chaplains. But going to Power Memorial did get me off the hook when the police finally arrested me for shoplifting at a record store on Flatbush Avenue. The judge inquired of my school affiliation and, noting my status as a freshman at Power, gave me a suspended sentence. What I didn't tell the judge was that I had flunked three classes the first time around and I was repeating my freshman year.

They Will Be Victors

School didn't get any better. Even in my second go 'round as a freshman, I was repeating three classes. For one of my tests I had to memorize ten Latin words and explain what they meant. I failed all ten words. In accordance with the school's discipline procedure, the teacher whipped me ten times across each hand—one time for each missed word—with a leather strap. And just like on that graduation day back in middle school, I swore that this would be the last time anyone would do that to me. When one of the black-robed Brothers entered the room to see if my discipline had been properly administered, I spit and threw a chair at him. The brother ducked just in time for the chair to crash through the window onto Amsterdam Avenue. I turned and walked through the door and out the building, knowing before even having done it, that I was going to be expelled.

CHAPTER 2

BREAKING AWAY

ANY CHANCE I HAD of going to college went out the window along with that chair. After getting thrown out of Power Memorial High School, I convinced myself I didn't want to go to college anyway because it meant waiting too long to make real money—and I wanted to make it *now*. Petty larceny didn't seem like a long-term option either, especially to a budding sixteen-year-old criminal mind.

On one of my delivery days for Carl the Butcher, he told me about the Food & Maritime Trades High School in lower Manhattan.

"Look, Bobby," he said, "did you know you can make $120 a week as a butcher after you graduate?" That sounded like a lot of money compared to what my father made. "Not only that," he said, "they pay you to work in your senior year."

Carl was a fat guy with jet black hair. Even for a butcher it seemed like he lived high on the hog. Every Saturday I washed his Cadillac and he let me drive it around the block. He had a place in upstate New York, and I found out later that he also had one in Queens' notorious Ozone Park. It would still be a few years before I pieced together how Carl managed to live so well.

So when Carl took it upon himself to encourage me to look into the Food & Maritime Trades, I paid attention. And it sounded like a pretty good deal. The school was down by the Hudson River, near the wholesale meat market on 14th Street. As it turned out, transferring there from Power Memorial not only freed me from the hell of the Irish Christian Brothers, it also lopped an hour off my subway commute from Brooklyn.

But the best part was that I connected with another transfer student named Stanley Farrow. Eight months younger than me, Stan who lived in Brooklyn's Brownsville neighborhood, wanted to get out of Jefferson High School as much as I wanted to get out of Power Memorial but for a different reason; although he was as smart as a whip, he was bored. He had no more interest in academics Jefferson High style than I had in the Irish Christian Brothers style of discipline. Like me, he wanted to make real money and couldn't be bothered with college.

In many respects Stan's life seemed almost a mirror image of mine. Like me, he came from a big family that included six boys. His father, an upholsterer, found himself out of work nearly as often as my father did, which put the family's economic burden on Stan and his two older brothers. As a kid, he'd fight for the busiest street corner to set up his shoeshine box, and at the end of the day he and the other shoeshine boys would flip their coins into a cigar box in a bid to double or triple their money. Whatever Stan made went into the family coffers. When he got older, he delivered meat for the neighborhood butcher.

Every morning I would meet Stan on the Number 4 train from Brownsville and we'd ride to school together. In the afternoon we'd ride home together. As seniors we did our field placement at the 14th Street market together, which meant we had to be there at four o'clock in the morning. To do that I would catch the 3:15 a.m. train at the Kingston Avenue Station and then I'd find Stan fast asleep in the rear car. From there we would continue the trip in silence.

The Food & Maritime Trades School drew mostly black and Puerto Rican kids—gang members and school dropouts—from every New York borough. In today's vernacular, you could say that the school had a "very diverse student population," and we learned that if you hooked up with the right people, you got along fine regardless of race. For the first two years you did your academics in the morning and practiced your trade in the afternoon. In your senior year you got a half-day field placement at the 14th Street wholesale meat market or the 12th Street wharf.

One afternoon my parents stopped by the school to check on my progress. My teacher, Mr. Seinfeld, told them, "Your son is very, very bright. I honestly think that, with the right guidance, we could get him into Cornell University's Hotel and Restaurant Management program. He should definitely go on to college." My mother cut him off and said, "No, he's going to be a butcher." My father, as usual, remained silent—defeated. And I thought to myself, "Maybe *she* should try taking the 3:15 a.m. train."

I got to be pretty good at boning hips and fillets, but Stan picked it up a lot faster than me. Still, we both managed to snag jobs at the 14th Street market after we graduated, and we started at $120 a week—just like Carl the Butcher said.

Meanwhile my family's apartment at St. John's Place, along with most of Bedford-Stuyvesant, had been taken over by the blacks and Puerto Ricans. Although my parents couldn't afford it, they decided to move to Flatbush. They said they needed a bigger apartment. The night I graduated from the Food & Maritime Trades School, my mother came into the room and shook me awake.

"Look, Bobby," she said, a frantic tone in her voice. There was always a frantic tone in her voice. "You have to stay home."

"Why?" I mumbled. My brother, sleeping next to me in the bed, stirred.

"You gotta give me and your father money so we can stay in this apartment."

"Why?" I mumbled again.

"Whaddya mean why? Because this place is more expensive than the other one, and you're going to make more than your father. Because we need the money is why!"

No fucking way am I staying home, I thought. As soon as I get my own place I'm out of here. I turned over and pretended to go to back to sleep.

Stan Farrow would prove to be a lifelong friend and soulmate. Not only did we work across the street from each other at the 14th

Street market; we hung out, we ate, we slept, we did everything together. We were as inseparable as two friends could be.

We started a part-time business together, a home delivery operation that supplemented our $120-a-week paychecks. Every afternoon at the 14th Street market we'd buy leftover meat at wholesale, carry it home on the train, and sell it to people in the neighborhood. We were budding entrepreneurs. In due course my brother Tommy, who followed us through the Food & Maritime Trades School, joined us in the venture. In 1966, Stanley pushed his number up and was drafted by the Army and sent to Korea. It would be almost two years before we would see each other again.

It didn't take me long to find out there was more to the meat cutting business than I learned at trade school, and it had nothing to do with meat cutting. I had known the Costellano brothers, Peter and Paul, ever since I started making deliveries for Carl the Butcher in Brooklyn. Every so often one of them would come into Carl's butcher shop with a package under his arm and say, "Hey, Carl, I need to see you in the back." I had no clue what they were talking about, and it wasn't my place to ask questions. All I knew was the Costellano brothers never bought any meat.

I didn't learn until I started working at the 14th Street market that Paul Costellano was a rising force in the Gambino crime family which, through many enterprises legitimate and otherwise, controlled virtually all the butcher shops in New York City. I also learned that butcher shops throughout New York City were fronts for the Gambino crime family. The Gambinos, through the Costellano brothers, used the shops to launder money from various illicit enterprises. Carl's shop was a minuscule part of the Gambinos' city-wide money-laundering operation, and woe be to any butcher who didn't play along. It was also at the 14th Street market that I first heard of Elvin Lee (Big El) Bynum, a big-time drug smuggler and Black Mafia kingpin, with whom I would later cross paths.

Four years out of the Food & Maritime Trades School, I had gone about as far as a butcher could go working for somebody else. I contemplated whether it was worth starting my own shop, which would mean having to deal with the Gambinos.

Breaking Away

One thing seemed certain—I needed a change. I married Patty Reilly on May 19, 1965. Over the next four years, we would have two sons—Craig Steven Wollack, born March 9, 1968, and Robert E. Wollack III, born November 20, 1969. At the same time there was a war going on in Vietnam. It didn't matter whether I agreed with it or not. I just knew that this wasn't the kind of change I was hoping for. My brother Tommy was already there and had written home about how terrible things were.

But I still wanted to live life on the edge. I took the Civil Service Exam for the New York City Police Department. If I was going to be drafted into the military, I wanted to get the best training possible ahead of time to improve my chances all around for survival. So, I signed up for Co E 19th Special Forces Group, ABN of the New York National Guard, a.k.a. the Green Berets, and got shipped off to Fort Bragg, North Carolina, for several months of training. During training, I found out that my scores on the NYPD exam had been stellar. Coupled with my military training, I had positioned myself perfectly for a career as a cop. My Green Beret stint was nothing spectacular—but I did go to West Virginia and Utah for mountain exercises. I was a pretty damned good paratrooper and if I had to go to Nam, I was confident that I would be prepared for anything.

As it turned out there was plenty of action at home. The raging fires of racial tension that rolled over Watts and Detroit were heading east and war protests were on the rise across the country. The New York Police Department, bracing for the impending civil unrest, needed a few good men for their Tactical Patrol Force. The pay wasn't that great—$6,000 a year—but the benefits were good and so was the job security, such as it was for a cop. There was a "twenty-and-out" retirement plan that paid half salary. And I was twenty-three, recently married, and had a kid on the way. I had responsibilities.

If riot control was going to be my piece of the action, so be it. At least I would be staying home. And my Green Beret training was just the ticket I needed for the NYPD Tactical Patrol Force.

What I didn't know was that it would also be my ticket to something far more dangerous.

CHAPTER 3

RUNNING WITH THE DEVIL
La Cosa Nostra

HOW THE NEW YORK Police Department came to be called *New York's Finest* has always been a mystery to me. Although it claimed to be the nation's number one crime fighting institution and boasted the largest police force in North America, no other police department in the country—at least when I hired on—matched its record for corruption.

In the 1870s the NYPD came under the control of Tammany Hall, the legendary Democratic Party machine made up mostly of Irish immigrants. For more than a century Tammany Hall called the shots in the city's politics. Promotions and appointments, including those in the police department, were based on patronage—and Irish ethnicity—more than on performance or merit, which may explain why many New York cops are Irish to this day. (The patronage system is gone now, but traditions persist.) If illegal liquor needed to change hands or a ballot box needed to be stuffed, a New York cop's way of dealing with it was to take a bribe or look the other way, depending on his political allegiance.

They Will Be Victors

Shortly before the turn of the nineteenth century, conditions began to improve under a new police commissioner named Theodore Roosevelt. But his reforms turned out to be short-lived. After his ascendancy to the Presidency of the United States, Roosevelt reported that between the two positions, being New York City's police commissioner was the tougher one.

By the time I became a cop in 1967, the lawlessness within the department rivaled that of the streets. Evidence of this can be found by reading the newspapers of the day. A page one story appeared in the *New York Times* on April 25, 1970, under the headline: "Graft Paid to Police Here Said to Run into Millions. Survey links payoffs to gambling and narcotics—some on force accuse officials of failure to act."

New York City had its own race riot in 1964 after a white cop killed a black teenager. The riot started in Harlem and worked its way into the familiar streets of Bedford-Stuyvesant, leaving looted and burned-out businesses and terrified residents in its wake.

All you had to do at that time was look around or read the latest *New York Times* op-ed piece to find out why there was so much civil unrest—high unemployment among blacks, de facto segregation in housing, failure to enforce civil rights laws, and half-hearted prosecutions in black murder cases. To add fuel to the fire on the home front, the Vietnam War was at its peak and resistance to the war had reached a fever pitch.

On April 4, 1967, at New York's Riverside Church, Martin Luther King had given a speech called *Beyond Vietnam* to a group of clergymen. King told how the war devastated the hopes of America's poor. "We are taking the black young men who had been crippled by our society and sending them eight thousand miles away to guarantee liberties in Southeast Asia which they had not found in Southwest Georgia or East Harlem," he said. "So we have been repeatedly faced with the cruel irony of watching Negro and white boys on TV screens as they kill and die together for a nation that has been unable to seat them together in the same schools." King's speech at Riverside Church didn't achieve the immortality of his *I*

Have a Dream speech delivered on the steps of the Lincoln Memorial, but it signaled the coming of a sea of change in America's attitude toward the war.

This was the social backdrop for my journey on the path to becoming a member of the NYPD. For my orientation to the Tactical Patrol Force, I was assigned to an asshole cop named Jerry from Long Island. Our tour was 6 p.m.—2 a.m., four days on and four days off. The first day, he took me to a bar where we had a couple of drinks and a sandwich. When I reached into my pocket to pay, he leaned over, touched my arm, and said, "Whaddya doin' stupid—this is on the arm." We left and went across the street to a "bodega"—a Puerto Rican grocery store—where he picked up some cigarettes. He flipped me a pack and we began our beat walk. Again, no money exchanged hands. About an hour later, we took our "meal time" and went to the movies. One evening shift I asked him why we weren't writing any summonses, and, in response, he brutally kicked me in the shins with his pointy Italian shoes. About five minutes later Sergeant McGowan came by and scratched our memo book (a twice-a-shift ritual to ensure that officers were on the job). I considered whether I should report the exchange with my partner, but I knew I was still on probation, considered the "code of the blue," and wrote it off to hazing. I had lived through what Arthur Niederhoffer, sociologist and former NYPD officer observed: that "policemen preferred to perjure themselves rather than be known as informers."[1] I was experiencing some ambivalence—the confusion that comes with wanting to eat well versus wanting to sleep well. The whole ordeal took me back to my days at Nate's Candy Store. Whatever my internal conflict at the time, the perks that came with being a cop created a lifestyle that I quickly became accustomed to.

On the evening of April 4, 1968, when news came of Martin Luther King's assassination in Memphis, all hell broke loose. Stokely Carmichael, Chairman of the Student Nonviolent Coordinating Committee (SNCC), as quoted in the *New York Times* April 5, 1968, declared: "When white America killed Dr. King, she declared war on us. . . . Get your gun." Before even finishing my training stint at the New York Police Academy, the two main forces behind the country's upheaval—racial unrest and the Vietnam War—came together in an explosion of protests. Across the city, buildings burst into flames. It was my coming out as a member of the NYPD Tactical Patrol Force.

Three weeks later, another uprising would occur with more serious consequences for me and my fellow officers. It happened at Columbia University on Manhattan's upper west side in the spring of 1968. A student activist named Bob Feldman discovered documents in Columbia's Low Memorial Library linking the university to the Institute for Defense Analysis (IDA), a weapons research think-tank that did business with the U.S. Defense Department. His discovery touched off the first protest in which students demanded that Dr. Grayson Kirk, Columbia's president, sever the university's ties with IDA. Following a peaceful demonstration inside the library, the administration placed on probation six anti-war student activists—called the *IDA Six*—for violating the school's ban on indoor demonstrations.

Meanwhile, Columbia's decision to build a gymnasium in Morningside Park, the barrier separating Columbia from Harlem, made matters worse. In what became known as the *Case of Gym Crow*, the university tried to assuage angry Harlem residents by allowing them to use the gym—through a back door. The disingenuous plan backfired, and black residents and students tore down a fence at the construction site and attempted to burn the building down.

For a week my partners and I on the Tactical Patrol Force stood our ground around the campus perimeter, hoping the sight of our night sticks and tear gas canisters would keep the students at bay. Instead they kept taunting us and throwing paper bags of human excrement at us—students at this great university that many of us had dreamed of going to. Our orders from Mayor John Lindsey and Chief Inspector Sanford Garelick had been to hold our position around the perimeter and not to interfere with the students.

But on April 30, Garelick cut us loose, and we beat the shit out of everybody in sight, including innocents who unknowingly got in our way. For eight days we had allowed the students to taunt and tantalize us. Now it was our turn to get back at them.

When all was said and done, seven hundred students had been arrested, one hundred and fifty received minor injuries, and seven of my fellow cops went on disability—one with a broken spine, another with a punctured lung. As my tactical patrol unit got ready to leave, I looked up at the statue of Minerva, the Roman Goddess of Enlightenment, on the front steps of the Low Memorial Library. A poster propped up in her lap said, *RAPED by the COPS*. The message tore into me and awakened me to how polarized our country had become, rounding out my initiation into riot control for New York's Finest.

Far away from campuses and battlefields, life on the streets of New York City continued. Ethnic neighborhoods grew and the subculture of the streets changed with the times. The Italians were to the Mob what the Irish were to Tammany Hall. The Gambinos were among the most powerful families in the national crime syndicate and maintained their base of operations right in my hometown of Brooklyn. The family's organized crime activities included, among other things, racketeering, conspiracy, loan-sharking, money-laundering, drug-trafficking, gambling, extortion, and murder. Carl the Butcher, my old boss at the butcher shop, had said that you couldn't find nicer people.

Carlo Gambino, a Sicilian immigrant born in 1902, entered the United States as a stowaway. As a young man he learned quickly how to turn Prohibition into profit, buying illegal whiskey in five-gallon cans for $15 and stashing them away till they fetched $50 each. During World War II he made a fortune in a ration stamp racket.

One of Gambino's associates was his brother-in-law, Paul Costellano, a former butcher who, along with his brother Peter, got the Gambino family into the meat business. The Gambinos would set up people in legitimate businesses and use the businesses to launder money from drug smuggling and other illegal enterprises.

The idea, in case the IRS or some other government agency got curious, was to produce a receipt that would show the sale of a pound of heroin as a hind quarter of beef. It was a boondoggle for both the butcher and his financial backer.

It was tough making ends meet on a cop's salary, especially when you had a wife and kid to support and another kid on the way. My son Craig had been born less than a month before the riot at Columbia, and Robert would be joining us in November of 1969. And with our family growing, we needed a bigger place to live. We found it in Bayside, Queens.

As a tactical patrol officer, I was on the fast track, moving up the ranks, crashing through windows and barricades and making tons of arrests. At the same time, I was being groomed for a division called SIU, the Special Investigations Unit, to become an undercover cop. I had my first interview with the narcotics division. I then began training with the guys on the Tactical Patrol Force (TPF). Every night from that point on I would exchange my patrolman's uniform for street clothes and return to uniform only when I got called to put down a riot somewhere or to handle some other crisis situation.

When I *really* went undercover, I would dress up sometimes as a Rabbi or a bum. The *New York Sunday News* had an article in its May 11, 1969 issue with a page-five headline: *A Game of Cops and Rabbis Cuts the Mugging*. The article included a photograph of me and six colleagues dressed in Hassidic garb. The article explained that Hassidic Jews were frequently being attacked on their way to or from Synagogue, and that the use of the Tactical Police Force resulted in many arrests and substantially decreased the number of muggings and led to the formation of the plainclothes unit. I would also dress in drag (this was before the NYPD began to hire women to be police officers) and walk Brooklyn's streets at night and flash my badge to anybody who snatched my purse, slipped me drugs, or propositioned me for sex. The latter didn't happen very often because—as my partner astutely observed—I looked less like a woman than a fireplug wrapped in a skirt.

It was one of the many guises I put on to bust people—and God knows there was plenty of illegal stuff going on in Brooklyn that qualified. But the most prevalent illicit activity centered around drugs. Richard Mayfield [not his real name] whom I first met as my captain in the Army's Special Forces Unit, became a friend. He was also a sergeant in the 79th Precinct of the NYPD. It didn't take me long to figure out that Mayfield was taking bribes from Elvin Lee (Big El) Bynum. I knew of Bynum from my work with the TPF street crimes unit, where any junkie on the street could tell you about Big El. Besides his smuggling operation, which accounted for a large amount of the heroin brought into the country, Big El's stock-in-trade included extortion, hijacking, and gambling. He also operated numerous legitimate enterprises, including a men's clothing store on Fulton Street. He was a partner with the notorious Frank Matthews, and "between them, Matthews and Bynum probably accounted for the distribution of about one-third of all the heroin entering the country."[2] Bynum was also connected with Mafia soldier Joey "C" and the Luchesse crime family in the form of "Tony Ducks" Corallo. (However, until I recently read Goddard's book, I had no idea of the extent of Big El's operations.)

Big El was an imposing figure; he stood six foot three inches tall and weighed well over two-hundred pounds. He had a flat broken nose and piercing eyes. He walked with a limp—the result of an injury from a gunfight. Someone had broken into his hotel room in Hampton Bay, Virginia, to kill him. Being a killer himself, he was quick to pull up his mattress and protect himself. The story goes that he got off a few shots, too. Two days later they found the intruder in the oyster beds. Big El was called "the King" in the Norfolk, Virginia, area. He was not anyone to mess with.

With Mayfield on Bynum's payroll, it wasn't long before I was on the take too, not only helping him cover for Big El but doing my own thing. Niederhoffer observed that "the policeman frequently loses the ability to distinguish between law and license in himself."[3] Along the way we began to bust more people with cocaine but nowhere near as much as with heroin. We knew very little about cocaine, but at the time it was considered to be a non-addictive fun drug similar to the marijuana that we frequently enjoyed. Over time my cocaine use escalated, but not enough to compromise my work or my hustles. George Hanold, Mayfield's brother-in-law, told Richard he wanted in on the action. Hanold and I were the same age, but he'd been on the force two years longer than I. He retired from the force to become a coke dealer in Manhattan, and became our supplier of choice for our personal consumption.

We thought we were big stuff, my crew leader Dale Styne and I, and Big El was at the center of our game. When he needed guys who were bothering him to be taken off the street, he'd sell them an ounce or two of heroin or an eight-ball of cocaine, and we'd move in for the bust like clockwork. That's how the game was played.

Hanold figured out his own game—smuggling. He brought us his idea and introduced us to the great snitch Juan Valdez, famous for his role as the man in the familiar Columbian Coffee TV ads airing at the time. We became involved with Valdez, who led us to horse jockeys who used cocaine to keep their weight down. This would give the jockeys a great edge when racing, just like the horses were sometimes juiced up. Valdez's real name was Jose Duvall; he claimed that he worked for the late Eddie Egan, the famed detective who broke the French Connection. Valdez also claimed that Ira Blumenfeld, who was in charge of the entire NYPD narcotics division, was also on the take. Dale and I went to see Eddie at one of the bars he owned in mid-Manhattan and he validated that Valdez was indeed a reliable snitch.

In October of 1970, an incident at the TPF (Tactical Patrol Force) resulted in my transfer to the 70th Precinct on Flatbush Avenue, coinciding with Richard Mayfield's promotion to lieutenant and transfer to the very same precinct. As would become apparent later, this was more deterministic than coincidental. Regardless, at the time it worked out perfectly for us. I would drive Mayfield—an imposing figure of a man and Korean war veteran—around the streets of Brooklyn and surrounding areas collecting protection money—a little something for the fellas at the station house. While assigned to the midnight shift, I learned how to go "into the coop" to grab a couple of hours of sleep. We would find a place to hide the patrol car and sleep. One had to be careful and look out for "shoo-flies" (NYPD internal affairs officers—the most reviled of all policemen). They were called "shoo-flies" because most of them were recruited out of the academy and never became true street-cops. Therefore, they had no allegiance to the unwritten code of the beat-cop.

Most of the cops I worked with, including some of the feds from the Bureau of Narcotics and Dangerous Drugs (now called the Drug Enforcement Administration) were on the take to one degree or another. When it came right down to it, they were no more than gangsters and mercenaries themselves, and like myself lived life on the edge because that's where life was at. If you weren't living on the edge you weren't living at all, and that was the bottom line. Though not proud of this part of my life's journey, it represents meaningful experiences that would come to foster a deep sense of commitment on my part to helping people.

In reality I was just one of many cops at many levels that collected from Big El. I was nothing special. I was just a bit player in his drug smuggling operation that stretched from New York City to places as far away as Marseilles and Barcelona and South America. I never saw anything more than a few ounces of heroin when we did a drug bust. Whenever I went into Big El's clothing store on Fulton Street to do my business, I'd ask for *the man* and the store manager (a man named Buster Watson, a former trainer of boxer Floyd Patterson)[4] would show up from the back room with a smile and a sealed paper bag. I never witnessed Big El personally handling drugs or distributing money; all of my dealings were through middlemen. All I was concerned with was my take—as high as $700 a month. In between these extracurricular activities, I arrested countless individuals for serious criminal activity, and I became a decorated officer.

The chill of early December hung in the air. On one of our visits to Big El, Dale Styne, my partner, and I inquired of the sales clerk, "Is Elvin here?" She said, "No."

"When will he be back?" I said.

"Tomorrow," she said.

When I returned with Dale and Lieutenant Mayfield the next day, green lights and garlands filled the display windows, and a sign in the door said *Christmas Sale—50% off*. When we went inside, Buster was waiting with the paper bag.

Two weeks later, I got a call from Hanold. He sounded shaken and said he had been arrested and wanted my help getting a lawyer. I called Stanley and arranged to meet Hanold at the offices of Kane, Finger and Salaway in Queens. We had been doing a fair amount of cocaine through our dealings with Big El, and on the way over we did some to take the edge off. We first met Hanold in the bar below the attorneys' offices, and took a couple of stiff drinks. The feeling of being under the microscope is something that can't fully be described, but suffice it to say we were all at the rawest edge of our nerves.

We proceeded upstairs, and, in hindsight, made one grave mistake. We didn't pat Hanold down for a wire. But there really was no reason to. He was a brother. He had shown his loyalty in the past. And perhaps most importantly, the law related to wearing a concealed listening device had been revised, making the admissibility of evidence from a wiretap unclear.

In the attorneys' office, we had a joint consultation. Here sat three laymen consulting with attorneys on issues that would change the course of all our lives. We conferred with them in candid terms, as any reasonable person expecting the attorney-client privilege to be in force would do. We offered to help Hanold any way we could. It is my opinion that Hanold's wiretap violated my constitutional rights and this would later become the basis for my appeal to the U. S. Supreme Court. Some of what was said would come back to haunt Stanley and me.

Two days later Mayfield and I met, and he let me know that he had heard from Hanold that the word was that I was to be arrested. Mayfield was expecting no repercussions, and wanted assurances from me that I would back him up. This was never an issue. However, I did insist that he bring his brother-in-law to the table and that Hanold was his problem to clean up, and that the knife cut both ways. If I was going to stand up, Hanold had to stand up.

Five short days later I still had Christmas shopping to do. When I got off duty, I stopped at Macy's to look for last-minute presents, and then swung by Woolworth's to pick up Christmas lights. It was late in the afternoon of December 23, 1970.

I finished my shopping, hopped in the car, and made my way back to 69th Avenue, my street in Bayside, Queens. As I rounded the corner, I sensed something was wrong. I moved to get out of the car and had just emerged with the Christmas lights when three unmarked police cars rolled up—no flashing lights, no sirens—like Dickens's Christmas ghosts. With Hanold's arrest a few days earlier and the meeting with Mayfield, I was already waiting for the other shoe to fall. I was hearing footsteps as I looked around at the cars circling the entrance to my driveway.

The detectives and various law enforcement undercover agents got out of the cars. Six men approached me as I started—feigning blissful ignorance—for my front door. I knew immediately who they were.

"Are you Robert Wollack?" one of the plainclothes policemen from the unmarked car asked.

I mumbled that I was, trying to disguise the fact that my heart was pounding.

The man flashed his badge while another man produced handcuffs. "We're from the U. S. Joint Task Force on Narcotics," he said. "And you're under arrest."

They handcuffed me, placed me in the back in one of the waiting cars and drove me to headquarters in downtown Manhattan. When I arrived there, I was surrounded by more than twenty Task Force members, one of whom I recognized as being associated with Big El. I knew then that anything I said would be conveyed to Big El and I'd be signing my own death warrant, so I lawyered up. The questioning ceased, and I was taken to the West Street Federal Detention Center.

They Will Be Victors

The orientation to my temporary housing was one of the most humiliating experiences of my life. Pacing back and forth in my cell in the West Street Federal Detention Center in Manhattan wasn't the greatest way to spend the night before Christmas Eve, especially when you have a wife and two very young sons at home. Among the thoughts that invaded my mind was my father; he had died earlier in the year of leukemia. I missed him, but at the same time I was grateful that he would be spared the embarrassment of my arrest.

I stopped pacing and sat down on my bunk. I thought about everyone on the outside bustling around and getting ready for Christmas and rested my head in my hands. Thank God, I thought, my father hadn't lived to see this day. His life had been hard enough without having to bear the weight of a promising son being disgraced.

There were twelve other policemen whom I personally knew who were actively involved in the dealings with Big El, but they were never incriminated and were able to continue in their careers until they retired. One of my colleagues—Dale Styne—took disability leave, became a heroin addict, and ultimately died of AIDS. In fact, I had never worked with any police officer who did not violate the law in some way or other, including committing perjury, assault, or violating citizens' constitutional rights.

Updike's pitch was very matter of fact. If I helped him, he would help me by reducing the charge against me and by making my cooperation known to the sentencing judge. My refusal was equally calm and matter of fact; I simply told him I wouldn't do it. "Look," I said, "I'm not going to wear a wire for two reasons. First, if I get caught I'm dead. Second, it's not right. I accept responsibility for my own thing, but in no way am I going to snitch on my partners. We were in shootouts together and they were there with me and we watched out for each other. And now you want me to wear a damn wire? No way!"

I expected some pressure, some threats, and some third-degree tactics but there were none. Instead, Updike said he understood my decision and respected it. The meeting was over in less than fifteen minutes.

In retrospect and with the benefit of hindsight, I now realize that Updike was offering me a chance because of my youth, my family, my relatively minor role in the Bynum organization, and because I was a policeman. I didn't take advantage of his offer, but Updike's treatment of me with dignity and respect, both at this meeting and during and after my trial, were part of what enabled me to turn slowly but surely to a very different life from the one I had led prior to my arrest. My decision not to cooperate with Updike meant that I would face my trial and its consequences entirely on my own.

I was out on bail the next day. In short order the shame dissipated under the weight of practical challenges—old habits die hard—and the activity and sophistication of the Gambino's businesses and the tie-in with the meat business beckoned to me. Practically, I looked at it as a possible opportunity to defray some of my impending legal fees. Stan Farrow and my brother Tommy got their Army discharge, and, with a little help from Big El and Joey "C," a soldier for the Gambinos, the three of us started our own butcher shop on Brooklyn's Fifth Avenue. We joked that we were in the laundry business too. Who knew when you might come across some money that needed cleaning?

CHAPTER 4

THE TRIAL

GOING ON TRIAL FOR a felony in federal court is intimidating, to say the least. As a cop I had appeared in court many times to press charges against someone I'd arrested for offenses ranging from possession of drugs to armed robbery. With Big El serving as our informant, we had brought down countless numbers of bad guys, while quietly becoming one of them. Now I stood before Judge David N. Edelstein not as a witness for the prosecution, but as a defendant facing four felony counts. Sadly the case of *The United States vs. Wollack, Wollack and Farrow* included my brother Tommy and my long-time friend Stanley. The trial began on July 19, 1971 in the United States District Court in Manhattan.

The Feds' case premised that the three of us had conspired to obtain and distribute cocaine along with three other co-conspirators. My hope rested on whether Tommy and Stanley would be let off. Although there was no substantive evidence to warrant them being investigated by the Joint Task Force, the Feds were after them for whatever tenuous connection they could find linking them to the Gambinos and to Big El Bynum. The three of us were simply caught up in the web cast by the Joint Task Force which happened to coincide with the Knapp Commission—the infamous anti-corruption task force made famous by the movie *Serpico*. The Knapp Commission, which was established in April 1970 By Mayor John Lindsey, was focused on rooting out corruption in the New York City Police

Department. My arrest was by the Joint Federal/State Task Force, and I was able to avoid testifying before the Knapp Commission. I did not want to experience the fate of Serpico who was allegedly shot by his NYPD colleagues for being a "snitch."

My intimate involvement in the activities that Mayfield had coordinated and enlisted me in was slightly more apparent thanks to Hanold's betrayal. There was a series of changes to the law related to the statutes under which I was being charged; yet my attorney and I remained hopeful that the outcome would be favorable. However, with each passing day the weight of my circumstances grew heavier. It was as if I were being buried alive by the realization of what I had done, and by what I now faced as a result of those decisions. I wondered if I'd ever see my wife or boys again, except through a glass pane in a prisoner visitation room. My wife would prove to be a loyal companion during this critical time in my life. She would be a regular visitor and supportive spouse.

At the prosecutors' table sat an agent from the task force and Assistant U.S. Attorney Charles Updike. I was impressed with Updike's credentials (Amherst College, George Washington University, and a law degree from Harvard University).

My defense attorney was an elegant little Jewish man from Queens named Sidney Sparrow. I had observed his litigation skills during the many times I had testified as a cop in the courtroom. My original lawyers (the ones in whose office Hanold had worn the wire) were two former Assistant District Attorneys from Queens County. They referred me to Sparrow. What I had suspected—but had not been able to verify until I met with Charlie Updike years later—was that my original lawyers had been disqualified from handling my case. Both they and I had been recorded surreptitiously in their office and depending on how the trial proceeded, the information from that recording could have been allowed as evidence, thereby turning them into potential witnesses. The truth of the matter was that they had said some potentially incriminating things about themselves on that tape, and the Assistant U.S. Attorney moved to disqualify them from serving as my counsel. He did not want me to be able to argue later on that my defense had been tainted or ineffective because my counsel had a conflict of interest.

Tommy's and Stanley's attorney was Frederick T. Stant, Jr., a colorful, bald-headed man nicknamed "Bingo" because he'd won so many drug conspiracy cases, including a big one at the U.S. District Court in Richmond, Virginia. A favorite of the criminal justice lawyers, he came up the hard way, growing up on freight trains during the Depression. He eventually worked his way through Georgetown Law School.

The stage—replete with the apparitions of comedy and tragedy—was set. Taking his seat at the bench, Judge Edelstein shuffled through a sheath of papers, paused and looked at Tommy and Stanley and me at the defendants' table. "Gentlemen," he said, "you are charged with three counts of unlawfully selling cocaine and one count of conspiracy to obstruct justice."

I knew that if convicted under the current law, I could receive five to twenty years on each count. That meant up to eighty years in prison if convicted on all four counts—not a pleasant prospect. Behind me, in the spectator's section, were my wife and two sons. I wondered what my three-year-old son was making of all this. Sidney Sparrow thought the presence of my family in the courtroom would soften the jury's disposition toward me.

Numbness closed in on me like a fist when Charlie Updike began his opening statement. While there were three of us on trial, Updike directed his arguments primarily at me describing how I was "deeply involved in the narcotics traffic in New York City" and emphasizing how I had violated my trust as a New York cop. He stated that he had the evidence on tape, explaining to the jury how I had incriminated myself in a conversation with a fellow police-officer-turned-informant. The police officer, Lieutenant Mayfield's brother-in-law George Hanold, once so eager to get in on the action, had been indicted along with me on cocaine and conspiracy charges. He pled guilty and served two years in a federal penitentiary, receiving a reduced sentence in exchange for wearing a wire to obtain evidence and testify against me and my co-defendants.

In the value system that I knew as a police officer, Hanold had done the unpardonable by betraying a fellow cop. While Updike questioned him on the witness stand, the thought crossed my mind that his brother-in-law should have done damage control with him. It wasn't Mayfield's fault Hanold snitched on me, but under the rules of the game it was Mayfield's job to check him. But Mayfield never took action—likely driven by the influence of his family connection and coupled with the fact that Hanold had not included Mayfield in the net that was cast. "Some justice!?" I thought.

Sidney Sparrow argued that while I was indeed a drug user, I had done nothing illegal—that I got only what I needed for myself and that the prosecution had nothing to go on but George Hanold's word. The only hard evidence they produced was one-eighth ounce of cocaine and a $50 counterfeit bill.

When Sparrow called me to the stand, I testified that what I said on George Hanold's tape was nothing but cocaine-induced nonsense. It was a calculated confession intended to convey that I was incapable of doing anything, let alone having the wits to run a big-time drug trafficking operation.

When Updike cross-examined me, I testified that, yes, I had used cocaine as a cop—lots of cops were doing it—but in no way was I involved in drug trafficking. I told what I believed about Lieutenant Mayfield's dealings with Big El Bynum and the Gambinos, but that I couldn't prove anything. I testified that, "Yes, I was friendly with Elvin Lee Bynum and I have nothing incriminating to offer about him." All in all, Updike went easy on me. I sensed he already had what he wanted from another police officer that they had no doubt been able to wire.

The trial ran for ten days. Except for my testimony, my wife sat through the whole ordeal including fourteen hours of jury deliberation. When Judge Edelstein called the jury in for the reading of the verdicts, I resumed my seat at the defendant's table with Tommy and Stanley. Stanley's mother leaned over the rail separating us from the spectators and said, "Listen, Stanley, we all make mistakes. No matter what happens, we're here to support you." I thought, "If only my mother would say something like that, how

The Trial

different things might be." At this moment when the rest of my life was at stake, I didn't even know whether my mother was in the courtroom.

When the jury members resumed their seats in the jury box, Judge Edelstein asked the foreman, "Have you reached a verdict?"

"We have, your honor," he replied, passing the verdicts to the clerk.

Tommy's turn came first. The judge asked him to stand, and the clerk read each of the four counts followed by each of the four verdicts. The clerk's monotone voice belied the drama of the moment.

"Count one...not guilty," the clerk said, pausing. He then resumed the reading of the next three verdicts: "Not guilty...Not guilty...Not guilty." I saw palpable relief on his face. And as his verdicts were read, my confidence level grew ever so slightly.

It was the same with Stanley when the clerk read his verdicts: "Not guilty...Not guilty...Not guilty...Not guilty." Things seemed to be going well—how could there be a conspiracy when only one co-defendant remains to be sentenced?

Finally came my turn. Judge Edelstein asked me to stand and face the jury, and then he instructed the clerk to continue with the reading of the verdicts. The clerk flipped a page and continued:

"Count one, for unlawful sale of cocaine...Not guilty," he said.

"Count two, for unlawful sale of cocaine...Not guilty," he said.

"Count three, for unlawful sale of cocaine...Not guilty," he said.

Without breaking rhythm, the clerk continued in his monotone voice:

"Count four, for conspiracy to sell cocaine...Guilty."

A stunned silence fell over the courtroom. Or perhaps it was that dull thudding of the blood that rushes to your head when you are surprised, alarmed or in danger. I turned around and looked at my wife and tried to speak, but the words were caught in a vacuum where my breath should have been. The court officer slapped his handcuffs on me and led me away. My sister's scream pierced the courtroom:

"Bobby! Bobby! Bobby!"

35

I felt weightless, like a balloon tethered to its mooring, anxious to escape but unable to break free. Then I heard another voice in my ear—my mother's: "Run, Bobby, run!" It sounded like an echo, but it was real enough. The nightmare of that moment was real enough too.

Judge Edelstein remanded me to the West Street Detention Center in Manhattan—where I had first been sent upon my arrest—and set my sentencing for September 7, 1971. No bail this time—likely because my life was potentially in danger. As time would tell, this would prove to be all too true. However, jail wasn't exactly a "safe haven."

I went through the same intake process as I had previously—the one that all inmates go through: you strip yourself naked and expose your private parts including your buttocks which they ask you to bend down and spread apart. They also check your mouth, hair, and ears, concluding the dehumanizing search. I would experience this search many more times—each time I re-entered a jail or prison.

The nightmare continued. The day after the verdict, on July 30, my mother came to see me at the West Street Detention Center. She held in her hand a copy of the *New York Times*. "Just look at this," she said sharply. She flipped to an inside page and pressed it up to the glass pane that separated us. An article headlined, *Policeman Guilty in Narcotics Case*, appeared at the top. I started reading it through the glass:

> A suspended policeman was convicted in Federal Court here last night on a charge of conspiracy to sell cocaine while he was a patrolman in Brooklyn. The 27-year-old defendant, Robert E. Wollack, testified at his trial that he had used cocaine heavily while a patrolman and that many other policemen also used drugs, but he denied that he had operated as a cocaine dealer....

My mother pulled the newspaper away and leaned into the microphone. "Thank God your father is dead!" she said. Then she got up and left. If ever I felt shitty that was the time. Once more my

The Trial

eighth-grade graduation cap was being slapped off, and the sting of humiliation was being kept ever fresh. I told my wife to never again bring my mother to see me.

On the day of my sentencing my sons Craig and Robert—three and a half and two years years old respectively—were in the courtroom with my wife. The boys were more or less oblivious to the gravity of the situation. Daddy was going away on a long and wholly unplanned trip. I sat in the courtroom feeling desperately alone, in spite of a gathering of people who would come to be enduring figures in shaping my life going forward: my lawyer Sidney Sparrow, Prosecutor Charles Updike, and Judge Edelstein.

Updike approached the bench. "Your honor," he said, "I believe the defendant, Mr. Wollack, needs to go to prison for a period of time and pay for his crime. But I also believe that he can be rehabilitated, that he can straighten himself out, and that he should attend college and be given a second chance. I therefore recommend the minimum sentence of five years on the conspiracy conviction."

"Gentlemen," the judge intoned, "I have reviewed the recommendations and Mr. Wollack's letter and have reached my decision. . . ."

CHAPTER 5

THE MILAN CONNECTION

"IN THE CASE OF the *United States vs. Wollack*, *Wollack and Farrow*," Judge Edelstein said, his eyes fixed on the binder, "Mr. Robert Wollack has been found not guilty on three counts of unlawfully selling cocaine and guilty on the fourth count of conspiracy to do so, which conviction carries with it under Title 26, Section 7237(b) a minimum sentence of five years and a maximum sentence of twenty years in the Federal Bureau of Prisons."

The judge continued reading: "The court has carefully considered the arguments of the prosecution and the defense regarding an appropriate prison term for said defendant. The court believes the argument of the lead prosecutor regarding rehabilitation of the defendant has significant bearing on the terms of punishment. The court does not believe, however, that the minimum allowable term for this offense is appropriate given the defendant's position as an officer of the New York Police Department at the time the offense was committed.

"It is adjudged by this court," he concluded, "that the defendant be hereby committed to the custody of the Attorney General or his authorized representative for imprisonment for a period of six years on Count Four."

They Will Be Victors

The judge made it all sound so impersonal—the defendant this, the defendant that—as if all this had nothing to do with me. I felt that floating sensation again, drifting away as far as I could but unable to remove myself from the reality of what I faced. So what? I wasn't even sure if the judge had said "six years" or "sixteen years." It didn't matter anyway because, for the moment, it seemingly had nothing to do with me.

It took a few hours for reality to sink in. A six-year sentence, although a year above the mandatory minimum, was still far less than twenty, and Sidney Sparrow said it could be cut in half for good behavior. Moreover, I would receive credit for time already spent at the West Street Detention Center until the Justice Department made up its mind where to send me.

A federal sentence opened up the possibility that the facility to which I would be sent could be located virtually anywhere in the country. There were a countless number of federal prisons to choose from, and I didn't know where I'd wind up after the prescribed two weeks of psychological testing and assessment.

Another two weeks passed before I learned that my next "home" would be the Federal Correctional Institution at Milan, Michigan. Located fifteen miles south of Ann Arbor off U.S. Highway 23, it was a medium security prison of some six hundred male inmates. Back in the '30s it had been a "co-correctional" facility, meaning it housed women as well as men, and included famous "alumni" George "Machine Gun" Kelly's wife and John Dillinger's girlfriend. The FBI's infamous witness against the Mafia—Joe Valachi of the Genovese crime family—was secretly held at Milan Prison. Now the prison housed mostly high-testosterone men in their twenties whose crimes consisted of counterfeiting, bank robbery, drug trafficking, and other federal crimes.

The six-hundred mile car trip from New York was anything but a joy ride. One U.S. marshal would drive while the other kept an eye on me. I sat in the back seat shackled in handcuffs, a belly chain, and leg irons. Every four hours or so the marshals would change shifts with another set of marshals; one pair would drop me off at a jail along the prescribed route, and another pair would pick me up to travel the next leg.

So it went for several days with stops in Pennsylvania and West Virginia between the long hours on the road. The marshals assigned to escort me on the night shift checked me into a local jail. The expressions on the marshals' faces belied some concern. My cell reeked of urine, and toilet paper littered the floor around an open nail keg, which served as the stool. A chain and padlock secured the door. The marshals deposited me into this hell-hole with an obvious degree of hesitation.

Fifteen minutes later the marshals returned. "Look," one of them said, "we haven't checked into a motel yet. We're going on to Columbus, Ohio." This small act of compassion—purely altruistic given the fact that it demanded they continue their journey later into the evening—left me greatly appreciative. I didn't know if they felt sorry for me, or if they didn't want the blame in case I got hurt on their shift. Either way, I welcomed getting back into the car—even if it meant being shackled again.

Over the course of the trip, I engaged in conversation with the marshals. On one occasion, I assured them that I would be making quick work of formulating an appeal. They looked at each other knowingly, and the one watching me turned and said, "Yeah, when we make our way back sometime next year, you'll be hoeing a row of cabbage!"

I arrived at Milan in the fall of 1971. While many in Michigan were enjoying the outdoor colors of the fall season, my world had suddenly turned gray and my mood was matched by the same dull, flat indoor space that I entered.

My initial worries were not so much about myself as they were about my wife and two boys. In spite of herself, my mother offered to take them in until other arrangements could be made, or the money I left with them ran out.

Meanwhile, I adjusted well enough to life at the Milan Penitentiary. Daily routines included three counts during which guards ("hacks" as they were known) would count the inmates during mid-morning, mid-afternoon, and at night when everyone was in their cells.

I learned a lot of jargon during those first days. Inmates who caused trouble were sent to "the hole"—placed in isolation. Homosexuals were called "gumpies," and your cell was referred to as a "crib" or "house." Close friends within the prison were "homies," and a "homeboy" was an inmate who was from the same city or geographical area you were from. The term "off the hook" meant to stop talking because of a chance of being overheard by a snitch. "On the outs" referred to a person who was "short" which also meant that he was being released from prison in the near future. The "world" was the outside.

The importance of assimilation dates back to the arrival of immigrants on Ellis Island. Like America to the immigrants, prison was an entirely different world to every new arrival. Learning this vocabulary—only a fraction of the vernacular familiar to inmates and guards alike—was essential to every inmate's smooth transition into prison life. If you couldn't speak the language, you were out of the loop. And that was definitely not a place you wanted to be.

Within a day or two of my arrival, the guy in charge of food services—who apparently had seen the word *butcher* on my job skills form—offered me an opportunity to get assigned to the meat cutting part of the kitchen. That was a godsend on a couple of levels. First, I could get paid—albeit at the paltry level of $25 per month—and I had access to everything I could eat: eggs, cheese, bread, vegetables, pickles, olives, and occasionally lunch meat. I was also able to pick up a little cash on the side. Every Saturday I'd put on a long army coat, march into the kitchen, and fill my pockets with cheese sandwiches. Then I'd sell the sandwiches for fifty cents each to inmates in my block, my entrepreneurial spirit again coming into play.

Every inmate had a niche—a money-making scheme that he carried out on the side. Mine was cheese sandwiches. Other inmates sold things like cigarettes ("squares"), candy bars, even clean underwear, because the prison issued you only five pairs every week, and if you played handball, basketball or lifted weights, you needed

The Milan Connection

seven or eight. The easy way for a lazy inmate to make money was to sit around in the same underwear all week, and then sell—in effect "rent"—his unused underwear to prison jocks like me. Necessity truly was the mother of invention, and the subculture worked to improve everyone's "standard of living," if you could call it that.

I was next in line to be in charge of the butcher shop operation, but I had to wait until a guy named Vaughn—a Vietnam vet who was doing time for shooting a lieutenant—got released. Vaughn had taken revenge on the lieutenant for letting his men get killed. He had three months to go. Somehow he had gotten picked to work in the meat-cutting department before me. The only problem—besides his Post-Traumatic Stress Disorder symptoms—was he did not know how to cut meat. When I told him I'd been cutting meat all my life, he said, "Can you teach me so I can get a job?"

"No problem," I said, knowing this would get me unlimited access to the meat locker.

"Just one condition," he said. "I get all the booty going out of here. You ain't gettin' nothin'! But when I leave this place, you get it all." The deal was done. Three months later, Vaughn was released and found a butcher job at an A&P. I still have his thank-you note.

My position in the hierarchy also put me in touch with the Black Muslims. Notorious for being close-knit and non-communicative with whites, one of them approached me one day in the yard. "Hey devil honky, I hear you got all the cheese. What a brotha gotta do to get some?" I goofed on him for a second—"Hey bro', I thought you guys didn't eat meat." He looked at me like I had lost my mind. Then I said, "Forget it man, what can I do for you?" From then on it was "Salaam Alechem." Now I'm not saying we became best friends, but we arrived at a mutually beneficial understanding.

These direct interactions with the black culture, in conjunction with those from my youth, would form a foundation that would enable me to relate to and assimilate with the young people who I would come to serve. During the next year and a half, I also had a chance to teach meat-cutting to two black guys from Chicago named Shep and Tommy. They were members of the Blackstone

Rangers and had been involved in a series of bank robberies. I also trained several other inmates throughout my time as manager of the butcher shop. I gained a lot of satisfaction from these opportunities to help people, and I would later look back on them as my first taste of social work, albeit at an informal level.

Prison life is always filled with tensions. There are tensions between inmates and guards, and between men who come from various sections of the country. But the greatest source of potential conflict lies between ethnic groups. During mealtimes black inmates chose to sit in a specific section of the dining hall. An inmate who wasn't black dared not sit with them unless invited to do so and even then it was a tenuous situation. I vividly recall how close we came to experiencing a full-blown race riot during one particular mealtime. You could literally feel the tension; it was palpable. I was fully alert to the danger, my antennae vibrating. Suddenly one person hurled a salt or pepper shaker, and in an instant anything that wasn't bolted down was being hurled back and forth in the racially divided dining-hall. Verbal insults flew with the debris adding to the violent agitation, and I felt my heart pounding. A small prison guard whom we called "Beanie" due to his physical stature—he stood about five feet and four inches tall—climbed up on a table and shouted with a commanding voice, "STOP!" His first command was quickly followed by another, "STOP!" For a moment there was total silence pierced only by the breathing of the throng; with each collective breath came a lessening of the pressure in the atmosphere—the barrage of pelted cafeteria remnants, verbal insults, and hostile glares being gradually replaced by the clicking of eating utensils against plates. Soon everything returned to normal.

Each morning I woke with apprehension about the unknown challenges of a new day and my personal chances for survival. It didn't take long for me to realize that what I needed for my overall well-being was a clique—a group to belong to—like the gang I had belonged to in Brooklyn. Prison was no different. There I quickly realized that I had nobody to watch out for me or to be a buddy with. I needed somebody I could look out for as well. Survival in prison depends on running with a pack, so I knew I had to find a group. I hadn't forgotten the whispered threat that was made to me by two federal agents of the Joint Task Force during my interrogation—"Because you wouldn't cooperate with us, you will be lucky to survive one year at the pen!"

I soon made some friends including some black guys from New York City who knew my story and chose to watch my back. And I watched theirs. That's how I survived. That's how we all survived. I also made other friends whose influence and loyalty would become life-long.

About a month into my stint, an inmate a few years younger than I—he was maybe twenty-three or twenty-four—started working out with me in the weight room. He was soft-spoken, average height, wiry, and had a ruddy complexion. I studied him for a few days—like I did every inmate—before finally introducing myself.

"I'm Bob Wollack from Brooklyn," I said, extending my hand.

"Jim Walsh from St. Paul," he said. "People call me Pete."

"What are you in for?" I asked, it was always the first question you asked an inmate.

Pete told me about how he had arrived in March after serving in the 25th Infantry Division in Vietnam. I learned that he had a sister and that his father worked as a railroad switchman. He also mentioned that he had gone to an all-male Catholic military school in St. Paul called Cretin High. He enlisted in the Army right out of high school so he could get his military service out of the way. Then he was sent to Vietnam. I sensed he was suffering from the same thing a lot of returning Vietnam vets suffered from—what we now call Post-Traumatic Stress Disorder. Unfortunately, nobody understood much about it then.

As for what brought Pete to Milan, it will suffice to say that he got mixed up with the wrong crowd after moving in with some Army buddies in San Antonio following his tour in 'Nam.

A few weeks after our initial meeting, Pete came into the weight room with an inmate I hadn't seen before. "Bob," he said, "I want you to meet Bill Tilton from F Block. He just arrived here. We went to high school together in St. Paul."

They Will Be Victors

"No shit," I said. Wiping my hands on my shirt, I got up from my weight bench and shook his hand. Bill was several inches taller than me, a bit on the gangly side, and wore an ear-to-ear grin.

"You know about the *Minnesota 8*," Pete continued. "Well, he's one of them." Bill Tilton was a year older than Pete. They had known each other only peripherally at Cretin High School, but were obviously thrilled—and to a larger extent relieved—to run into each other at Milan. Bill was near to graduating from the University of Minnesota with a degree in economics and had already been accepted into law school when the feds arrested him. He had been arrested inside a Selective Service Office in Alexandria, Minnesota, from which he and others had intended to steal the files of young men eligible to be drafted and then dump the files into the Mississippi River. It wasn't something he accomplished by himself. The *Minnesota 8*—a group of college-aged kids that raided draft offices around the state—had effectively halted half the draft in Minnesota.

"We were decent burglars," he said, a sly grin breaking out on his face. "But we were a little weak on security, since the FBI was there waiting for us." He quickly added, "But don't think I'm a draft dodger."

"You're not?" I asked.

"No," he said. "The draft is okay under certain circumstances, but not for this stupid and aggressive war." Prison clearly had not changed his opinion.

Both Pete and Bill had wound up at Milan because of Vietnam—Pete because he was sent there as a soldier; Bill because he tried to prevent young men from being sent there as soldiers. Either way they were screwed. But I liked them both. We connected and I felt like I had found some friends that I could count on and who also would be able to count on me. There are two kinds of people in the world—those who believe that every occurrence is simply a random event, and those who believe that things happen for a reason. I count myself among the latter. And this belief would prove to be true decades later when our paths—Pete's, Bill's, and mine—would lead us to heights far beyond the setting that brought us together.

CHAPTER 6

A PRICE ON MY HEAD

MY FIRST SIX MONTHS at Milan went well enough. Every morning I got up at 5:30, went over to the kitchen, and cut meat until 11 o'clock. Every so often Pete Walsh—who worked in the guards' mess—would pop into the kitchen looking for fresh veggies. In the afternoon we played handball and lifted weights. Gradually, I felt my strength returning. I had lost a lot of muscle due to the trauma I had endured following my arrest. Some evenings after dinner, I worked in the law library writing writs for fellow inmates. I also taught vocational education courses, specifically reading, writing, and reading comprehension.

My friend Bill Tilton was assigned to the prison warehouse with a couple of hillbillies. This, I imagined made for less-than-stimulating intellectual conversation. But he never complained. Whenever we walked the prison yard he let me pick his brain. The Second Circuit Court of Appeals, on January 5, 1972, affirmed my guilty verdict and I needed Bill's advice. Did I have a chance with the United States Supreme Court? Suppose I appealed on the grounds that my Fourth Amendment rights against unreasonable search and seizure had been violated? Bill had already failed in his own appeal. Nevertheless, it was my opinion that Tilton & Wollack made the best jail-house lawyer team at Milan federal prison.

We communicated with a constitutional lawyer, Herman Schwartz, who taught at the University of Buffalo Law School. However, as Bill had predicted, the Supreme Court refused to hear my case. Only two U. S. Supreme Court Justices—Marshall and Douglas—consented. The requirement to hear a case was that four of the sitting justices must agree to do so. Yet, the fact that two justices saw merit in my case speaks to the quality of the arguments we presented. Still, with good behavior I figured I might get out in four years, maybe even three. Meanwhile, I resigned myself to the fact that prison was going to be my life, and I was determined to make the best of it. I had food to eat and a group to belong to. Despite being locked up, I decided that life in the slammer could at least be made tolerable. That's when I was reminded that control is an illusion. I was also reminded "that what goes around, comes around." While it was my feeling that my constitutional rights had been violated, candor required me to also admit that as a cop I, along with some of my colleagues, had violated the constitutional rights of many citizens. All in all I learned an important lesson about the value of our United States Constitution.

I had just slipped my last tray of sliced ham into the kitchen locker one morning when I was confronted by a guard. He said that he needed to escort me from the kitchen to the front office. "Wollack," he said, "there are two gentlemen who want to see you."

I recognized my visitors as the two federal marshals who delivered me on the last leg of my trip to Milan back in October. Now it was April 1972. Barring probation, I had five-and-a-half years to go on my six-year sentence.

"Mr. Wollack," one of the marshals said. "We have a subpoena for you."

"For what?" I asked.

The marshal handed me a sealed envelope. I opened it and read the document. The U.S. District Court in New York City wanted me to report as a witness in the case of *The United States of America vs. Elvin Lee Bynum et al*. The trial would begin in two weeks. The *et al* included Joey "C" and about ten or twelve other defendants—all charged with conspiring to obtain and sell narcotics.

Once again I found myself in the back seat of a federal marshal's car, Don McLean was belting out "Bye-Bye, Miss American Pie" on the radio, and I was accessorized in the prison jewelry that restrained my movements. I made the long trek back to New York City, but this time as a witness rather than a co-defendant. I had to be available in the event the prosecution wanted me to testify in what was then one of the biggest drug-dealing trials in the city's history.

I was returned to where the nightmare had begun—the West Street Detention Center. Every morning at 6:30 the marshals would come by to haul us over to the Federal Southern District Courthouse. I'd sit in the basement holding area for the duration of the day while court was in session, then be shuttled back to the West Street Detention Center for the night.

Four days passed…then five…then six. Every morning at 8:00 two agents would show up in the basement of the courthouse and escort other defendants in the case up to the courtroom. Then they would bring them back down late in the afternoon—like human yo-yo's. Throughout the trial, Big El and Joey "C" remained out on bail. I couldn't get a firm handle on what was transpiring in the proceedings at the courthouse. Nor did anyone tell me whether I had been subpoenaed by the prosecution or the defense. All I knew was that Charlie Updike, who prosecuted at my trial, was the lead prosecutor at this trial, and that I was being called as a witness, not a defendant. The protection against double jeopardy gave me some consolation as to my fate in this particular matter.

I was already serving out my time—I certainly didn't want to do it at the West Street Detention Center. I had seen enough of the place, and it was filled with bad memories from my own trial. The courthouse basement wasn't much better; we were placed in a temporary cell along with about fifteen other men with nothing to do and we were served only a baloney sandwich for lunch. I tried to find enough room so I could do push-ups in an effort to keep in shape.

Another day passed. Still nothing happened.

The next morning, when the Task Force agents came down to escort the defendants to the courtroom, I decided I'd had enough. "Hey, man," I shouted, "what the hell am I doing here in this basement? I want to be back at Milan with my guys."

That evening, I was the last one left in the temporary holding cell. I called the guard and asked him to call Updike's office and ask, "What the hell am I doing here; I am not testifying against any one about anything!" After about fifteen minutes, two agents appeared. "The prosecutor will see you now," one of them said.

"Do we need to cuff him?" the other one said.

"No, we shoot rabbits when they run."

"Look," I said, "you guys don't need to fucking worry about me. I ain't going nowhere."

So up the stairs we went to Charlie Updike's office—all eighteen flights. It was the best workout I'd had since Milan.

When we entered Updike's office, he came out from behind his desk and shook my hand. I hadn't seen him since my trial.

"You look good, Bobby," he said. "You put on weight, you're off drugs. That's a good thing."

The idea of reciprocating with a "Good to see you too Charlie" never crossed my mind.

"What do you want from me?" I said.

"Well, nothing so far."

"So why did you bring me in?"

"We had to have you on hand to testify in case your name came up."

"Well, has it?"

"Not yet. But we have somebody here who wants to talk with you." Updike called toward the door. "You can bring him in now."

"Bobby, I think you know George Marble [not his real name]," Updike said.

A Price on My Head

George Marble was a tall, handsome ex-Marine who owned the famous Alice's Restaurant in upper Manhattan. He was also Joey "C"'s driver. I had met him only once or twice before when he and Joey the Butcher stopped by the butcher shop on their money-laundering rounds. Joey called him "Georgie Cuffs" because he had a nervous habit of tugging at his shirtsleeves. I remembered Joey telling me how he bailed poor Georgie out of a failed business venture by lending him money to pay off his creditors and then drafting him as a player in his drug-dealing game. Georgie who had gone to college had started out straight enough. His Alice's Restaurant on Manhattan's upper eastside, which opened after the movie came out, had a flurry of customers at first but faded from the scene along with the movie, leaving him in debt to Joey "C." Now I sensed he was being suckered in again, but I wasn't prepared to hear what he was about to say.

"He wants to tell you something," Updike said, turning to Georgie who was immersed in his trademark cuff-tugging.

"Bobby," he said, "did you know Big El Bynum and Joey "C" had a contract out on you?"

It was a bombshell I had not anticipated.

"That doesn't surprise me," I said, trying to conceal my disbelief. Now that I was up to speed on why I was where I was, I worried about how much they thought I knew about their drug dealings, and prayed to God I didn't get called to testify. But here I was waiting my turn in Charlie Updike's office only a short walk away from the court room.

Georgie continued: "I think it will surprise you to know who they wanted to carry it out."

"Who?" I asked.

"They wanted *me* to do it."

"Bullshit."

"Let me finish. Big El wanted to get you to go to the corn-beef and tongue plant on Utica Avenue (in Brooklyn) for a conversation. Then he wanted Joey and me to be waiting in the back of the meat plant where they told me to knock you out, slip you into a plastic bag, shoot you, place you in the trunk of a car and drive the car off somewhere to be parked. I was informing for the Task Force, and when the order to hit you came down, I immediately alerted them. Updike made sure that Big El, Joey, and I—and some other guys—were arrested before we were able to get to you."

It sounded too surreal—too absurd. "So now what?" I said.

"Show him what he wants to know," Georgie said, motioning to Updike and another Assistant U. S. Attorney. I was then shown the transcript from the grand jury affirming just what George Marble had said.

George looked over at me. "Hey, I'd jump out this window if they told me to," referring to his allegiance to the Task Force.

"So why don't you jump, Georgie? We're eighteen floors up. Why don't you fucking go ahead and jump? I already got my time. Charlie, what's up with this shit? Look, I *really* don't want to testify; I can't. I told you that before. Why do you think I'm in prison now? It's because I refused to cooperate."

"Okay, Mr. Marble, you can go now," Updike said.

After Georgie left, Updike turned to me. "He was telling you the truth, Bob."

Even before Updike confirmed it with his unwavering gaze, I knew Georgie wasn't making any of it up. But I couldn't testify without writing my own death sentence, and I'd already established the fact—with six years of my life—that I was not going to roll over on anybody. So I said, "That guy is the slime of the earth. I don't believe him for a minute (I lied for emphasis). Look, Charlie, I don't have anything to give you. I was just a bit player in this whole drug scheme, and I'm not testifying against anybody."

If Updike was frustrated with me, he didn't show it. A part of me wants to believe he actually admired me for the courage to accept my own responsibility without dragging other people down to save myself. I figured he had what he wanted from Georgie Cuffs anyway—if he could believe him.

"Well, Bobby," Updike said, "once the trial is over, you'll go back to Milan and continue lifting your weights and finish out your time. Maybe when you get out you can help reform the system."

Updike continued: "See you later, Bobby. Take care and good luck."

This meeting was the second time that Updike had offered me a chance to cooperate. As with the first time, there was no pressure except his telling me that I really didn't owe any loyalty to a couple of guys who wanted to kill me to spare themselves prison time. But I knew I was going back to prison and figured they probably wouldn't be far behind me. I was beginning to move on with my life and didn't need the complications that cooperating with the Joint Task Force would have entailed.

Again, what stuck with me from this encounter was Updike's treatment of me with dignity and respect. We both knew that I was a convicted felon who was at that very moment serving his sentence. And yet the opportunity to cooperate was offered in a straightforward and matter-of-fact way and my second refusal was accepted with the same calmness and grace as the first. In short, although we both knew I was a convict, I also felt like a human being with real choices. People who feel self-worth believe that they can become positive participants in our society. I came to learn later that just as dignity and respect had been important to me, they were important to the troubled young people I would ultimately devote my life to helping.

After the trial was over—about five days later—Joey "C," Big El, and the other defendants were all placed in the West Street Detention Center. Joey "C" (another butcher who was in league with the Gambino crime family) occupied the bunk above me and "Big El" Bynum the bunk beside me. There I was—incarcerated with some of the most dangerous criminals in New York State—the very guys who had conspired to have me brutally murdered.

One day we were in the center's kitchen, and I looked over at Joey. "Georgie Cuffs told me about the hit you and Big El put on me," I said. "Is that true?"

He didn't reply, but his look was an affirmation.

"Why'd you do it?" I asked.

Joey "C" didn't look the least bit fazed. "We hadda whack everybody who could be a snitch," he said. "If you was in my shoes, wouldn't you do the same?"

I asked about Bunnie, a guy up from Philadelphia whom I had grown to like, and who I knew had connections to Big El.

"Yeah, too bad about Bunnie. Look, ain't nothing personal."

Joey handed me a wooden spoon. "Now help me make the spaghetti sauce."

CHAPTER 7

TURNING POINT

THE TRIAL ENDED WITH guilty verdicts for Big El Bynum and Joey "C" and twelve other defendants. I never did find out who subpoenaed me—whether it was the government or the defense—but it didn't matter since I never took the witness stand. Big El drew a forty-year sentence and died in prison. Joey "C" drew sixteen years and was eventually released. I often wondered if Big El thought living like a millionaire for the decade he dealt in drugs was worth the price.

Back at Milan, I began to take a fresh look at my own life. Compared to Big El or even Joey, I didn't have it so bad. I was just a bit player in their drug-dealing game, someone who shammed his way in, someone who thought he was bigger than he really was, someone who wanted the good life but didn't want to bother working for it.

I wondered why some people just go with the flow while others blaze their own trails, why some just march off to war because

They Will Be Victors

Big Brother tells them to while others say, "Hell no, I won't go." I started reading Rollo May and other writers you could take something from, books like *Man's Search for Himself*, and *Man's Search for Meaning* by Victor Frankl, the Austrian psychiatrist who survived the Nazi Death Camps and wrote his book in 1946. I read Erickson and other books by psychiatrists; I read books about crime along with fiction, and biography. One of the books that also impressed me was *The Politics of Heroin in Southeast Asia* by Alfred McCoy. This book outlined the involvement of the CIA and the U.S. government in moving heroin through Southeast Asia, which contributed to the addiction of many of our own soldiers. History, as it is inclined to do, would repeat itself during the Iran-Contra scandal as the sale of illegal drugs and weapons to fund subversive U.S. government operations continued then and probably still does today.

These books helped me refine my thinking, expand my conceptual and social horizons, contemplate the meaning of my existence, and consider how I fit into the big picture. I began to ask myself questions like, "Why am I here?" and "What is my purpose in the world?" With the most basic of Maslow's "deficit needs" being met for me by my institutional surroundings, I was able to catapult through literature toward achieving Maslow's "self-actualization" level.

Rollo May said we pass through five stages as human beings—*innocence*, where as infants we have only physical needs; *rebellion*, where we want freedom but don't understand the responsibility that goes with it; *decision*, where we try to break away from the past and seek our own way in life but still want to rebel; *ordinary*, where we learn responsibility but find it too demanding so seek refuge in conformity; and *creative*, where we face our destiny with courage, no matter what it brings. I'd already passed through the first two stages. Now I was struggling with the third—*decision*.

I asked myself, "Why did I become a cop in the first place? Was it because a cop's uniform gave me power? Or was it because I could make the world a better place?" In his book *Behind the Blue Shield: Police in Urban Society*, which is a sociological inquiry into the workings of police departments, Arthur Neiderhoffer, a former New York cop turned sociology professor and attorney, says that every cop is cynical after five years—cynical about the world in general and about the system that they are forced to work within. In my case it only took a year and a half. Eventually all cops break the law—some in small ways, others in grand fashion—whether it's perjury or physical abuse or something else. They can't win cases if they don't, and that's why they put the meanest, toughest, dirtiest cops in the worst precincts. Yale Kamisar, a law professor at the University of Michigan, observed that: "The police fear—and not without cause—that the public will blame *them* for an increase in crime. Whenever the newspapers carry a sensational headline about the rising national tide of juvenile delinquency, or about some shocking local youth-gang depredation, the question likely to be raised in countless homes is: 'Why don't the police put a stop to it?' But no police force can put a stop to it."[5] The occupational socialization process fosters in the officer a sense of justification in using force and toughness in the performance of his duties, even if that force might be used illegally. My own observations indicate that very few young policemen can resist the urge to adopt an authoritarian, oppressive approach to dealing with would-be perpetrators.

Even though I had Milan to thank for two of my best friends, Pete Walsh and Bill Tilton, I knew that prison life wasn't a career plan that fit with my goals. The sooner I got out the better. To the system I was just a broken machine that needed fixing. More than anything I wanted to be free—not just from prison but from my past. This would be a part of my psyche that would lead to lingering personal pain but ultimately would provide some of my greatest personal satisfaction and self-repair.

I was soon to be unexpectedly presented with a path to reflecting on and contending with my past that would come to be the bedrock of my healing. Two years had gone by since my arrest the night before Christmas Eve 1970. I remembered pacing the cell that cold December night while my wife and my two sons waited for me to come home and put up the Christmas lights. Now I was locked up in a federal prison six hundred miles away—Craig was four and a half and his baby brother Rob was almost three. I wondered if they needed their father as much as I needed them. The answer was self-evident—every child needs a responsible and caring father.

The separation weighed on me like a huge rock. Each day I struggled to put it out of my mind as I plunged into the day's routine—up at 5:30 sharp, in the kitchen at 6 where I cut meat until 11, then to the weight room to work out with Pete, then lunch, back to the weight room, and finally to the prison yard where Bill Tilton and I would exercise our brains discussing everything from politics to Proust. Believe me, it is one thing to do these things by choice and it's another to do them by default. When your world is the size of a large city block and it's surrounded by electrified fences and barbed wires, the thinking man—the restless man—makes the best of it.

When I left the mess hall, a poster by the door caught my eye:
CHRISTMAS MASS
DECEMBER 25, 1972 – 6:00 A.M.
CHAPEL – D BLOCK

I was intrigued—my mother's devotion to the church was seemingly different from what the sign offered—and the next morning I checked it out. When I entered the day room, the Mass had just begun. A prison chaplain who was a Lutheran pastor and a Catholic priest were preparing for the Catholic Mass. The chaplain's assistant, who was serving as an altar boy, and I were the only inmates who were present at the service. There were also about eight or ten civilians from Ann Arbor who were involved in prison ministry. I hadn't been in "church" since my wedding. The Mass began and much to my surprise, the Mass was being said in English—not in Latin. It was the first time that I had heard the Mass being said in my own language. Right before Holy Communion there is the exchange of the peace when we say to each other, "May the peace of the Lord be with you." These visitors smiled at me and one by one shook my hand and hugged me as a part of the exchange of the peace. The physical contact was at once both foreign and affirming. How was I to understand these wonderful people who had chosen to come to this isolated place at 6:00 in the morning to be with me? We proceeded to the table that served as the altar to receive Holy Communion. I hesitated at first, silently questioning my faith and my own self-worth, and then knelt down beside them. As the pastor and priest in turn served the elements, each one placed his hand on my shoulder—it was as if the hand of Christ rested on me reassuring me that my sins would be forgiven. For the first time in my life I felt I had met true Christian people who actively believed the message of Jesus Christ—people who weren't phonies and hypocrites but lived out their faith in real ways. They had come to a prison on a cold Christmas morning to give hope to a lost soul like me. They emulated Jesus himself who went to the edge of a cliff to rescue a lost sheep. For the first time at Milan federal prison, I cried.

If there was ever a turning point in my life that early morning Christmas Mass in 1972 was it. I never did find out the name of the pastor or the priest. But, from that point on, I determined to make the most of the time I had left in prison, however long it might be. And I resolved to develop my spiritual well-being along with my mind and my body—my own personal trinity.

For many others in many ways 1972 was a turning point. I remembered my grandpa Frank Costello telling me how grateful people across Europe were to Americans after we helped them to defeat Adolf Hitler and Nazism; and then we helped them rebuild under the Marshall Plan. But the Vietnam War, that had dragged on for nine years, didn't resonate at home the way World War II had. We had witnessed the Battle of Hue and the Mai Lai massacre and the Kent State University killings. Richard Nixon had just been re-elected, and the Watergate scandal was starting to unfold. If we hadn't lost our innocence as a nation—not that we ever had it—we certainly had lost our standing in the world.

But there was something we hadn't lost that affected me directly. Thanks to Ramsey Clark, who had served as U.S. Attorney General from 1967 to 1969, I was the beneficiary of an increased commitment to the rehabilitation of inmates in many of our federal prisons. Clark's reforms included individual and group prisoner therapy, family therapy, schooling, and vocational testing—all testaments to his personal character and our national commitment to human and civil rights, and the idea that individuals can, in fact, be rehabilitated. I took advantage of all of these. Twice a week a recent graduate of the University of Michigan School of Social Work—his name was Mark Glesener—would drive down from Ann Arbor to conduct group therapy for the inmates. He was also my caseworker. Every so often he would be joined by his professor, Chuck Wolfson, who conducted family therapy sessions for inmates and their spouses to help them re-adjust to life on the outside. Meanwhile, I had arranged for my wife and sons to move from her mother's place in Florida to an apartment in Ann Arbor so she could attend Professor Wolfson's therapy sessions with me.

Wolfson had grown up in New York and his father had been a cop, and this shared context would lend itself to fruitful dialogue and promote meaningful progress in my life. He had earned a Master's Degree in Social Work at Wayne State University in Detroit and had risen to full professor at the University of Michigan where he headed the criminal justice program. Mark Glesener was Wolfson's protégé and had just earned his M.S.W. degree specializing in group treatment methodology. Glesener's master's thesis was *The Utilization of the Ex-offender as a Para-professional in Group Therapy*.

Before long Wolfson and Glesener became my role models. I began to think of going into the same line of work. If I couldn't make the world a better place as a cop, maybe I could do it as a social worker. I felt I had found a path that would answer the question of my purpose in the world.

More and more, I looked ahead to the day when I would be out of prison. When I wasn't cutting meat in the kitchen or attending therapy sessions, I learned to be a scholar. Reading opened up a whole new world for me. I devoured books in prison and I taught and encouraged other inmates to read. I soaked up history, biography and fiction like a sponge. I read everything from Hemingway and Faulkner to Freud and Carl Jung. I read every issue of *Newsweek*, *Time* and *U.S. News and World Report* that I could get my hands on. If it was Pete Walsh who motivated me in the weight room to build up my body, it was Bill Tilton who motivated me in the library to read and stretch my mind. He had me read the seminal *The Pentagon Papers* after Daniel Ellsberg came to visit him. I remember sitting in front of a black-and-white television in the day room of D Block watching our POWs step off the plane onto the tarmac on their way home and thinking, "Bill, you were right all along about Vietnam." It wasn't until January 1973 after nearly sixty-thousand American deaths and two million Vietnamese deaths, that a cease-fire had finally been declared. Bill Tilton's experience and perspective helped me to recognize and appreciate the social justice implications involved in the Vietnam War.

It was an unfair war that was bleeding United States government resources—resources that should have been going toward rehabilitating deteriorated urban centers and supporting the poor and under-served in these communities—communities that I was soon to become a part of.

Milan's Warden Hughes was a decent and fair-minded man of medium-height, balding, and well-dressed. He had a habit of looking over the glasses perched on the end of his nose. He was the perfect champion for the innovative approach to prisoner rehabilitation that had been implemented at the facility. He took a personal interest in my situation, and appreciated my ability to manage the meat-cutting program and teach other men the techniques of meat cutting. He also understood my circumstance and, as a result, he personally accompanied me to my parole hearing—a step that, to my knowledge, was very unusual for him. His presence was instrumental, and I will forever be indebted to him for this selfless act. The parole officer, a consummate bureaucrat, was brief and blunt in his remarks. His demeanor belied a sense that Hughes had perhaps taken the liberty of advocating for me with the parole board before the hearing. In essence, he lectured me that I had ruined my life forever. Then he said, "Oh, and by the way, you are not to reside in the state of New York." My release date was scheduled for two months down the line.

They Will Be Victors

With a heartfelt promise to stay out of trouble, I bid the parole board that approved my release the fondest of farewells. It was into this harsh and often senseless reality that I would be released from prison two months later. Milan's shadow would fade into my past forever. I had to acclimate myself to a reality that didn't even offer the comfort of geographic familiarity. Michigan might as well have been Madrid. In June the warden put me on a work release assignment with an inmate named Donald Story. I called him "Big Don" with good reason, although he was as gentle as a puppy toward me. When I asked Big Don what he was in for, he chuckled, "Well, it's like this. I needed some money so I went into a bank. When I finished my transaction I came out. The cops didn't approve of the withdrawal."

Every day for the next two months a guard would drive Donald and me to Tecumseh, a town near Milan, where we worked side-by-side at the Budd Wheel Company feeding metal rims into a pressing machine. After each day, our hands would be bloody from handling the sharp-edged rims. We worked so hard that on day four, the union steward came by and cautioned us about working too hard. We had to slow down our production so as not to "set the bar" too high for the others. We were in great shape and happy to be working in the real world. It was attitudes like the steward's that would ultimately lead to the demise of the competitive advantage that the American automobile industry had enjoyed through the early 1970s.

A few days before I got paroled, I encouraged Big Don to get in touch with me after he got out of the joint. I was paroled on August 23, 1973. Over the years Big Don pulled off a number of similar "transactions," earning him several more years in the slammer. I wouldn't hear from Big Don again until 1999, when he got out for good and resolved to turn his life around. He was finally able to make good on his promise to contact me after his release. Life had changed a lot since last we spoke. I was in a position to offer him a job and I did so without hesitation.

But back in 1973 things were still in a formative stage where my life was concerned. What was past was, at least for the time being, left in the past; and my energy was being directed to what was to come. As Rollo May would put it, it was time to be *creative*; I knew I had to face my destiny with courage no matter what the future held.

PART TWO

STARTING OVER

"A responsible person does that which gives him a feeling of self-worth and a feeling that he is worthwhile to others. He is motivated to strive and perhaps endure privation to attain self-worth."

William Glasser, M.D., *Reality Therapy*

CHAPTER 8

UNDERSTANDING DREAMS

THEY TELL YOU SOMETHING when you leave the joint: *Don't look back*. For the first time since my trial I could ride in a car unshackled by either chains or supervision. More than that, for the first time since my trial I could hold my younger son Rob on my lap (he was three-years-old) without a prison guard hovering over us. The significance of physical touch in a child's development is well-documented. The dehumanization of imprisonment is multifaceted and greatly transcends simple freedom of choice. Prison is a place of sensory deprivation. The importance of physical touch to your humanity doesn't stop at childhood. Holding my child was the beginning of my rebirth as a human being.

My wife pointed the car out of the prison parking lot. Craig, now five, sat in the back seat. I wondered what he and his brother made of their father sitting in front next to their mother. This was a man whose face they had seen only through the glass pane. This stranger would now be competing for their mother's attention, setting rules without having earned the right to do so, and intruding on their lives.

Don't look back, they say. But at that moment the impulse was too powerful. Time is the most precious resource we have. It can't be manufactured or synthesized, you can't invest what you have to get more, and you have neither control over its duration nor forewarning of its expiration. But the choices each of us makes will directly impact how our time here on earth will be spent. For two-and-a-half years my wife had stood by me, raising those boys while she worked as a secretary, moving six hundred miles from what she and they knew as home so she would be closer to me in prison and could attend Professor Wolfson's therapy sessions. Her participation as a willing recipient of my ill-gotten gains made her participation in the therapy process understandable and, at a moral level, compulsory. As I thought about these things, it was all I could do to choke back tears.

All the while as we headed up Highway U.S. 23 to Ann Arbor my wife was silent. She hadn't spoken a word since we left the prison parking lot. Finally she said, "Bobby, what are you going to do now?" Her eyes remained fixed on the road.

It was a question I had been thinking about for a long time. I had read, I had learned, I had found some inspiration. I wanted to blurt out, "Become a social worker and help troubled kids stay out of jail," but even to me the idea sounded desperate, pathetic, and ridiculous. "And just how do you expect to do that?" she would say. "Don't you have to go to college first? And how are you going to support your family in the meantime? I've been doing it for two-and-a-half years. Now it's your turn."

I imagined her saying these things, and I understood why she'd be well within her right to doubt and question me, so I replied simply, "Go back to meat cutting, I guess." It was something I knew how to do, and it would pay the bills. It was the Plan B that circumstances required before I could begin to work on Plan A.

Within a few days I landed a meat cutting job in Saline, a town near Ann Arbor. It didn't take me too long to save enough money to make a down payment on a used Dodge Dart. The 1973 oil crisis was at its apex and the price of gas was "soaring" to fifty-five cents a gallon. When the oil crisis eased and I could afford a longer commute, I took another meat cutting job—this one was forty miles away at Detroit's Eastern Market. My pay was about $250 a week—not bad for an ex-con a few months out. A lot of things had changed while I was locked up, but one thing that remained constant was Mafia control over the meat business—in Detroit as it was in New York.

Their willingness to hire me was exposed as more than pure altruism when one of the crew at the market approached me and said, "Bobby, we did a little homework and we were wonderin' if you might wanna run some numbers for us?" Some guys go to the joint but when they get out, they decide that the high lifestyle is worth paying the price so they return to a life of crime. But, that wasn't me! I wasn't even inclined to give the appearance of any interest. I also knew the inquiry wasn't a question likely to go unrepeated. I uttered the words, "I quit." And I wondered where the words had come from. The ride home was sobering, but it felt more like a step forward than a step back. However, not everybody saw it that way.

When I got home and told my wife what had happened, her reaction was—well—practical. "You what?!" she screamed.

"I quit my job," I said.

"Are you crazy? What are we going to live on?"

"I don't know, but I was faced with getting back into what I just paid a heavy price for being part of in the first place. I need to move on with my life. We need to move on with OUR lives."

"Well then I'm moving out, because I'm not supporting you and the boys both."

"You know something?" I said, without considering the consequences of what I was about to tell her. "It really doesn't matter, because I'm not going to make it on the outside if I don't do what I need to do. I'm smart, I learned things in prison that I didn't know before, and I'm going back to school whether you like it or not, because I know what I want to do, and I know that's the only path to real success for me or anybody."

They Will Be Victors

My wife was incredulous. "But you can't be serious about social work!"

"I *am*. Maybe more serious about it than anything I can think of in my recent past."

"How much does a social worker make?" She asked.

"The money isn't important. Working with kids, keeping them out of jail, and knowing that I'm doing what I really was put on earth to do—that's what I really want to do."

"What about your own kids?" she replied.

"My own kids? Who do you think I'm thinking about? This isn't about me alone! Don't you understand dreams? God has a plan for everybody, and I swear as I'm standing here that this is the path I have to take. It's gonna lead us all to a better place as a family." I persisted.

"How can you dream of a job that pays less than the one you've got? Look, I'm tired of working as a secretary and raising the boys myself—they hardly know you. It's time you pick up the slack. If you don't, it's over between us!"

I knew our marriage was in trouble, but I had to make a choice. I could either get my job back at the Eastern Market and risk returning to a life of crime or I could go to school and pursue my dream.

The next day I called Mark Glesener, who had been my therapist at Milan. When I told him what happened, he said, "Bob come to my office and let's talk."

A few days later I pulled up to the Frieze Building on State Street which housed the University of Michigan School of Social Work. Mark was waiting for me along with Professor Chuck Wolfson.

"Sorry to hear about your marital troubles," Wolfson said after we exchanged greetings. "We'll support you in whatever way we can." He nodded to Mark, who took over the conversation.

"Bob, if you're serious about social work, we figured out how you can get your M.S.W. degree in five years while you continue to work full-time."

"Where?" I asked.

"Huron Residential Services here in Ann Arbor," he said.

"They have a group home on Vaughn Street with eight kids, all adolescent boys. They need someone to look after them on the 3 to 11 p.m. shift."

"Mark and I agreed to recommend you for the job," Wolfson said.

My feelings of appreciation and hope were tempered by a self-esteem that was still in the post-prison rebuilding phase. "But I have no experience."

"You'll learn on the job," he said confidently. The stigma of prison obviously didn't play much in Chuck's value system. I took comfort in this.

"How much does it pay?"

Wolfson looked at Mark who replied, "Seven thousand a year."

I did a quick mental calculation. It came to $135 a week, about half of what I had been making at the Eastern Market. But it put me light years ahead of where I was relative to achieving my dream.

"I'll take it," I said.

"That's not all," Mark said, nodding to Professor Wolfson who explained the rest of the plan.

"If you keep your grades up, we'll see to it that you get into the School of Social Work after three years. We know you can do it because you got straight A's in all of the courses you took while at Milan." Thanks to Ramsey Clark's philosophy which still permeated the federal prison system, I was able to earn ten college credits from Washtenaw Community College and Eastern Michigan University. My gratitude for this opportunity would become evident in years to come.

"You mean for a master's degree?"

"Exactly," he said, "We think you can do it. You have the real world experience plus the academic ability."

"So when do I start?" I asked somewhat incredulously but no less enthusiastically.

"First you need to finish your undergraduate work," Wolfson said. "They just hired a new professor at Eastern Michigan University, Don Loppnow, whose field is sociology and criminology. He's teaching a course on working with adolescents. It will help you at Vaughn House." Loppnow would come to serve as the university's Provost and Acting President in later years.

Several days later, with the facilitation of Wolfson and Glesener, I met with the Associate Executive Director at Family Group Homes, Inc., John Yablonky. The meeting was cordial but appropriately probing. John inquired about my skills, my attitude, and my experience. The groundwork that Chuck and Mark had laid, coupled with John's sensitivity, made the interview meaningful but not overly interrogatory. John concluded the interview with an unexpected welcome to Vaughn House.

"You start next week on the 3 o'clock shift—we're short-staffed." John and I would remain colleagues for the next thirty-five years (and counting).

Having become gainfully employed—in no small part due to my mentors' recommendations—I proceeded to enroll in Professor Loppnow's classes. It is interesting to note that I later was to become his teaching assistant. My path was set. Apparently and unfortunately, so was my wife's. When I told her the news, her response was, "Well then, I'm filing for a divorce." I passed the remark off as an angry outburst. Sooner or later, I told myself, she would come around. With the investment she had made to stay close during my incarceration, I couldn't fathom how she would deny me the opportunity to be a father to my sons and deny them the opportunity to get to really know me.

Bill Tilton, in town for a concert, came to my house and tried to persuade my wife that the path I had set was the right one for all involved. "Bob needs to go to school or you'll be visiting him again behind a glass pane." Bill had long told me that I was as smart or smarter than anyone he'd met in college and that's the route I should take, not going back to simple meat cutting, the limits of which might easily tempt one to return to crime for extra income. Where Patty was concerned, his comments fell on deaf ears. But Bill and I continued to talk—he impressed upon me that I had no other choice. Paroled from Milan just ahead of me, Bill was painting houses back home in Minneapolis before starting law school in the fall—four years behind schedule. Despite the delay, Bill would come to be the first ex-offender to be admitted to the Bar in Minnesota—a move facilitated by his former prosecutor, now a federal judge, who had come to sympathize with Bill's perspective on the travesty that the Vietnam War had come to represent.

In the summer of 1974, I visited Bill and stayed at his mother's house near the St. Croix River. We had a reunion of sorts over the Fourth of July which included Pete Walsh, "Captain" Jim Meyers, and a lot of Bill's activist friends from St. Paul/Minneapolis. I used to run for exercise and also as a way of clearing my brain. I took a run during the visit to Bill's and recall thinking, "This is Shangri-La." The weekend served as the perfect launching pad from which to begin what would become my new career. Captain Jim's path had not changed quite as dramatically as mine had. We found out much later that his trip to Minnesota had been financed by an "unauthorized withdrawal" from a bank back in Michigan.

When I got back to Ann Arbor, I was refreshed and ready to begin. I pulled my Dodge Dart into the driveway at Vaughn House. My supervisor introduced me to the eight residents, all boys, including a fifteen-year-old black kid named "Red" because he had red hair and a hot temper, and sixteen-year-old Harold, the most eager-to-please of the group. After the introductions, my supervisor turned to me and said, "See ya—good luck," leaving me to fend for myself. That was the sum of my orientation, but my duties were clear enough: cook dinner and keep the kids occupied.

Most of the kids, suspicious of me at first, stood back and watched while I took Harold on in a one-on-one basketball game in the driveway. Gradually the other kids—Big Ron, Terrence, Terry, Tony, and Tavy—joined in while Charles (who was developmentally disabled) cheered from the sideline.

When it came time for dinner, I prepared roast pork with all the trimmings—at least my meat cutting experience was useful. I told myself it was probably the best meal these kids had had since coming to Vaughn House.

After dinner I expected the boys to clean up, but before I knew it they had all left the house leaving me with a pile of dirty dishes. The program rules specified a 10 o'clock curfew. Naively, I figured they would clean up when they returned. But as soon as they returned, they all bounded up the stairs and bedded down for the night. I stood there looking back and forth between the empty staircase and the sink overflowing with dishes.

When my relief worker, a bespectacled U-M nursing student named Stan Slaughter, showed up for the midnight shift, there were no kids and plenty of dirty dishes. Stan looked at me, his eyes bulging through his thick glasses, and snarled, "Look, man, I'm not taking my shift till you get rid of those damn dishes!"

"But all the kids took off," I said.

"Well, if you can't get them to do the dishes, you'll have to do them yourself. I'm not taking my shift until you do." Stan popped a beer and disappeared into the next room with his textbook and began studying.

It was half past midnight when I finished the dishes, and then I sat down with Stan and we talked about the job. He was full of information. He loved working the midnight shift even though he was a half hour late most of the time. He gave me some practical advice. Establish relationships, foster trust, play ball with them in the backyard, and above all don't let 'em out of your sight until they do the dishes!

When I got into the car and headed home, I asked myself, "What was I getting into? Did I make the right decision? Was I really cut out for this kind of work?"

The next morning I called Chuck Wolfson and asked for his advice.

He, too, had some sound advice. "You've gotta offer them something that will serve as a reward—you have to give them incentives," he said. "Have you read the book, *Positive Peer Culture?*"

"No," I said.

"It just came out. It's by a couple of social workers named Harry Vorrath and Larry Brendtro. It has some good stuff in it that will help you."

Understanding Dreams

Later that morning, on my way to Professor Loppnow's class, I picked up a copy. If nothing else, I figured it would be useful for his class. As I began to read, I realized the book was about more than giving kids incentives. It described how kids develop self-control and become sensitive to people around them. It explained how with proper guidance they can become stronger individuals, not by being forced to comply with rules and regulations, but by developing skills to solve their problems. It talked about the importance of peer influence as a motivator for behavior. It was a notion I was all too familiar with in the negative and one that held a sense of promise—both for my young charges and for me personally—that really resonated with me.

It took me a few days to finish the book. Meanwhile, back at Vaughn House my self-inflicted dishwashing detail was quickly wearing thin. After dinner on the third night, I was mentally prepared to apply my first formative experiment from the book.

"Look," I said to the kids before they ran off, "I got a quarter in my hand, see?" I held it up between my thumb and forefinger like a magician. "This will go to the first one who volunteers to do the dishes." Today a quarter might buy you ten minutes at a parking meter; back then it bought you a pack of cigarettes.

And like magic, Harold's hand shot up.

"You got it," I said.

"Yes!" he shouted, and he jumped up and gave me a high-five.

During my career in social work with troubled youth, I would find myself the recipient of physical assaults on many occasions. I have been kicked, punched, scratched, and even spat on—and I never retaliated. This is in sharp contrast to what I would have done as a policeman. By virtue of their position and training, police are indoctrinated to believe that they have the authority to use physical force—even severe assaultive force—to maintain authority. Police historically used night-sticks, flashlights, or other weapons and forms of violence to exercise their authority. They often find themselves in situations where the threat is vague, concealed, or indeterminate. A social worker or a child care worker, by virtue of their inherent knowledge of the cases they encounter, and, in keeping with their training and code of ethics, could never get away with this inappropriate response. It is the social worker's job to use these events as teachable moments for demonstrating to youth that problems are best solved not by physical force but by communication, respect, responsibility, and negotiation. This element of my career would come to be perhaps the most supremely satisfying—that I could help young people and maintain order with my wits and my compassion, rather than with the proverbial stick.

And this simple victory with the kids emboldened me, and I started holding group meetings in which I let the kids sound off about everything from curfews to TV time. It was my first meager attempt at group therapy. I had a long way to go before I could match the skills of my mentors, but at least it was a start. I had made the most important decision of my life—to help kids in trouble get back on their feet. However, I still had many unanswered questions about myself, about social work, and about the future.

CHAPTER 9

THE RIGHT CHOICE

GLASSER TALKS ABOUT CHOICES – how being free means being responsible and how being responsible means making the right choices. Out of his own experience working with delinquent youth, he developed a new approach, *Reality Therapy*. It is characterized by a direct personal approach that requires the youth to confront his behavior and be challenged to change. It insists that the youth accept personal responsibility for moral choices and reject excuse-making.

In prison everything you do is monitored, structured, and controlled. The visible limits of the facility burrow deep below your own physical manifestation. Every sense is stifled by the sameness of every day. The smells are the same stale, institutional potpourri of feces, urine, body odor, and bleach. The absence of color in the environment defines the emptiness a thinking man confronts. The sounds are repetitive and the responses border on involuntary. Every transition in your day—from getting up at 5:30 to lights out at 10—is signaled by a bell or loudspeaker that ultimately elicits a Pavlovian act. There are no decisions—none required, none desired.

I think it may have been John Rayoa who coined this saying, "Experience is the hardest teacher—he gives the test first, and the lesson later." Responsibility didn't figure in my early choices and my freedom was something I took for granted. Prison made the connection between choices and responsibility incontrovertible. And it took freedom from some kind of philosophical theory to the rarest and most exquisite human treasure.

Against my wife's wishes I had taken the job at Vaughn House so I could pursue my dream. But the question still gnawed at me, "Had I made the right choice?"

Pete Walsh, my friend and weight-lifting partner from Milan, had made the same choice I did—to pursue a career in social work. After his parole which came about the same time as Bill Tilton's, Pete got his own on-the-job training as a bus driver for the Washtenaw County Juvenile Detention Center while taking classes at Washtenaw Community College.

My wife moved out, I moved in with Pete, and life moved slowly forward. The divorce decreed that she had custody of our two sons and I had weekend visitation rights. Often I would take the boys over to Vaughn House to hang out with the older kids. The visits made Craig, now six, feel like a grown-up. "Daddy, when can we go back?" he'd ask. So back we would go the following weekend to hang out, throw the basketball around, or just watch TV.

On the first anniversary of my parole, I couldn't imagine anyone savoring freedom more than I did—a feeling accentuated by the time spent with my sons over the last several months, although our time together was limited. The slow but steady progress at Vaughn house convinced me that, all things considered, I had made the right choice. But making the right choice is frequently not the path of least resistance. And staying the course can be harder than anything you had considered when the choice was first made. I returned the boys to their mother on that first anniversary day, and was unexpectedly confronted with just how real the lingering and unforeseen effects of decisions are. "Bobby," she said, sweeping the boys inside the door. "There's something I need to tell you." I tried to read her during that brief pause.

The Right Choice

"I'm moving to San Diego and taking the boys with me." It sounded as distant and impersonal as someone announcing they were running up to the store for some milk and eggs. I was incredulous. I uttered something helpless and desperate, and Patty responded with her own brand of incredulity, dumbfounded at how I could have expected anything different to transpire. She closed the door and, as I turned away, all of my instincts were screaming to turn back, but my mind acknowledged the futility of my situation.

On Labor Day they left in her car. I hadn't cried such bitter tears since my father died. My mind raced with the small details of her decision—"Why San Diego? Was it because she couldn't stand another Michigan winter? Was it to put distance between us? Was it because she was afraid of me or afraid of the potential conflicts that might coincide with my continuing presence in my sons' lives? Was it because she had found someone else? In hindsight my perseveration was an exercise in self-distraction, and it was ultimately irrelevant—no answer would suffice. I resigned myself to this most brutal of punishments—even in prison I had had some level of contact with my boys—and vowed to myself that the day would come when we would once again connect as father and sons.

The finality of my wife's decision drove home the irreversibility of my own chosen path. I had dedicated my life to social work, and had come to terms with all the questionable choices and attendant consequences that had led up to this point. I had a sense that my understanding of my purpose in this world was clearer now that it had ever been before.

I plunged back into Professor Loppnow's classes and persuaded him to sponsor an independent study opportunity for me at the W. J. Maxey Boys Training School, a large juvenile correctional facility built in the 1960s and operated by the Michigan Department of Human Services on a site south of Brighton, Michigan. Loppnow himself had worked as a prison counselor before becoming a college professor. His father, a Moravian bishop, had instilled in him the value of looking out for other people. I reflected on this and wondered if my mother in her own peculiar way had instilled the same value in me. After recruiting a group of residents from the facility, I introduced them to group therapy and applied more of the conceptual constructs from *Positive Peer Culture* to my work with these young men.

At the end of my junior year at Eastern Michigan University—just as my mentors Glesener and Wolfson had predicted (and in no small part facilitated)—I was accepted into the University of Michigan School of Social Work. I was the first student to enter their graduate program without previously having earned a bachelor's degree.

I started at the School of Social Work in September 1976 with Chuck Wolfson serving as my graduate advisor. Many people have helped me through the years in many different ways, but I owe a unique and profound debt of gratitude to Chuck Wolfson for his role in setting me on my career path.

"Bob," he said, after calling me into his office the first day of the new term. "I've arranged a field placement for you while you work on your master's."

"Where?" I asked.

"Before I tell you, does the name Jim Minder ring a bell?"

"Minder...Minder...Jim Minder," I muttered, trying to recall where I had heard the name.

"This might refresh your memory." Wolfson pulled a newspaper clipping out of a manila folder and handed it to me. The headline read, *U-M Genius Can't Stay Out of Jail*. It described how Jim Minder, while a University of Michigan student, paid his way through school by robbing banks.

"What's this from?" I asked.

"The *Detroit Free Press*, fourteen years ago," Wolfson said. "But he turned his life around. When he was in prison, he started taking correspondence courses. That's how I got to know him. I told him he should use his talents and intelligence to do something constructive."

This was a refrain that I was all too familiar with and that over time I had become more comfortable ascribing to myself.

Wolfson continued. "After his release, he got a master's degree in social work—that was in '71, five years ago." Then he added with a sly smile, "I was his advisor."

"Oh, I get it," I said. "You're on a personal mission to turn ex-cons into social work wunderkinds."

"Well," he said, his tongue rolling in his cheek, "you're only the second one, so don't think you're anything too special."

We both had a hearty laugh.

"Anyway," he continued, "after Jim finished his master's degree, he went to work for a Catholic nonprofit agency, Boysville of Michigan. Now he's the associate executive director, and he needs a youth treatment specialist at one of his group homes. I think you'd be a perfect fit."

"Where is it?" I pressed.

"Ecorse."

"Ecorse! What an ugly name."

"Wait till you see the town."

The next day I drove out. Ecorse was just as Wolfson described it. Located downriver from Detroit, it consisted of drab single story bungalows surrounded by factories and warehouses. Even on a sunny day the town looked gray. When I turned off Jefferson onto Outer Drive, I had no trouble spotting the building—a 1920s era red-brick two-story building with a Gothic arched entrance. It didn't look anything like Vaughn House, let alone a building that belonged in the neighborhood. A makeshift sign out front proclaimed its function:

XAVIER CENTER
RESIDENTIAL HOME FOR BOYS
A SERVICE OF BOYSVILLE OF MICHIGAN

"This used to be a Catholic convent," Minder explained after we made our introductions. "I got Boysville to lease it from the Archdiocese of Detroit. I figured why not put it to good use. It had the room we needed and the price was right."

Minder didn't strike me as a bank robber—rehabilitated or otherwise. What I saw was a man in his mid-forties, gentle, cerebral, affable, and totally at peace with himself.

"You know how I got here," he said. It was more a statement than a question.

"Well, Chuck Wolfson filled me in."

"I'm sure he didn't tell you everything. He's a good man—Wolfson. But let me tell you what you need to know about me before we work together. I don't want there to be any surprises."

Jim Minder proceeded to tell me his life story—how his parents divorced when he was three, how his mother couldn't afford to raise him and sent him to live with his eighty-year-old grandmother in Massachusetts. When she died, he got shunted around from relative to relative, and when he was in high school, he started hot-wiring cars and stealing food off grocery shelves. By the time he started college—a miracle in itself—he had been arrested three times. When his father, who eventually took him in, went to work for Ford Motor Company in Dearborn, Minder transferred to the University of Michigan. It was around that time, he said, that he bought his first gun, a Smith & Wesson .38 revolver, and he began his robbing spree. During his holdups, he'd wear a silk stocking over his head and have to reach inside it to straighten his glasses.

"You see too many movies where the robbers go in screaming and yelling," he said. "I would just quietly tell them it was a robbery and show them my gun, and that was it."

Jim's idea at first was to rob a bank or two and then retire. But when he found out how easy it was, he kept on going. Eventually the law caught up with him and retired him to the State Reformatory at Ionia for ten years where he joined the debate team. In 1962, during a debate against a team from the University of Michigan, he escaped, and in so doing earned another five years in prison.

Finally in the late 1960s, he resolved to give up his self-destructive ways. "I told myself, this is ridiculous—the person getting beat up is me." He got the University of Michigan to count his correspondence credits toward a bachelor's degree. In 1969, upon his release from prison, he had earned a bachelor's degree in sociology and was ready to start work on his master's at the U-M School of Social Work. "That's when Chuck Wolfson entered the picture," he said. "I tell you these things about me because he told me a few things about you."

Compared to Minder, I was nothing—just small potatoes with my drug conspiracy conviction and two-and-a-half years in the joint. He was a latter-day Dillinger and had done fifteen years. The thought inspired me—if he could make it on the outside so could I. It dawned on me that Wolfson's matching me up with Minder for my field placement was calculated, brilliant, and not entirely without risk to Wolfson's reputation. His confidence and courage would prove to be well-founded.

Affecting a confidential tone, Minder cupped his hand under my elbow and winked, "It takes two rehabilitated crooks to trust each other—real-life honor among thieves. Come on, I'll show you around."

I plunged into my field placement with a passion. No father and son could have connected like Jim Minder and I did. I became his protégé in practical terms while I continued to follow Professor Wolfson's academic lead. I suspect he took a great deal of pride in his two "rehab projects" hitting it off so well. Not only did Minder have a way of relating to juvenile offenders—after all he had been one himself—but he had a gift of entrepreneurship that one wouldn't readily expect of someone who had been locked up for fifteen years. Xavier House was only one of three Catholic convents he had converted into group homes. He had opened two others—one in Saginaw and one in Alpena.

But for reasons not entirely clear to me, the powers-that-be at Boysville started dropping hints they wanted him to leave. I suspect that they viewed his entrepreneurial zeal as a threat to their conservative, religiously-driven approach to their program operations. Therefore, Minder's days at Boysville were numbered.

In January, four months after I started my field placement with him, Minder resigned and started his own agency, now known as Spectrum Human Services. Like Boysville, its mission was to help wayward kids get back on track, but his clients included girls as well as boys. I knew Jim was leaving—he had told me before Christmas break about his plans. He wanted me to follow him to Spectrum, but my relative inexperience led me to conclude that stability was a better choice for me. He had managed to obtain a license from the State of Michigan to operate group homes without disclosing his criminal history. "If you're clean for five years, you're off the hook," he said. "I've been clean for ten—ever since I served my time for cutting out on the debate team at Ionia."

Then he added, "Remember the name Harold Gazan. He's the one in Lansing responsible for the regulation of child welfare and adult foster care facilities in the state; it's his staff that licensed me. A good man, Gazan. He might help *you* some day." These words would prove to be prophetic.

There was a rub to Jim's pursuits. Although he had a license to operate group homes, he didn't have a contract from the state, and without a contract from the state he had no revenue coming in. "Any day now the contract should be approved," he kept saying. Within a year, Jim had persuaded me to follow him to Spectrum Human Services and to become a group leader at St. Bridget's in Detroit (a converted convent), where I worked with girls and boys. My culinary background also left me in charge of all the cooking. I continued to learn under Minder, but came to question whether it was worth the risk. Weeks passed...then a month...and then another month. Still no contract, which meant I didn't get paid. To complicate matters, although I was in graduate school, I lacked a bachelor's degree, which limited my ability to get promoted.

When the third and fourth months passed without a contract, I finally went into Minder's office and said, "Jim, I can't stay unless you pay me. Huron Residential Services wants me back in Ann Arbor to run Vaughn House. It's a step up from what I did there before, and they offered me a nice increase in pay." I stayed with Minder through the spring semester and then assumed my new responsibilities at Vaughn House. Minder had hired Roger Swaninger, Felton Rogers, and me at the same time. Roger was hired to be the program director, and he would ultimately become the Chief Executive Officer of Spectrum Human Services.

As a footnote, Jim Minder did ultimately pay me once he received his money from the state of Michigan. We would remain friends and colleagues throughout our careers.

CHAPTER 10

THINKING OUTSIDE THE BOX

IT DIDN'T HIT ME UNTIL after I left Jim Minder's office how brief a time we had worked together—only eight months. But in those eight months I had learned the *business* of social work—the risks and rewards of starting up an enterprise, the pride of entrepreneurship, the satisfaction of putting your own touch on helping kids.

Apart from how to run a business, I still had a lot to learn about the *clinical* side of social work. Every day I spent on the job, every hour I spent in class, every book I read in my field—from B.F. Skinner's *Science and Behaviorism* to William Glasser's *Reality Therapy*—brought me closer to realizing my dream. Every day I looked for ways to help disadvantaged and delinquent kids get a second chance. I kept asking myself, "What worked? What didn't work? What could be improved?"

When I returned to Vaughn House in May—this time as house supervisor—I still had a year to go on my master's degree. Yablonky, who was still serving as associate executive director, paid me $10,000

They Will Be Victors

a year—not bad for a full-time student—and agreed to let me try some new ideas. One of them was a point system for rewarding positive behavior. The idea came in part from a course on behavior modification I had taken from Professor Edwin Thomas, plus some adaptations of various principles I had learned from my reading of B.F. Skinner, and lastly from my working with the kids at St. Bridget's for Jim Minder where I was able to test and refine the point-system concept.

My point system was based on the premise that behavior is learned through both positive and negative reinforcements, an idea which forms the foundation of behavior modification. Positive reinforcers might include tangible items such as money and snack foods, along with intangibles like praise or providing the youth with certain privileges or increased personal status. Negative reinforcers (such as rules) serve to encourage positive behaviors. The reminder that a certain behavior is not accepted and if continued or repeated will result in a loss of a specified privilege is a negative reinforcer. The point system is a powerful means of modifying behavior because it uses both positive (rewarding of points) and negative (the removal of points) reinforcers based on specified standards of behavior. Punishment (such as the loss of certain privileges) occurs when rules are violated. The use of both positive and negative consequences must be handled within a well thought-through structure that is openly and clearly shared with the youth so that they understand ahead of time what the results or consequences are. Fairness along with care and concern must predominate in the use of such a program and staff need to be carefully monitored to ensure the integrity and the consistent application of the system. Whenever a negative reinforcer is used such as taking points or privileges away from a youth, it is very important that the staff person at that moment provide the youth with a clear understanding of the reason for the action being taken. I made sure that I had the youth's attention—that he was making eye contact with me. I would first identify the specific behavior that required me to take points away and then briefly explain how he could find his way back. The development of an effective point/level system substantially reduces the temptation for staff to use abusive, informal, or unauthorized means of controlling maladaptive behaviors.

I had observed among the boys and girls I worked with during my six months at St. Bridget's that positive reinforcement not only made youth feel better about themselves, but they got along better with their peers and with adults.

It didn't take an Einstein to figure that out; nevertheless, it took tons of research by B. F. Skinner and others to convince the experts that certain principles of behavior modification were powerful social work tools in working with troubled youth. For me it was a matter of common sense. The challenge was how to apply common sense to modifying adolescent mal-behavior. So I developed my point system.

Although some of the youth that were at Vaughn House during my prior employment were grown and gone and a few new kids had moved in, most of the kids I had worked with before were still there—Big Ron, Terrence, Charles, Cliff, Tony Sablowski, and Red—who let me know in no uncertain terms that since he was eighteen now he wanted out. My first day back it was obvious there was no more structure now at Vaughn House than there had been before. Nor had anything been done clinically—either through group therapy or individual therapy—to help the kids adjust to life on the outside. The result was nothing short of chaos.

I remembered my first day at Vaughn House three years ago when I tried to get everyone to like me so I could form positive relationships with them. I also recalled that they all ditched me after dinner and left me to clean up, but then after studying about behavior modification—I dangled a quarter at the dinner table to entice one of them to wash the dishes. But now I was three years older and wiser, and I had a sure-fire plan that would get them to do what I wanted.

"Look," I said, calling my first group meeting to order, "there are going to be some changes around here."

"Oh, jeez!" I heard Red mutter to the kid sitting next to him.

"Listen up," I said. "I have a poster here that's going up on the wall. I'm going to list seven things on it that I want you to do every

day." I held the poster up. "Number one." Below the heading, *Target Behaviors*, I wrote:
1. Wake-up, 1-5 points.
"You all wake up in the morning, right? At least you're supposed to," I said.

"Charlie lays there and plays with himself," Terrence broke in, punching Charlie's shoulder. Charlie protested over the teasing of the group.

"From now on its everybody up at 7:15," I said, "except on weekends—then it's up at 9:00."

"Shit, no way," Red muttered.

"What the hell do you mean, *1-5 points?*" Big Ron asked.

"I'll get to that in a minute." I turned back to the poster and wrote:
2. Appearance, 1-5 points.
"Appearance? Big deal! When's the last time Cliff got a haircut?" Terrence said. "I'm not even sure it's him under that shag."

Next I wrote:
3. Room, 1-5 points.
Now it was Cliff's turn. "Have you seen Terrence's room? It looks like the city dump."

Between the kids' grumbles and wisecracks, I listed the rest of my *Target Behaviors* along with the points I assigned to each one:
4. School attendance, 1-20 points.
5. Lights out, 1-5 points.
6. Chores, 1-7 points (3½ for morning, 3½ for afternoon)
7. Rules, 1-5 points.

"Now, about the points," I said, indicating the first item on the list. "Take *Wake-up*. The person on morning shift will call you once. If you get right up and show up for breakfast on time looking clean and mean, you get five points."

"What if you're late?" Tony asked. It was the first time he had spoken up.

"For every minute you're late, you get a point taken away," I said.

"What are the points for?"

"Good question, Tony. You can use them to buy things at the canteen like a candy bar for twenty points or a Coke for forty-five."

"A Colt .45?" Terrence shot back.

"I said a Coke, Terrence. Or it can be a Pepsi or 7-Up—forty-five points. But no Colt .45, sorry." I explained to the kids how they could collect points to buy more expensive things like sneakers and rock concert tickets. Each item purchased required a specific number of points.

"Look at this graph, Tony." I pulled out another poster and wrote in a vertical column on the left-hand side the numbers 5 to 0 in descending order. Then across the bottom I wrote "S-M-T-W-T-F-S" representing the seven days of the week. At the top I scrawled in the behavior that I wanted to use for illustrative purposes. The behavior I focused on for the poster was *Wake-up*. I explained, however, that to implement the point/level system would require a separate chart to be completed for each of the seven behaviors that we would be concentrating on. Each boy would be measured to the same seven behaviors and each would have seven charts. The sum total of the seven charts would be added at the end of each week to determine their point totals and when they would be eligible for advancing to another level of added responsibility.

"Let's first take *Wake-up*," I said. "Tony, let's say on Sunday you show up for breakfast three minutes late." I drew a point where Sunday and the number two intersected. "On Monday you show up in the nick of time. That's five points. On Tuesday you show up four minutes late, you earn one point. Wednesday you fall back further and show up five minutes late—you get zero points. Thursday you're on time, Friday you fall back to two minutes, and Saturday you're on time. This is what your chart would look like at the end of the week." I held the poster up for everyone to see.

The poster I made was to illustrate the concept. I also explained that the point system was part of a level system (a series of graduated levels—each with additional privileges—which were based on the points earned and accumulated over an extended period of time). This point/level system became the basic framework for my rehabilitative strategies with troubled youth.

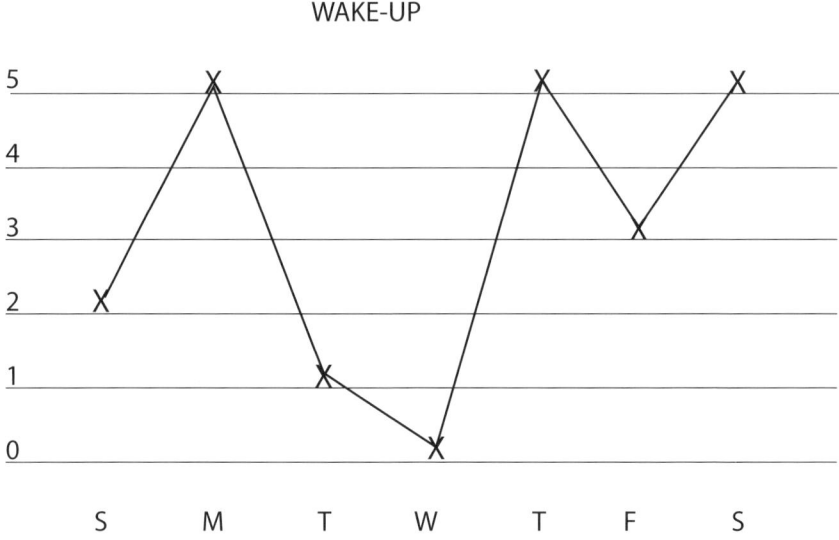

"So Tony, how many points does that give you by the end of the week?" I asked.

Tony studied the poster for a minute and answered, "Twenty-one."

"Correct," I said, "just enough to get you a Snicker's bar and one point to bank."

When the wisecracks stopped, I took that as a good sign. Maybe the kids just needed to know what was expected of them. And once they knew what was expected of them, wouldn't they do what any ordinary person would do? These were all ordinary things anyway, things any ordinary person would do in an ordinary day.

But what I overlooked was the fact that these kids were anything but ordinary. Most had been neglected or abused as children. Many had police records for vandalism, shoplifting, or car theft. These were kids whose behavioral and social problems society had failed to address—poverty, racism, lack of education, unemployment—kids whose parental role modeling had been non-existent or inconsistent at best and whose anti-social behavior was the natural outcome of their growing-up years. These were kids that society had already given up on.

Now they were my responsibility. After everything that had gone on in their young lives, after everything that had made these kids anything but ordinary, how could I show them that I wasn't just about rules and regulations and behavior points? How could I show that I cared about them as human beings?

When I finished explaining my point system, the group was silent. I thought, maybe I'm getting through to them. I waited for someone to respond.

"This is bullshit!" Red exploded, popping out of his chair. "Come on, you motherfuckers, let's get out of here." Five or six others followed him out of the room and through the front door. They came back that night.

When my eleven o'clock shift relief arrived, I changed into my track shoes and ran a ten-mile lap around town. Running that night was just like crossing the St. Croix River in Minnesota that Fourth of July weekend when I went to visit Bill Tilton, and it helped clear my head.

After a few days Red cooled off and life went on. So I began to contemplate whether it would be a stretch to offer Red the peer manager position. That would give dramatic punch to positive reinforcement in the point system. Every night at group meeting I would report on everyone's point tally. One by one the kids caught on, and getting points became competitive: Who would *win* the most points by the end of the week? It was amazing what a little positive reinforcement could do.

Even so, I sensed something was lacking. It was one thing to change a kid's physical behavior; it was another thing to change his psychology. My own work with kids had borne out what B.F. Skinner and other behaviorists had concluded: that delinquent behavior could be modified through incentives and rewards. But did that go far enough? Didn't that amount to treating the symptoms of an illness, not the causes?

They Will Be Victors

Sigmund Freud, whose ideas dominated social workers' thinking through most of the twentieth century, said in effect you couldn't help who you were, that you were molded from day one by events outside your control, and that mostly you weren't conscious of those events even though they controlled your thoughts and feelings and actions. What that boiled down to was—you were a victim of early childhood circumstances and there wasn't anything you could do about it, so you needed to accept the way you were because it wasn't your fault.

Then along came William Glasser, a young psychiatric resident at UCLA with the ink on his M.D. certificate not yet dry, who found that Freud's ideas didn't work well with delinquent kids. Youth need self-respect, and self-respect comes with living responsibly not by saying "poor me, poor me" and blaming the past.

In his landmark book, *Reality Therapy: A New Approach to Psychiatry*, published in 1965, Glasser described his frustration in trying to apply Freud's ideas to his delinquent charges at a school in California:

> A car-stealing juvenile delinquent...treated by a psychiatrist for years on the basis of mental illness, will not change as long as he is allowed to play the misunderstood or mistreated delinquent child who doesn't understand all that happened to him...Therefore, to do Reality Therapy, the therapist must not only be able to help the (youth) accept the real world, but he must then further help him fulfill his needs in the real world so that he will have no inclination in the future to deny its existence and to violate its laws.[6]

Didn't it make a lot more sense to deal with the present, not the past? The past was immutable. You couldn't change it. But you could change how you dealt with the present. As a budding social worker intent on changing the status quo, I decided to integrate the principles of Glasser's ideas to my approach to group therapy.

It was the fall of 1977; I had two semesters to complete before earning my master's degree. I ran some of my ideas past Chuck

Thinking Outside the Box

Wolfson while attending his Social Work 646 class. When I told him about my point system and how I wanted to supplement that with reality therapy, he said, "Bob, you're thinking outside the box. Why don't you do your term paper on it?"

I went to work. For the next several months, between classes and my eight-hour shifts at Vaughn House, I labored over the most important paper of my academic career. I compared my point system to other group treatment approaches, and noted how even it fell short of addressing a person's sense of human connectedness, his sense of responsibility, and ultimately his sense of well-being.

"In contrast to the psychoanalytic approach," I wrote, taking my own little swipe at Freud, "reality therapy emphasizes the here and now.... What happened in the past is insignificant because regardless of how much we know about past traumas and parental relationships, the past cannot be changed."[7]

The key challenge was how to translate Glasser's ideas into therapeutic principles that I could apply to my own work with these troubled kids, principles that would go beyond changing their *external* behavior and change their *internal* being as well. I started with five principles: *Involvement, Communication, Responsibility, Behavior, Education*.

In due course I would modify and expand the list to include seven principles, but I had discovered in Glasser a bold, new approach to treating troubled adolescents. The paper ran thirty-one pages. It had been a lot of work, but I knew even though I was just a graduate student that I had made a major contribution to the literature in my field and I was proud of it.

All the paper needed now was a dedication. Before I turned it in to Professor Wolfson, I dashed off the following:

> *Chuck, my friend and mentor, to you I dedicate this*
> *brilliant piece of work and believe me I busted my ass.*
> 7 December 1977
> *Ann Arbor*

Wouldn't you know that *The Dedication* was the part he liked best! But we have to tip our hat to Freud's concept of ego—even a professor-mentor is human.

CHAPTER II

SAINTS, HEROES, AND ROLE MODELS

TO SOMEONE LIKE ME who grew up in a Catholic home and attended a Catholic school, there is no higher human achievement than to be declared a saint. In my book—I called it "Robert's Book of Mere Mortals"—it's a higher status than I give to kings, prime ministers, or even presidents. The problem is, saints are easier to venerate than to emulate and so many of them end up as martyrs, which is why we name feasts and festivals after them—not to mention rivers, mountains, islands, cities, schools, churches, streets, hospitals, convents, and group homes for delinquent kids.

The next level down is the heroes. In that category I put generals like Washington, Grant, and Eisenhower, and athletes like Muhammad Ali, Babe Ruth, and Lou Gehrig. I also include in the category of heroes people who have made a genuine and enduring difference in society—Lincoln, Gandhi, John and Bobby Kennedy, and Martin Luther King, Jr. Like many of the saints before them, they ended up as martyrs.

The next step down is the role models—people we emulate because it's within our power to do so. We know them as flesh-and-blood human beings, not icons whose names we see on schools and churches and street corners. In that category I put my mentors Bill Tilton, Mark Glesener, Chuck Wolfson, and Jim Minder.

I recall admiring the skilled athletes of my day who became my heroes. When I was a kid my grandfather Frank Costello would take me to see the Brooklyn Dodgers play at Ebbett's Field. On one of these occasions, I was actually picked up and held by Jackie Robinson. As a young adult I had seen the great Muhammad Ali in the ring three times—against Jerry Quarry, Oscar Bonavena, and Joe Frazier.

But none of these events matched the awe that I experienced when I first witnessed the spectacle of the one-hundred-thousand-plus noisy spectators jammed into the "Big House" for the Big Game against Ohio State on November 22, 1975. The Big Ten championship was at stake, and so was the Rose Bowl.

When I entered the stadium, the University of Michigan Marching Band was parading down the field with their maize and blue banners and blaring brass instruments, warming up for the halftime spectacle. I turned to the girl next to me—a U-M student who'd invited me along—and said, "Man, this is really great!"

Once the game got underway again, it got even better. The Wolverines, led by their freshman quarterback, Rick Leach, came back from a 7-7 halftime deadlock to take a 14-7 lead. Meanwhile the Wolverine defense led by Don Dufek, their All-American safety and team captain, held Ohio State's great senior running back Archie Griffin to less than one hundred yards for the first time in his college career.

But with three minutes to go in the game the Buckeyes' quarterback Cornelius Green handed off to his fullback Pete Johnson on fourth down and Johnson bulled his way into the end zone to tie the score. The Wolverines were mounting an offensive push on the next series of downs on a roll to break the tie, when Coach Bo Schembechler inexplicably called for a pass on the Michigan 40. Ray Griffin, Archie's brother, intercepted Leach's pass and ran it back to the three. With two minutes to go, Johnson notched his second touchdown of the game and put the final nail in the coffin: Ohio State 21, Michigan 14.

Saints, Heroes, and Role Models

In hindsight it was the consummate clash between two Big Ten teams whose rivalry was nothing short of legendary. All the cheering and yelling had left my vocal chords in shreds—same for the one-hundred-thousand-plus other spectators. But the silence following Johnson's touchdown was surreal. Regardless of outcome I was from that day forward a rabid fan of the Maize and Blue and of Coach Glen E. "Bo" Schembechler. And freshman Rick Leach—our future board member—would never lose to Ohio State again, and went on to break many Michigan records and become All American in football and baseball—the only Michigan player to ever be All American in both these sports. In Leach's senior year, the rivalry with Notre Dame would be rekindled. Even with the legendary Joe Montana at quarterback, the Fighting Irish couldn't overcome Leach's offensive onslaught of two touchdown passes and one running TD, and the Wolverines walked off the field with a 28-14 victory in South Bend.

The kids at Vaughn House were instant fans, and I had created a cheering section as avid as that of any other Wolverine boosters in town. Most of them knew the starting players' names by heart. Some of the players, including George Przygodski and Don Dufek, lived right up the street from 1001 Vaughn.

After the season ended I went over to their place and knocked on the door. Prsygodski answered.

"George, I'm Bob Wollack," I said. "I'm with Vaughn House down the street. Do you know anything about it?"

"Yah, I do," he said. "I see kids coming and going there all the time. Aren't they juvenile delinquents? You look too old—"

That made me laugh, and I cut him off in mid-sentence, "Actually, I was a juvenile delinquent," I said, "but you're right—I'm too old for that now. I'm a student at Eastern Michigan and next year, with luck, I'll start working toward a master's degree in social work at Michigan."

George seemed interested so I continued: "Right now I'm just a youth care worker—a glorified baby sitter," sensing that being a little self-deprecating might appeal to George, "and I sit with these kids eight hours a day. I was just wondering if you'd be willing to stop by sometime and say hello to them. They're all Wolverine fans and they'd dig it if —"

"Let me get my jacket," he interrupted. Two minutes later we were on our way to 1001 Vaughn, laden with maize and blue T-shirts that said "University of Michigan Wolverines" on the front. When we arrived the kids attention alternated between the T-shirts and the presence of a real live Wolverine football player in their midst.

A few days later George came back with his roommate, Don Dufek. They brought tickets for an upcoming Wolverines basketball game. Tony helped me cook up a steak dinner with all the trimmings. The kids were even more impressed when George and Don offered to help wash the dishes. I held up a quarter and said, "Thanks, but I got the kids trained to do that." Laughter filled the room.

Before the semester had ended, several more Wolverine football players got in the habit of stopping by—Don Dufek's brother Bill Dufek, John "Flame" Arbeznik, Mo Morton, Rob Lytle, and Tim Davis. I don't know if my cooking had anything to do with it, but every other week or so they'd show up just in time for dinner.

Tough, macho football players were just the role models the kids at Vaughn House needed. These were guys they looked up to and wanted to emulate. When I told Larry Tokalkski about their visits, he said, "Hmm, you might have something there." Larry was the coordinator of Project Community that connected social work students from EMU with student athletes from U of M. He was a teaching assistant at the University of Michigan majoring in sociology.

"That's what I was thinking—role-modeling is about acquisition and imitation. The whole impact on a behavior modification level would be great for these kids—a bunch of big dudes who were making something of themselves through sports and academics," I said.

Back then I was a long way from practicing reality therapy, let alone developing a point system for modifying human behavior. But I sensed I was already innovating, building on the theories to develop new practices. Why not take another step? Why not have the athletes spend time with these kids say, once a week as a class project? Why not give them two hours' credit and have them write a paper at the end of the semester?

Besides Rick Leach and his 1975 teammates, other Wolverine greats went through the Project Community program—men like Jerry Meter, Tim Mileta, the Lioni brothers, Mel Owens, Bob Holloway, Walt Downing, Harlan Huckleby, Russell Davis, and Mike Turgovoac (now the defensive coordinator for the Carolina Panthers). Through these relationships I was fortunate to become acquainted with Coach Schembechler as well.

When I returned to Vaughn House in 1977, I was halfway through my requirements for earning a master's degree and fancied myself an academic. Project Community was a combination of academics and practical field studies. It had synthesized the concepts of modeling, behavior modification, reality therapy, and everything else I learned in school. For reaching adolescent boys, I found using these athletes as volunteers and role models worked as well as any application of B.F. Skinner's or William Glasser's theories.

I kept these role models before the eyes and minds of the Vaughn House kids. Many of these individuals became my lifelong friends—people like Don and Bill Dufek, Tim Davis, George Przygodski, Mo Morton, John Arbeznik, Rick Leach, Stanley Edwards, Anthony Carter, Mike Day, Rob Lytle, John Wangler, and U of M Cross Country Coach Ronnie Warhurst, who went on to become the head track coach. Many of these trusted associates would be pivotal in helping me to found the agency that would represent my legacy and, in many respects, my redemption.

Rick Leach went on to play big league baseball for the Detroit Tigers and Toronto Blue Jays, and Don Dufek played pro football for the Seattle Seahawks. As starters on the University of Michigan's football team in the mid-'70s, they were household names in Ann Arbor. Project Community as a formal program eventually ended, but the idea of connecting collegiate athletes with troubled youth would remain a foundation of my approach to social work and community outreach. It would result in lasting friendships and serve as the launching pad for something powerful.

CHAPTER 12

DREAMS OF MY SONS

LIFE AND DEATH TOGETHER represent the quintessential mystery of being human. As I progressed in my career and developed innovations to help troubled youth, I met young men who would touch my heart in deep and meaningful ways. Among them was a boy whom I first met at Vaughn house in 1975. This was Tony Sablowksi and he was still there when I returned in 1977. His shock of tousled red hair hung over his often-furrowed brow. Tony was a serious-minded thirteen year old who was likeable, approachable, and very bright. Despite being born to parents who never cared for him, who abused him and his brother to the point that foster care was their only viable option, Tony remained upbeat, optimistic, and essentially happy. He had really gravitated to Project Community, and became a fixture at the Arch Street Athletic Club where he would hang out with the Wolverine athletes.

As it happened, Tony was drawn to another redhead like himself—John "the Flame" Arbeznik—a Michigan student and athlete. They took to each other like brothers and Tony flourished under John's mentorship. That spring Tony's grades in middle school—straight A's all the way through—warranted special recognition. He was selected by the school to travel to Orlando for a trip to Disney World. We were all proud of him and took up a small collection so that he could get some souvenirs and have the kind of experience every child would like to have. But a terrible tragedy was about to happen.

Tony would never have the chance to celebrate his accomplishment. Crossing into Georgia, the bus pulled off the highway. The driver was unable to maintain control on the off ramp's curve and the bus rolled over. The ever-vivacious leader, Tony had been riding in the front seat so he could watch the road disappear as his dream came closer. But his dream ended, along with that of three other young men whose lives ended suddenly and far too soon.

I received a call that afternoon from the treatment director at Family Group Homes. She was aware of how fond of Tony I was—he had become in many respects like a son to me—and the gravity in her voice was palpable. "Tony was killed in a bus crash in Georgia," she said. A cavity opened up in my soul, the breath and blood and spirit draining from me in a vacuum of grief. But the calling of the social worker requires setting personal needs aside and responding to the needs of others. I drove to Vaughn House knowing that youth and staff there would need reassurance and support.

All four of the victims of the accident were laid out together in an auditorium at Eastern Michigan University. The community was devastated at the loss of such promising young men. Hundreds of well-wishers, friends, and family members walked solemnly past the caskets—looking for answers to unuttered questions. Tony's face bore the same expression it always had had in life, but the staff were thinking, "Couldn't he at least have made it to the celebration?"

After the public ceremony Pete Walsh, John Arbeznik, and I went to Tony's wake and funeral. Tony was eulogized by the Reverend Jimmie Ward, Jr., who had worked with Tony at St. Francis Home. Jimmie was a man who spoke with passion, caring, and sensitivity. He gave Tony the respect he was due—not as an abused or abandoned child but as a light in the lives of all those he touched. I made a commitment to myself to keep Tony's memory alive, and this commitment would be fulfilled in the years to come.

I graduated with honors in April 1978, less than a month after Tony's death. Though the event was bittersweet, I was now equipped with a Master's Degree in Social Work (MSW) from the University of Michigan, and I was ready to begin my career as a professional social worker at both an experiential and academic level.

While graduation often brings with it the stress associated with becoming a professional in need of employment, I had the good fortune of having two job offers pending—one with Family Group Homes (FGH) and one with my old mentor, Jim Minder. Despite a compelling offer from Jim, I opted for the director position of FGH's two group homes in Ann Arbor—Vaughn House and Miller House. Within a year I opened a third group home. Along the way, I continued to apply the social treatment concepts that I had learned from my mentors, as well as the Seven Principles and the point system I had developed on my own. I added more *targeted behavior*s to the list I started out with. Every day I would have my house supervisors track our clients' progress on everything from greeting skills to school grades, and every week I would have them give out rewards based on each kid's performance.

I kept looking for new treatment approaches, new ways of doing things. I asked myself, "Did my first attempt at putting Glasser's ideas about reality therapy into working principles go far enough?" In my paper for Professor Wolfson's Social Work 646 class, I had identified five guiding principles—*involvement, communication, responsibility, behavior, education*. But what about *reality*—one's willingness to face the real world? Or respect—treating others as you would have them treat you? Or *negotiation*—the ability to get what you wanted without hurting anybody else?

Most important, what about *love*? Don't you have to love yourself before you can love someone else? A lot of people don't believe that, but I do. It has nothing to do with narcissism but everything to do with self-esteem, self-affirmation, and self-realization. And this is reflected in the way we relate to other people. Love—love of self, and love from others—was something I needed so badly when I was a kid and after my release from prison. It was what I needed more than anything in order to put my past behind me and rebuild my life. So out of my application of reality therapy, I refined my five original foundational building blocks and finally settled on seven principles, which I put in logical sequential order. For the past thirty years, these principles have proven to be effective for both residents and staff. Those principles, and their preamble, are as follows:

To Be a Success in Life, Follow These Principles:
 1. Reality
 2. Responsibility
 3. Respect
 4. Communication
 5. Negotiation
 6. Education
 7. Love

St. Paul—one of the chief saints in my pantheon of mortals—says in his first letter to the Corinthian Church that love is the greatest human virtue next to faith and hope. But I rank it as the greatest human *need* as well.

By the fall of 1979, I had spent five years at Huron Residential Service, and I wanted to be closer to my sons, Craig and Rob. I was also ready for a change.

I learned about an opening at VisionQuest, a social service organization headquartered in Tucson, Arizona. VisionQuest operated a program called Wagon Train, which gave troubled teens a chance to find purpose for their lives by exploring the wilderness on horseback and in covered wagons. It was a unique therapeutic approach that I had read about and was interested in. The Wild West was something I'd only seen depicted in John Wayne movies, and the idea of "living" in such a place and time—even a sanitized version of it—held great appeal to a kid who had grown up in Brooklyn.

Dreams of My Sons

Tucson would bring me two thousand miles closer to my sons, and I was extremely anxious to be as close as possible. I was living with wonderful memories of my previous chance to spend time with them. I had willingly spent the money to buy tickets for both the boys and me to go to the 1979 Rose Bowl. It was a glorious California day and the festivities and the game were thrilling to Craig and Rob and to me too. However, we were utterly disheartened by the defeat of Michigan by USC because of the so-called phantom touchdown. It happened on the second down at the Michigan three-yard line when Heisman Trophy winner and USC tailback Charlie White dove through the heart of the Michigan line in an attempt to score. During the ensuing action, White lost the ball and Wolverine linebacker Jerry Meter (now the treasurer on the Wolverine Human Services Board of Directors) came up with an apparent fumble recovery on the one-yard line. However, the line judge determined that White had crossed the goal line before losing control of the ball. This play is considered one of the most controversial calls in the entire history of the Rose Bowl. The Wolverines lost the game to USC 17 to 10. It was a bitter disappointment. Nevertheless, the Rose Bowl would make a never-to-be-forgotten impression on the boys and I longed to once again spend quality time with them. Now Craig was eleven—almost as old as some of the kids I took care of at Huron—and I missed him more than ever. "As his father, I should be taking care of *him*," I thought. Rob was nine, and I hadn't seen him for a full third of his life.

Sometimes I would dream about my sons as I remembered them from my incarceration at the federal detention center in Manhattan—Craig looking at me through the glass pane in the visitors' room while I talked to him on the phone; Rob sitting on my lap in the car going home on the first day of my release. Sometimes I would imagine how they might look now, and I would see flashes of them in my dreams. And then I would dream of them as they had looked on that Labor Day when their mother put them in the car and left for San Diego.

They Will Be Victors

I arrived in Tucson and went right to work. My job title was treatment director, and I was to be responsible for the clinical operation of VisionQuest's Wagon Train. Each wilderness trek lasted fourteen days. Usually I would ride horseback, but I also did a lot of walking while the kids alternated between riding horseback and riding in a covered wagon. Before sunset we'd find a clearing, cook our dinner over an open fire, and camp out for the night. The ruggedness of the terrain, the rustic living, and the simple act of being outdoors converged to make the experience one of the most enduring and profound of my professional career to that point. We never encountered bandits or Indian warriors, but it wasn't hard to imagine them charging at us with their six-shooters or bows and arrows. When the two weeks were up, we would head back to the base camp and I would get two days off.

Despite my best intentions and planning, two days simply were not enough time to drive all the way to San Diego and back—an eight-hundred-mile round trip. I contemplated going there over Thanksgiving weekend—four days were better than two—but that got knocked out because the holiday fell in the middle of one of my scheduled Wagon Train adventures. My efforts to visit my sons were seemingly thwarted at every turn.

Grandpa Costello once told me, "Don't build your expectations so high that you'll be disappointed." It was good advice but it was something I failed to heed. My own VisionQuest adventure was more than a disappointment; it was a disaster. I got to see my boys only once—and then it was only for a few days over Christmas. And I found VisionQuest's treatment of its clients nothing less than appalling.

Case in point: When I returned to Tucson after the holidays, I observed two staff members slamming a kid's head against the wall, and shattering a mirror as shards of glass splayed out like shrapnel. I had seen incidents of staff-initiated abuse before. The precipitating problem was that the VisionQuest philosophy promoted the withholding of psychotropic meds from the kid's therapeutic interventions. Many of these youth had serious emotional problems and posed a physical risk to themselves and others. There was a compelling reason why they were prescribed these medications. Without their medications, many of them became extremely agitated and sometimes acted out violently. One staff member that I was acquainted with was so severely injured by a youth that she required reconstructive surgery. Nevertheless, the staff violence I witnessed toward youth was intolerable; I was obligated—at a moral and legal level—to act, and I filed a complaint with the State of Arizona's Department of Economic Services—a complaint that was supposed to be *confidential*. Then I boarded a plane for a scheduled trip to Michigan for Bill Dufek's wedding, expecting to return to Tucson a few days later. My plan to return would be short-lived While staying with Pete Walsh, I received a call from one of VisionQuest's managers, informing me that I needn't bother coming back to work.

A decade ago I had gone to prison for doing the wrong thing. Now I got fired for doing the right thing. I knew I had done the right thing and I felt betrayed by the fact that my reward was apparently a pink slip. Regardless of this unfortunate outcome, the VisionQuest experience would prove to be instructional and give me an unique perspective in designing wilderness and high adventure programming for troubled youth. And this would translate into a salient competitive advantage.

After I hung up the phone, my thoughts diverged from my own circumstances to contemplate the fate of those young people who would continue to be subjected to violence as a means of controlling their behavior. I wondered what Glasser and all the other human behavioral experts would say about that.

CHAPTER 13

THE BROOKLYN COWBOY

I FLEW BACK TO TUCSON to retrieve my car and personal belongings. The two-thousand-mile return trip to Ann Arbor was one of the longest in my life. Each mile marker I passed along Interstate 40 took me that much farther away from my boys in San Diego. Not only was I without my sons; I was without a job. For the second time since leaving Milan, I was starting over.

Pete Walsh proved to be a godsend, by letting me move in with him and his new wife. But he let me know in his own quiet way that she wasn't thrilled with the arrangement, that it was only temporary, and the more temporary the better. I felt like a stray dog, trying my best to be good natured and friendly no matter how discouraged I felt.

Although Pete and I had gone through graduate school together after our release from Milan, he saw more money-making potential in real estate than he did in social work. So after receiving his M.S.W. he traded his social work certificate for a real estate license, brokering deals for a Remax agency in Ann Arbor. I sensed after moving in with him that neither his marriage nor his real estate venture was destined to last, but I knew enough to keep my mouth shut.

As soon as I found a job I packed my belongings and moved into the downtown YMCA. The job was at a state-run psychiatric hospital in Northville—a town near Ann Arbor—where I worked as a ward therapist with adult schizophrenics.

For someone starting over for the second time, it wasn't a bad gig. It was the least stressful of any social work job I ever had because I worked the eight-to-four shift and had plenty of time to fish in the evening at the Huron River. After getting thrown out of Tucson, I decided that life up in Michigan was as good as I'd find it anywhere. Besides, I was making more money in my new job than I ever had before. I was at peace and was content to stay put.

But as the saying goes, life is what happens while you're planning other things. After six months on that job, I got a phone call from Ed Overstreet who was the executive director of Boysville of Michigan—Jim Minder's boss when he ran Xavier Center in Ecorse.

"Chuck Wolfson told me you're back in town," he said. "Can you come out to Clinton so we can talk?"

"About what?" I asked.

"I can't tell you over the phone. But Chuck said I should talk to you."

Clinton was a village of two thousand souls in southeast Michigan, more than half of whom were residents of Boysville's boarding school for troubled teens. Founded in 1948 as a joint project of Michigan's five Catholic dioceses, the school occupied a site once owned by Henry Ford who, when he abandoned his plans to build a factory there, gave the property to the Archdiocese of Detroit. The school was the largest of Boysville's statewide operations and also housed its headquarters.

When I arrived at Overstreet's office, he said, "We have a problem at one of our group homes."

"Which one?" I asked.

"St. Cecilia's," he said, "on the west side of Detroit. We have twenty-two kids living there, ages thirteen to eighteen. They're all victims of abuse and neglect, and most of them have police records."

His description could have fit the kids at Vaughn House or VisionQuest just as well. "So?" I interjected.

"The problem is we've had eighteen counts filed against us during the past year and we're about to lose our license," he said.

"Eighteen counts? For what?"

"Child abuse—by the staff at St. Cecilia's. We need to clean the place up."

I thought of the broken-mirror incident at VisionQuest and wondered if troubled kids at St. Cecilia's or anywhere else, so many of whom had been abused before coming into the system, would ever get a break. Wasn't juvenile delinquency the natural outcome of abuse and neglect? Reflecting on how content I was with my relatively stress-free job at Northville Hospital, I asked, "So why are you calling me?"

"I want you to clean it up."

"I'm happy where I am," I said.

"I don't doubt that," he said. "I know you're unique and innovative, and Chuck Wolfson and Jim Minder said you were the kind of person we needed to do this job."

I didn't say it out loud, but as Overstreet was speaking, I thought about how much I missed working with troubled kids. Of course it was stressful, sometimes even dangerous, but for me there was no higher reward than helping a sixteen-year-old kid break away from crime or drug addiction, go back to school, and turn his life around.

"I'm making $23,000 a year at Northville," I said. "Can you match that?"

"No problem."

"Can you give me a car?" I pressed.

Overstreet hesitated for a few seconds. "No problem," he said.

"One other thing," I said. "I want to have free rein to make staff changes."

"You've got it."

When I left his office, he shook my hand and congratulated me on accepting the job. Then, almost in passing, he said: "I hope you don't get shot." I didn't know who he was talking about—the staff or the kids. Either way, I knew I had to keep my eyes wide open.

I started at St. Cecilia's in August. Like other group homes in Detroit, this one had been a convent that closed when the Archdiocese ran into trouble recruiting nuns. Moreover, white flight that began in the '50s and escalated after the city's 1967 riots had left the surrounding neighborhoods predominately black. The convent, which had opened in the mid-'50s to educate and house Catholic nuns, reopened in the late '70s with a new mission for the changing times: to house and re-educate delinquent, predominantly black teens.

The building itself was early '50s in style—a bland, two-story, brick dormitory-type structure. As I approached the building, I encountered two kids smoking pot on the front steps. I walked past them without a glance or a word. I figured I would have to deal with it, but now wasn't the time. Two wings flanked the main entrance. The only decorative feature outside the building was a Moline cross carved between the words "St. Cecilia" and "Convent" on a marble lintel over the front door.

The entrance led into a foyer and central dining room with a living room on each side. Straight ahead, a stained glass door opened into a chapel with a low ceiling that jutted out the back of the building. Two stairwells, one on each side, led to the bedrooms on the second floor.

One thing I had learned on my Wagon Train stint was how the symbols of one's occupation convey authority. What is it about a cop's blue uniform or a priest's white collar that commands respect? On my wilderness treks I found that leather boots, a studded belt, and a ten-gallon hat did the same thing. So along with a new job, I asked myself, why not take on a new persona to get respect? I'm not talking Rodney Dangerfield here; I'm talking the Lone Ranger. Sprouting a mustache for good measure, I swaggered into St. Cecilia's in my cowboy garb.

I called the staff together for introductions. I took the opportunity to set the tone going forward. "I'm aware of the abuses that have been going on here and that will stop immediately. Violence is never a solution in helping troubled kids. I'm bringing in some new people to help me get things back to where they need to be."

The first person I hired was an ex-Detroit cop named Felton Rogers, who quit the force after the 1967 riots to become a social worker. Felton had been an all-state football player and high jumper at Detroit's Eastern High School and then gone on to play tight end at the University of Iowa. His quiet, six-foot-four presence exuded authority like a latter-day George Washington. We had worked together at Vaughn House and St Bridgit.

The second person I hired was Jimmie Ward, the Reverend who had eulogized Tony Sablowski back in 1978. He had a heart of gold and a tongue to match. If Felton had the gift of silence, Jimmy had the gift of gab—and the charisma that goes along with being a Pentecostal preacher.

With Felton Rogers and Jimmy Ward on board, I had the support and loyalty I needed to begin making the changes that were needed. The situation was so surreal that I actually ended up firing the director that I had been hired to replace. I was working with Boysville's central administration to get the building up to code. I was immersing staff in my therapeutic beliefs and approaches. I was applying the Seven Principles and the point system and beginning to see results. And, I was getting the right people on the bus and the wrong people off.

But some people just refuse to change. The day before Thanksgiving—a month and a half into my tenure—I caught a staff member slapping a child, and I fired him on the spot. At 2 o'clock the next morning I got a phone call from the night supervisor.

"The building is on fire," he said.

"What??" I exclaimed in disbelief. I had heard him right the first time. Immediately, I called Felton Rogers and told him I would come by to pick him up in five minutes. By the time we arrived, the fire had been extinguished but the damage had been done. The fire which had begun in the two downstairs living rooms had worked its way up the two stairwells to the second floor. "Arson!" The investigator's report proclaimed the cause of the fire, "Arson!" The curtains in both living rooms had been set on fire.

By the grace of God, the only casualty was a broken leg. The night supervisor had all twenty-two kids crawl from their second story bedrooms and jump to safety onto the chapel roof, but the building was gutted. Ironically, the only area that escaped the flames was my office. I shudder to think what might have happened had the fire not been discovered in time. While the fire marshal insinuated that he knew who committed the crime, he also expressed doubt that they would be able to prove it in court.

I wasn't inclined to accept that as closure, so I arranged a meeting with the alleged perpetrator, myself, and another employee at the home, Lynn Clay. We made it clear that we knew he had done it, and we didn't want to see his ass anywhere near us, our kids, our families, or our neighborhood. Otherwise we warned him that bad things were gonna happen to him. He came back with some half-hearted threats of his own, but by the end of the meeting we were confident he had gotten the message. Afterward I had to admit that it felt good to go back to the "street"—especially if it meant that kids would be safer.

The next eight months posed the biggest challenge of my career: what to do with the twenty-two kids displaced by the fire. There wasn't any doubt about the plan to rebuild St. Cecilia's, but how could I run a program without a building? And how long would it be before we could move back?

The day after Thanksgiving I went to see Monsignor Thomas Finnegan, the pastor of St. Cecilia Parish and President of the Board of Directors of Boysville. The monsignor, a gregarious man with a shock of white hair, seemed to take the fire in stride. "Putting all things in perspective, this is nothing compared to the '67 riots," he said. "Sure the kids can stay here while you rebuild. They can sleep in the gym, as long as they clear the floor during the day."

"That's very generous of you," I said, "but that's not quite what I had in mind."

"So what are you proposing?"

"To have them be able to study and eat in the basement and shoot hoops in the gym when they're out of school," I said.

"And where will they sleep?" he asked.

"The Boysville campus has extra dormitory space," I replied.

"Have you thought about how they're going to get between here and there? It's an hour-and-a-half each way."

"We'll need you to let us use a few vans," I said matter-of-factly.

For the next eight months we transported the kids back and forth between St. Cecilia's in Detroit and the Boysville campus in Clinton—a three-hour round trip—and we kept the program going without missing a beat. Felton Rogers and I even put together a basketball team for the boys. We played throughout the entire eight-month period—in recreation centers, at the state juvenile correctional institutions, and anywhere we were able.

Our boys from the group home were invited to use the St. Cecilia Catholic School gym which was located across the street. The athletic director for the St. Cecilia School was Sam Washington. He not only enabled us to use the gym, but he became personally involved with many of the youth from the group home. Sam Washington was no ordinary person. He was known throughout the Motor City as the great Sam Washington—renowned for his work in building Detroit's summer recreation programs. He attracted kids from all over southeastern Michigan to come and play in his summer basketball leagues.

Sam graduated from Detroit's Western High School in the early '50s where he played football with George Perles (who eventually coached the Michigan State University Spartans). They were both inducted into Western High School's Hall of Fame at the same time. Sam attended Ohio State University for two years where he continued to play football. He then played for the Canadian Football League before returning to Detroit. He spent the remainder of his career working as the athletic director for St. Cecilia Catholic School where he also drove their school bus. He believed in Detroit and loved kids.

After the disastrous Detroit riot of 1967, he was determined to provide something positive for the neighborhood youth to do. That is when he began to organize neighborhood sports activities and leagues—football during the fall of 1967 followed by basketball during the '67-'68 winter season. In the summer of 1968 he established his summer basketball leagues. Dave Bing (then an NBA player, and later to become a successful businessman and serve as mayor of the City of Detroit) volunteered during that first summer and he in turn attracted other NBA players. Soon, Sam had NBA stars from around the country who coached and played with high school and college-age kids in the tiny St. Cecilia gym, one wall of which was the out-of-bounds line. These summer leagues soon served as a magnet for scouts and coaches from some of the most prestigious college basketball programs in the country. Sam helped with fund-raising for rebuilding St. Cecilia. He was a great person.

Sam died in 1989, but he is fondly remembered for the mentoring he provided to many young men, some of whom resided at St. Cecilia House. Sam was inducted into the Michigan Sports Hall of Fame in 2007.

When St. Cecilia Group Home reopened the following summer, we had not only kept the twenty-two kids we started out with, but we had added six more. The six additional beds amounted to what could be described as Michigan's first emergency shelter beds. We agreed to take referrals at all hours, and to provide safety, warmth, and stability to youth facing dire circumstances. With the help of Al Lawrence, Carol Mayday, and others out of Wayne County Office of the Michigan Department of Social Services, we were able to offer this unique resource to the department and to the kids we were dedicated to serving. When I got permission to add another caseworker, I already knew who I wanted for the job. The only question was, would he accept?

I dialed a number I'd dialed a hundred times before, and a woman answered in a carefully rehearsed voice, "Thank you for calling Remax. To whom do you wish to speak?"

"Pete Walsh, please."

CHAPTER 14

TAKING RISKS

"PETEY, I NEED YOU," I said.

It's not easy to make a career change, or to take a leap of faith. But Pete knew about the fire, and he knew I wouldn't be calling if I weren't serious. Besides, social work was what Pete had been trained to do. He had an M.S.W. and he wanted to try a different path. But thanks to the 1981 recession, Michigan's real estate market was on the rocks—and so was his marriage. "When do you want me to start?" he said.

"Right now," I said.

Besides collaborating with me on a couple of research projects—first when we were both in undergraduate school and then later as graduate students at the University of Michigan School of Social Work—Pete had done a year's work-study with me at Vaughn House. One of the projects we collaborated on was a study of the federal Narcotic Addict Rehabilitation Act and its effectiveness in the federal penitentiary at Milan. Our data indicated that the program resulted in positive outcomes. The statute derived from Ramsey Clark's initiatives when he was the U.S. Attorney General. Pete didn't demonstrate the same passion for social work that I did, but

They Will Be Victors

I knew he could excel as a group leader at St. Cecilia's. Besides, we were like brothers. Ever since prison, our lives had proceeded more or less in tandem. We had roomed together, gone to school together, worked at Vaughn House together, and received our M.S.W.s together. We also met our future spouses around the same time. Pete had sworn off matrimony after his divorce, but after meeting Lorraine all bets were off. Within a year they were married.

Meanwhile, a twenty-eight-year old social worker had made the same vow after her first marriage ended. The first time I met her—April 1st, 1982—was in the Grand Ballroom of Detroit's Renaissance Center. After attending an all-day conference sponsored by the Child Welfare League of America, Pete and I—a couple of eligible bachelors looking for action—were gazing across the dance floor when I spotted a dazzling redhead talking with someone I knew. I charged across the floor and interrupted their conversation.

"Diane," I blurted out, "Introduce me to this beautiful woman."

"Oh, I'm sorry, Judy," she said, slightly annoyed. "This is Robert Wollack. He's the program director at St. Cecilia's."

"Judy Fischer," she said, extending her hand, "I'm a social worker at Hawthorne Center" which was the state's premier psychiatric hospital for severely emotionally disturbed children and youth located in Northville.

"You must be Clarence Fischer's daughter," I said.

"I am." Her eyes brightened.

"Well, he did a great job of putting this conference together," I said, not letting go of her hand. "Come with me to the other side of the floor. I want you to meet my friends. Excuse me, Diane."

She was the most beautiful woman I had ever met. I pulled her over to the table where Pete and a few others were sitting. When I introduced her to my friends, she said, "So how do you know each other?"

Pete dead-panned, "From prison."

Judy laughed. "April Fools' right?"

"No fooling," I said. "Old poker-face here—he's not a joker." I faked a right hook to Pete's chin.

"Well, isn't that interesting," Judy said. "Tell me more."

The fact that I knew Clarence Fischer gave me an edge with his daughter. Clarence was second-in-command at Lutheran Child and Family Services in Detroit and the co-founder of the country's first black adoption agency. I had met him on several occasions at professional conferences, and respected his work.

After I told Judy my story, she told me hers. "I grew up in a very open family," she said. "We talked about everything at the kitchen table—my mom and dad and my two sisters and I." Usually the dinnertime conversations had to do with helping people. She described how one Christmas eve, the doorbell rang and her family found three abandoned children at the front door. "Social work was our life," she said. Judy started working at her father's agency when she was twelve. Later she attended Concordia College in Ann Arbor and went on to get her bachelor's and M.S.W. at Wayne State University.

That first evening, we danced until the band packed up. Then we went out for drinks and talked some more, and at three o'clock I walked her back to her parents' room.

We got married nine months later, on New Year's Eve, 1982, at Hillside Manor a restaurant in Plymouth, Michigan. Monsignor Finnegan presided over the ceremony with a Lutheran minister, Pastor Eimen, the father-in-law of Judy's sister, Jane. My sons Craig and Rob, fourteen and twelve, stood up with us along with Judy's two sisters. After the reception the boys returned to California, and Judy and I flew to New York to watch the ball drop at Times Square.

My boyhood buddy Stan Farrow was there to greet us. A few blocks from the U.S. Second District Courthouse—the place that marked an earlier, less celebratory milestone in my life—Judy and I waited in the Times Square crowd for the ball to drop. I thought back to the night twelve years before when I had been arrested and about the conspiracy conviction that sent me to a prison in Michigan. Now here I was back in New York City where it all started, with my new wife. I was wondering if my second life—my second chance in Michigan—was an act of providence. Did God put me there for a purpose? I never thought of myself as a theologian, let alone a very religious person, but more and more I found myself thinking like one.

Back at St. Cecilia's I did my cowboy thing, showing up for work in my boots and hat. The kids, who'd seen their own share of John Wayne movies, had acquired a certain amount of respect for my western persona—as the saying goes, the clothes make the man. But it also caught the attention of the powers-that-be in Lansing, including Joe Jerome, a contracts manager for the Michigan Department of Social Services.

An ex-marine and Vietnam vet, Joe knew as well as anyone what it took to get St. Cecilia's up and running after the fire. He saw how my point system and seven principles worked, how the kids behaved more like ordinary human beings and less like delinquents, and how much better they fared after they ventured out into the real world. Our success rate—the number of kids who didn't wind up back in the system—went up from twenty-five percent to seventy-five percent.

One thing that helped the kids blow off steam was a competitive basketball program Felton Rogers and I organized. Every Friday night we'd drive the St. Cecilia kids to a different campus—Adrian Training School, Boysville in Clinton, the W.J. Maxey Boys Training School near Brighton—to take on rival basketball teams. If I didn't like the way Felton coached—being the quiet person he was, he didn't yell at his players or the referees nearly enough to suit me, so I would make him sit down and I'd take over. Everyone in the gym, whether they were paying attention to the game or not, noticed the change in volume after I took over.

In February of 1985, four-and-a-half years after I started at St. Cecilia's, Ed Overstreet, my boss, called me into his office. "I'm putting Pete Walsh in charge of St. Cecilia's," he said, waiting to see my reaction.

I gave him a dead-pan look—a trick I'd picked up from Pete—and waited for Ed to continue.

"All right," he said, breaking into a smile, "I'm promoting Pete, but I'm also promoting you—to Region Two director. You'll oversee

St. Cecilia's and three other group homes, including one for girls on Six-Mile and Telegraph. It's called Cabrini Center."

"Girls? I've never worked with girls before," I said.

"These girls are the same ages as the boys you work with—thirteen to eighteen. They have the same problems as the boys — they're all delinquents. Every one has been remanded to us by the courts for one offense or another—mostly prostitution, but also for petty larceny, assault, drug-dealing, disorderly conduct, you name it."

"How many are there?"

"Twelve."

It would prove to be the worst career move I had made to that point, rivaled only by my VisionQuest experience. But then, when you're offered a promotion early in your career, your choices are more limited. In retrospect, I should have turned it down. I was no more trained to contend with the unique emotional and behavioral problems attributable to adolescent young women than I was to be a nun. My cowboy persona, my using athletes as role models, even my point system and seven principles, didn't readily translate to this population. Despite these challenges, I wasn't ready to admit failure. But as often occurs in transitional leadership, those being led resist change out of fear. As feedback reached the ears of the administration, they became concerned.

Ed Overstreet called me back into his office. "Brother Francis, my boss, wants you to think about going back to St. Cecilia's," he said.

"Why?" I said.

"Because he thinks your temperament is better suited to that environment."

"That's bullshit!" I said. "I can do the job as well as anyone."

"Brother Francis thinks Pete can do it better," he said.

"Pete Walsh? I brought him to St. Cecilia's. You're gonna promote him over me?"

"Brother Francis likes him because he's mellow and quiet. He thinks he'd be a better fit."

"Brother Francis is a scumbag!" I shouted.

Overstreet looked at me, startled.

They Will Be Victors

"Look, Ed, my results speak for themselves. I got your success rate up from twenty-five percent to seventy-five percent, and some girl who isn't doing what she's supposed to do is screaming and you guys are punking out on me. Give me a break, man. I put my ass on the line for you."

I knew I had to do some quick thinking. "Here's the deal," I said. "I'll stay on as regional director for six more months, till December 31st, but that's all. Otherwise I'm going to sue your ass for $75,000."

"And when the six months are up?"

"I'll figure it out," I said.

"Well, let me talk to Brother Francis," he said.

When Overstreet got back to me, I didn't get the $75,000 I'd secretly hoped for, but I did buy six more months as Region Two director. I had a plan, but would six months give me enough time to put it in motion?

Ever since working with Jim Minder I knew in the back of my mind that I wanted to start my own program. Despite his early contract difficulties, I saw how successful he had become running his own agency. At first only Pete Walsh was privy to my plan and that was for a good reason. We were doing this venture together. Neither of us fully grasped the risk it entailed, even though we knew that two-thirds of all new businesses in this country failed within the first year. Could we beat the odds?

Pete and I drew up a list of all the things we had to do to get started. The first was to talk to Minder. Exactly what did we have to do, what hoops did we have to jump through to start our own agency?

"First," Minder said, "you have to acquire a building, and to do that you have to go to the banks and get loans."

"How do you do that?" I asked.

"Put your homes up for collateral," he said, "or get someone to buy the building and lease it back to you. Second, recruit a board. Third, write your by-laws and file your papers—make sure you're registered as a non-profit organization. Then get your state license—you're dead in the water without it—and get a contract from the state before you accept any kids. That's where I made my mistake."

As Pete and I listened to him, Minder seemed unconcerned about the fact that he was giving advice to potential competitors. When I called that to his attention he said, "Look, there are more troubled kids out there than any of us can handle."

"What about our criminal records?" I asked.

"Ah, you might have a problem there," he said. "You know Harold Gazan, don't you?"

"Only by name," I said. "He's the licensing guy in Lansing, isn't he?"

"Correct. Remember I told you he licensed me when I started out?"

"Yes, I do," I said.

"Well, at the time he didn't know I had a record. Then one day he got a call from a *Detroit News* reporter wondering whether I—the Jim Minder he'd licensed—was the same Jim Minder who'd been convicted of armed robbery." Nobody likes those kinds of surprises.

"So what happened?" I asked.

"He came to my office and demanded an explanation."

"What did you tell him?"

"I told him that I filled out everything the license application asked for. It asked if I had been convicted of a crime in the previous five years. I hadn't, so I was off the hook. But Harold demanded that my board put me on leave until his department did an investigation."

"And then you got your job back, right?" I asked.

"I did—after a month of hell. But now the game has changed. You have to disclose your criminal history no matter how far back it goes. If you were Cain and you killed your brother Abel, you'd have to report it."

When Pete and I left Minder's office, we had a much clearer picture of what we were up against. Already the odds were two-to-one against our venture succeeding beyond the first year, and that was under conventional circumstances. But with our prison records hanging over us, our odds made us a long shot.

Joe Jerome, the state contracts manager who had liked what he saw at St. Cecilia's after the fire, encouraged us to try. "Look," he said, "I saw what you guys did. If you want to start your own agency, go for it."

Item by item, Pete and I went through our check list. My tasks were to recruit the board, file the papers, and get the license and contract. Pete's tasks were to find a building and a way to finance it. His real estate background was perfect for that.

A few weeks later he said, "I think we have a building."

"Where?" I asked.

"The east side of Detroit—the old Guardian Angel Convent on Mayfield. The Archdiocese has it up for sale—$300,000."

"What about financing?"

"I had somebody in Ann Arbor who was interested, but he backed out," Pete said.

"Well, I have someone else in mind," I said.

"Who?"

"Bill Tilton. I'm seeing him over the Fourth. Maybe he'll help us."

Tilton had become one of his state's more successful trial lawyers. In addition, Bill had married a smart businesswoman from Oklahoma, Meredith Price, herself the daughter of a successful pipeline contractor. By then Bill and Meredith had enjoyed a couple of legal and business successes. I knew that Bill was willing to invest whatever he had in my venture to start my own program helping kids, so it was mainly a matter of winning over Meredith.

Those few days in July would prove to be significant, not only for myself, but for Pete and Bill as well. During the trip, Bill introduced me to his wife.

"This is 'RE,' my crazy friend from Michigan," Bill said. "He's going to do well."

His vote of confidence meant a lot to me—especially since he was putting his money where his mouth was!

Taking Risks

I returned to Detroit with a commitment from Bill and Meredith for a $300,000 cashier's check to present at the closing on the convent in Detroit. But without a license, there'd be no program, and without a program there'd be no need for a building. It was the proverbial "Catch-22," but sometimes you just have to push the envelope and hope for the best.

Meanwhile the clock was ticking. My job and my $40,000 salary would expire at midnight on December 31st. We needed corporate status, which meant we needed a name for our new venture. We needed money to pay for the furnishings. In short order, these items all fell into place. We applied as "Pioneer Human Services," but this was to be a brief interim step toward our ultimate moniker. We then made a plan to re-mortgage our homes—we were prepared to put our own money where our mouths were.

In August I received a letter from the Michigan Department of Social Services: "You are requested," it said, "to meet at the department's headquarters in Lansing at 10 a.m. Thursday, September 11, to discuss your license application and the implications of your criminal history." The letter was signed by Harold S. Gazan, Director of Audits, Investigations and Licensing Administration.

I took a deep breath, counted the days to September 11, and awaited my fate.

The Federal Correctional Institution—Milan, Michigan—my "home" from 1971–1973. (Photograph from website of Bureau of Prisons)

With Charlie Updike, the Assistant U. S. Attorney who prosecuted me—in his law office in New York City. (2008) (Photograph courtesy of Milton Nieuwsma)

Vaughn House—Ann Arbor. My first venture working with troubled boys. (Photograph Courtesy of Milton Nieuwsma)

With Bill Tilton, Sam McCargo, and Pete Walsh. Sam McCargo was the attorney who ably represented Wolverine Human Services in our litigation against Township officials. (Photograph from WHS Archives)

St. Jude's Home for Boys where Wolverine Human Services began–February 1987. This former convent was purchased from the Roman Catholic Archdiocese of Detroit with a generous loan from my friend, Bill Tilton. (Photograph courtesy of Milton Nieuwsma)

The Kingston Site of the Pioneer Work and Learn Center. (Photograph courtesy of Harold Gazan)

Detroit City and Juvenile Court officials and I flew by helicopter to observe the Pioneer Work & Learn Center in action and to discuss community racial attitudes toward the camp and its residents. (Circa 1989) (Photograph from WHS Archives)

A group of Vassar Campus boys on a back-packing trip to the Lake-of-the-Clouds, Porcupine Mountains, Michigan's Upper Peninsula—July 1992. These adventure experiences were used to build team trust and self-esteem. (Photograph from WHS Archives)

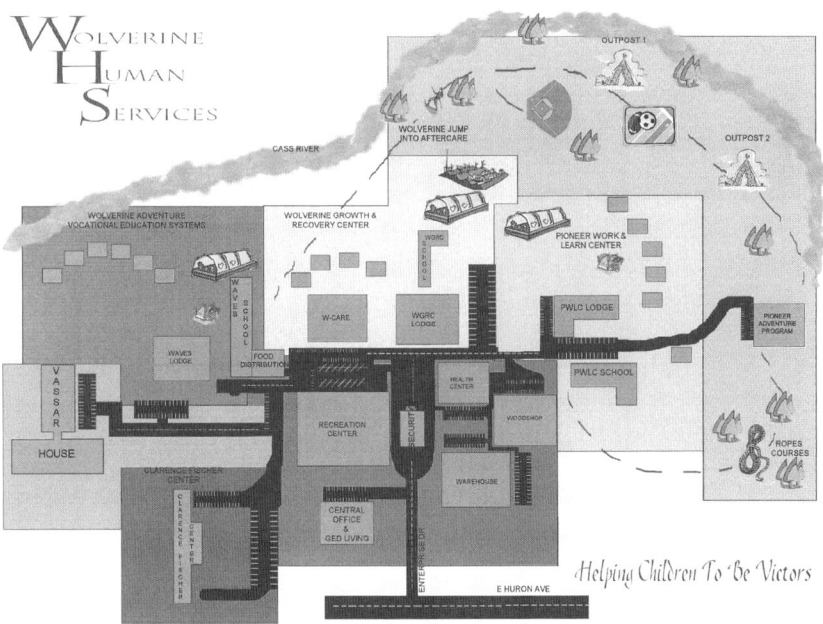

Map of the 135-acre Vassar Campus showing the most recent addition—Vassar House. (2008)

Group therapy session—Vassar Campus.
(Photograph from WHS Archives)

Standing in front our climbing-wall after having completed a demonstration climb—1994. Located on the Vassar Campus. (Photograph from a trade magazine: *Your Company*, Fall 1994, p 34.)

Typical Classroom—Vassar Campus.
(Photograph from WHS Archives)

One of three greenhouses that are now located on the Vassar Campus. (Photograph from WHS Archives)

Outdoor Adventure Center—Vassar Campus.
(Photograph from WHS Archives)

The Vassar Campus is comprised of 135 acres and is situated on the Cass River. Near the river is the Pioneer Work and Learn Center's camping area. This area is used by boys from the Vassar Campus as well as from our residential programs located in Detroit. (Photograph from WHS Archives)

This Vassar Campus extends to the bank of the Cass River. The photograph was taken from the Vassar property. (Photographs from WHS Archives)

The former St. Philip Neri Catholic Church was converted into a community center. This center was renamed the John S. Vitale Community Center in memory of John Vitale who was the director of our community center program. (Photograph courtesy of Milton Nieuwsma)

Victors Center—located on Detroit's east side. This is a non-secure facility for cognitively impaired boys. We established this program in 1988 in what was previously the St. Ambrose Convent. (Photograph courtesy of Milton Nieuwsma)

Getting ready to shoot some hoops with the boys at the Community Center. (Circa 1995) (Photograph from WHS Archives)

In 1991 Wolverine Human Services acquired St. Philip Neri Church and Convent. The Convent (photograph above) was turned into the Wolverine Diagnostic and Assessment Center. (Photograph courtesy of Milton Nieuwsma)

Governor Granholm visited the Community Center in August of 2003. (Photograph from WHS Archives)

John Vitale (known as the "gentle Giant") with two neighborhood kids at the Community Center which he directed from 1994-2000. He is bald as a result of chemo-treatment for cancer. The Community Center was named in his memory in 2000. (All photographs on this page are from WHS Archives)

Children playing on the playground of the Community Center.

An annual Christmas Celebration at the Community Center—with Bruce Kintz, Allen Jefferson, and neighborhood children.

With Mayor Coleman Young—January 1990.

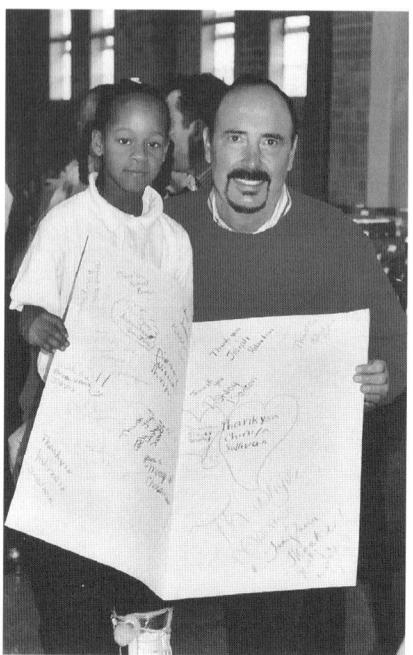

The children of the John S. Vitale Community Center presented me with a thank you card during the annual Christmas Party. (2006)

Neighborhood children enjoying the playground at the John S. Vitale Community Center.
(All photographs on this page are from the WHS Archives)

With my friend Harold Gazan. (2006)

Aerial View of Wolverine Secure Treatment Center and the fenced-in grounds.

WSTC—the large gym has three sections, one of which includes a boxing ring.

The Culinary Arts Kitchen—new wing at WSTC. (2008)

Points Store—where residents can convert their saved points to purchase or order items.

Culinary arts class displaying their vegetable carving skills. (2008)

Boys learning meat-cutting skills at the Meats Preparation & Distribution Center that is located on the Vassar Campus. (All photographs on this page are from the WHS Archives)

WSTC—new library and educational resource room. (2008)

The dedication of the Lt. Clarence Fischer Leadership Academy—August 30, 1998. Shirley Fischer cut the ribbon.

Color Guard—CFLA boys are in uniform. (Photographs on this page from WHS Archives)

Boys working on a landscape detail at Camp One—Vassar Campus.

Clarence Fischer, my father-in-law who ably headed-up Wolverine's Community Case Management Services Division.

Boys from the Clarence Fischer Leadership Academy (CFLA) marching to the parade ground in their summer uniform.

In my office on the Vassar Campus.

Boys in formation in their fall/winter uniform.
(All photographs on this page are from the WHS Archives)

With life-long friend Stanley Farrow and Jamo Wynn, one of our first graduates of the meat cutting, store management course. Jamo now is one of our full-time managers of the meat distribution center.

During September 2006, I named two cabins in honor of two long-time supporters of WHS. With George Mosher (left side of photo) and Earl Thomas (right side of photo).

Ground-breaking for Vassar House—April 2008. L to R: Judy Wollack, Unknown, Representative Brown, Matt Mitchell, Mike Jones, Derrick McCree, Pete Walsh, Dale Yagiela, and me.

With son Zack, good friend Bill Tilton, and son Matt. (2007)

Entrance to the newly completed Vassar House, a program for troubled teen girls. Opened in the autumn of 2008. (Photographs on this page are from the WHS Archives)

Bruce Kintz has been board chairman of WHS for more than 20 years. His leadership, counsel, and encouragement has been invaluable to me.

With early mentor and friend, Jim Minder and Roger Swaininger. (2007)

With Dennis Muchmore and Detroit mayor Dennis Archer. (Circa 2000)

Brian Griese & Charlie Batch—Annual Banquet Award Winners. (1998)

With lobbying mentor and friend, Jon Smalley of Muchmore Harrington & Smalley.

With Rick Leach, U-M football great from the late 1970s and a WHS board member, and former U-M Football Coach "Bo" Schembechler.

With friend and former chief financial officer, Bob Blumenfield. (2009) (Photographs on this page are from the WHS Archives)

I have been privileged to meet a number of our political leaders over the years. These are people whose leadership I have particularly admired. (These photographs are from my personal collection.)

With Judy at a reception at the White House with President and Mrs. Clinton. (late 1990s)

With Judy and Senator John Kerry during a wedding reception following the wedding of my friend and advisor David Katz and his bride Jill Alpert. (2004) (Photograph courtesy of Vince Brennan)

With Vice President Al Gore. (2000)

With son Matt, Governor Jennifer Granholm, Judy, and son Zack. (January 22, 2009 at an Inaugural Party for President Barack Obama)

With Jon Cisky and Joel Gougeon two loyal supporters and former state Senators.

The Rev. Craig Wollack is the Agency's chaplain. He is standing in the back row (third from the left) following a weekend chapel service. His four children are in the front row. (Photo from WHS Archives—April 2006)

My Family. L to R: Back Row—Robert E. Wollack III, Cheri and Craig Wollack, me, Judy Wollack, Matthew, and Zachary. L to R: Front Row—Cheri & Craig's four children—Cassandra, Caleb, Cierra, and Cole. (Photograph was taken on the Outer Banks, NC—August 2008)

CHAPTER 15

DAY OF RECKONING

OUR DUCKS WERE IN order for the meeting with Harold Gazan. On the morning of September 11, I met Pete at his home at 8 o'clock. He kissed Lorraine and his two baby daughters goodbye and we got into the car. During the ninety-minute drive to Lansing, Pete barely said a word. I wrote it off to nervous apprehension because I was feeling that way myself. If Gazan said, "No," then what? I had already made a deal with Ed Overstreet that my last day at Boysville would be December 31st. If we failed to get a license, I'd be out of work and I had a one-year-old of my own to support.

Joe Jerome, our advocate in contracts management, said not to worry, but I wasn't so sure. "Gazan's a tough cookie," he said, "a no-nonsense guy that doesn't play." I thought of Gazan's confrontation with Jim Minder. "A lot of people in the bureaucracy don't like him, but he's respected for his integrity," Jerome said. "Just play your cards straight—and pray."

We arrived a half-hour early at the Michigan Department of Social Services (MDSS) central office complex in Lansing, one block south of the State Capitol. We were directed to an eighth-floor waiting area. At

10 o'clock sharp a tall, gaunt-looking man with a stern face greeted us. "Hello, I'm Harold Gazan," he said, extending his hand. I had been informed by my sources that Gazan was viewed as possessing a strong personality. This was very much on my mind and I was wondering how Pete and I would be accepted by him.

Gazan introduced us to two other people who followed us into his office. Gazan was a deputy director of MDSS with responsibility for all of the public accountability programs which included the Bureau of Regulatory Services that Gazan had developed and previously directed as well. "This is Cindy Harrison who directs the Bureau of Regulatory Services, and this is David Fitzgerald from the Division of Child Welfare Licensing," he stated. Pete and I nervously shook their hands and we all sat down around a small conference table.

As a Catholic I had gone to many confessions—most of them as a child—but the priest had always been invisible. It was comfortable in its anonymity. Now here I was with my best friend and would-be business partner sitting face-to-face before three inquisitors with our checkered past about to be dredged up. I dreaded the questions that were about to come.

Gazan shuffled some papers and spoke first. "Welcome to this meeting, gentlemen," he said. I looked for clues in his demeanor. His tone was gentle, almost deferential, but so was Charlie Updike's before he sent me to prison.

"Our purpose today," Gazan continued, "is to discuss your license application to establish a residential facility for adjudicated delinquent boys—I've already indicated that by letter to Mr. Wollack—and to explore whether your felony records will be an obstacle to the State of Michigan granting you a license. Mr. Walsh, the felony reference applies to you as well, does it not?"

"That's correct, sir," Pete said, leaning forward.

"Do you have a facility in mind?" Gazan asked.

"Yes, we do, sir," I said, "the Guardian Angel Convent on Mayfield in Detroit. It was put up for sale by the Archdiocese of Detroit."

"But you haven't purchased it yet, correct?"

"That's correct," I said. "We have a purchase offer ready to submit with a registered check, but obviously—"

"I know," Gazan interrupted. "You need a license to operate it first. That's what we're here to talk about. Now it says here on your application, Mr. Wollack, that you were convicted of conspiracy to violate federal racketeering laws on July 29, 1971, and that you served two-and-a-half years at the Milan Federal Correctional Institution. Is that correct?"

"That's correct, sir," I said.

"Can you describe the events that led to your conviction?"

"Well, sir, I was an undercover cop in New York City. My partners and I would go on drug raids. There were nineteen of us from the 78th Precinct in Brooklyn, and we were on the FBI's suspect list for allegedly selling drugs we confiscated on those raids—mostly cocaine."

"'Allegedly,' you say. Did you in fact *sell* the drugs?" Gazan asked.

"My conviction, sir, was for *conspiracy* to sell."

"I see," he said. "What about your partners, the other eighteen cops?"

"They went free," I said.

"How so?

"The FBI wanted me to confirm their names, but I wouldn't play ball. I just couldn't do it. I accepted responsibility for my own behavior and paid my debt to society, but I refused to rat on my partners, so I went to prison."

"I see," Gazan said again, his face failing to register a reaction. "And Mr. Walsh, what about you?" "What did you go to prison for?"

"Well, it's like this," Pete said. I could see his hands tremble under the table. "After high school I joined the Army and got sent to Vietnam." Pete told the rest of his story, up to our meeting as inmates in the weight room at Milan. "It was in prison that we started to turn our lives around," he said.

"Is that true, or are you just telling me that?" Gazan asked. "Tell me, either of you, why I should grant you a license."

I knew I had to think fast. "You trusted Jim Minder," I said. "You licensed him, didn't you?"

That put Gazan on the defensive. "I didn't know about his criminal record at the time," he said. "That came out later."

"But he turned his life around, didn't he?" I said.

Gazan was silent. He looked at the application again and said, "It says here you both went to the University of Michigan School of Social Work and you each earned your master's degree in social work in 1978."

"That's correct," I said.

"A fine school. I went there myself, finished in '61," he said. "Do you know Professor Charles Wolfson?"

I looked down and saw that Pete's hands had stopped shaking. Gazan's personal comment and inquiry about Professor Wolfson somehow eased the tension.

"Yes sir, we both do," Pete said.

"He did my family therapy at Milan and later became my graduate advisor," I said.

"Mine too," Pete said.

"He was the best—turned our lives around," I said.

Gazan smiled. "It looks that way from the rest of your application. I've also heard about the good work you're doing at Boysville. Now if you'll excuse us, my colleagues and I would like to consult among ourselves. Would you mind stepping outside?"

Ten or fifteen minutes later—which seemed like an eternity—Gazan called Pete and me back into his office.

"Well, gentlemen," he said, "I just want to say first that I believe in rehabilitation. Your past criminal records will not be an obstacle to your obtaining a license."

"Thank you, sir, thank you," I said, letting out a deep sigh. It felt like a millstone had been lifted from around my neck.

Gazan continued. "Second, I want you to obtain as many letters of endorsement as you can from a variety of people attesting to your integrity. Should everything be in order and we grant you a license, then you'll need to apply to the director of the Office of Children and Youth Services in this department for a contract. Thank you, gentlemen, and good luck."

That was it. I left the conference more relieved than jubilant. We still couldn't operate without a contract—I had learned that lesson from Jim Minder—and without a contract I couldn't risk Bill and Meredith's $300,000 check on a building that needed to be renovated, not to mention the money we needed to furnish it. That was where the home equity loans came in—loans Pete and I took out, putting our homes up for collateral. It was a risky proposition to say the least, but a necessity.

The next day Pete called. "I gotta talk to you," he said, "right now."

I could hear the crack in his voice.

"Where?" I said.

"Let's meet at Capraro's Pizza on Telegraph Road," he said.

After we sat down and placed our orders I said, "What's up?"

Pete hesitated at first and then said, "Brother Francis came over to see me. He wants to make me regional director when you leave Boysville."

"What do you mean, when *I* leave? I thought we were *both* leaving!"

"He's been telling people we're going to fail—he even told Lorraine that. He said you can't do it alone. He wants me to stay," he said.

"Fuck him!" I said.

"He offered me a promotion with a substantial pay increase. I've got two new babies at home and—"

"Fuck it! Forget the whole damn thing!" I said. "If you want out now, after all we've been through, fine. We've been friends for a long time, and you gotta do what's right for you. But this is bullshit!"

I stalked out of the restaurant, leaving Pete to pay the bill.

I was devastated. It had never occurred to me that Pete would have second thoughts. Worse, Brother Francis Boylan, the executive director of Boysville of Michigan, had violated my close friendship with Pete. First, he had talked behind my back and told everybody that I would fail, and then he offered Pete my job at Boysville before I had officially left. On the other hand, I was not being fair in my attitude toward Pete. He was a loyal friend, and he was appropriately concerned for the well-being of his young family. He had a normal desire to ensure the security of his family by staying with Boysville, particularly after he was offered a promotion. I began to be troubled in my mind about our friendship and realized that I had been unduly harsh and unsympathetic in my response to him. It was really Brother Francis who was being disrespectful and underhanded. Now the pressure was on me more than ever to succeed. I knew I'd have to make it on my own, and there was no turning back—not for me.

When Pete called me a couple of days later, I was ready to give him a second chance. Look," he said, "after thinking it over, I have changed my mind. The more I thought about it, the more I realized Brother Francis was driving a wedge between us. I want to go with *you* and I'm still willing to join you in using my house as collateral for a loan."

At first, I responded with caution, but I was relieved to know that we would be working together again. Pete readily accepted the number two position in our fledgling organization. I was glad that he was willing to join me in taking a big risk, and we were determined to make our organization the best in Michigan. And, that was the last time either of us would have to deal with Brother Francis as our boss.

The Michigan Department of Social Services (MDSS) granted us our license to open the Guardian Angel Convent as a residential home for adjudicated delinquent boys. Now all I needed was a contract. There was no small controversy within the halls of the MDSS about granting a contract to an unknown entity. At the same time, there were people in child welfare licensing, as well as in contracts management, who had been very impressed with the creative approach I had used to keep the program at St. Cecilia operating following the fire. Harold Gazan had expressed his admiration for what I had done at St. Cecilia and was favorably disposed toward us. And somewhat conveniently for us, Ken Visser of the Office of Children & Youth Services was faced with the challenge of getting youth out of the overcrowded Wayne County Juvenile Detention facility as quickly as possible. He recommended to his boss Wayne Anderson that a contract be approved, and another hurdle was overcome.

On Christmas Eve day 1986, there was a knock on my office door at Cabrini Center. I had one week to go before leaving Boysville; one more week until my paychecks stopped.

"Come in," I said.

Joe Jerome entered. I was surprised to see him.

"What brings you here from Lansing?" I asked.

"This," he said, handing me an envelope.

I opened the envelope and pulled out an official-looking document. It had the Great Seal of the State of Michigan and two signatures at the bottom.

"It's your contract," Jerome said, "$900,000 for twelve months. You're in business. Congratulations!"

My eyes glazed over. Joe could not have known what that packet of papers meant to me. While he waited for me to say something, my mind drifted back sixteen years—to Christmas Eve of 1970.

"Joe," I said finally, "this sure beats sitting in a jail cell in Manhattan."

"What are you talking about?"

"Let's get Pete Walsh and celebrate," I said. "Then I'll tell you all about it."

PART THREE

MAKING VICTORS

"Being is manifested only in the process of actualizing its power. . . . Power becomes actualized in those situations in which opposition is overcome."

Rollo May, *Power and Innocence*

CHAPTER 16

THE LAUNCH

ONCE THE CONTRACT came through, I couldn't wait to get started. But things always take longer than you think they should. Not counting Christmas, I had thirty-eight days to get the building ready. All of the papers had been filed. We had our license and contract in hand, and the Archdiocese had accepted Bill Tilton's purchase offer. Now it seemed that all that remained to be done was some touch-up painting and some furniture purchases.

My board of directors was in place and it was an impressive team of professionals dedicated to helping kids. I had "Big Billie" Dufek, an All-American who had been drafted by the New York Jets and had played for one season before being sidelined by injury. He owned and managed a State Farm Insurance agency in Ann Arbor. He became our first board president. Vice president of the board was Ron Warhurst, who was the head coach of the cross country team and distance runners at the University of Michigan, and he ultimately became head track coach. Bruce Kintz, a young insurance executive, became the board secretary. Jon Walgren was our board treasurer. He was a mountain of a man and the only Michigan State University graduate on our board. Other board members included Don Dufek, the consummate strong safety and All-American from Michigan then playing for the Seattle Seahawks; Bob Ellis, who lived in Ann Arbor and was a small business owner; Howard "Howdy" Holmes, an Indy race car driver and North American Grand Prix winner and the CEO of the Jiffy Mix Company; Rick Leach, the extraordinary former quarterback for Michigan and four-year letterman in both football and baseball, at that time playing with the Toronto Blue Jays; Jimmy Libs, a volunteer assistant to Ron Warhurst and the owner of an insurance company; Jerry Meter, one of the finest human beings you'll ever meet and an assistant football coach and a track coach at the University of Michigan (he is now a sales representative for Steelcase); Jim Minder, President and CEO of Spectrum Human Services and a former mentor; and the Rev. Jimmy Ward, Jr., one of the great youth care workers in the Detroit area who left to go to Houston, Texas, but would later return to Michigan to work for me.

Of all these individuals, I owe special thanks to Bruce Kintz, who would rise through the board ranks to become chairman and serve in that capacity for over two decades. He remains one of my most available and trusted advisors on matters related to agency governance.

The Convent building located in one of Detroit's toughest neighborhoods was the latest casualty of the Archdiocese's decline. Built in 1950 to accommodate the rush of young women taking their vows, the two-story red-brick former convent featured an impressive arched entryway and a chapel with oak pews. It was in many respects a knock-off of St Cecelia. Its classrooms, central dining room, and two dozen bedrooms covered enough space—25,000 square feet—to fill half a football field. The building needed some sprucing up, and Bill's willingness to invest $300,000 in this building in this neighborhood can appropriately be described as a leap of faith. Not everyone was as hopeful.

The Launch

Returning from an inspection visit with the fire marshal, Pete said, "There's no way we can do it."

"Do what?" I asked.

"Turn the convent into a boys' home—that's what the fire marshal said."

"So what's the problem?"

"First, we need to put in fire doors and emergency exits. Second, if we have more than nineteen kids living there, we have to put in a sprinkler system."

I picked up the phone and dialed Earl Thomas, a building contractor who had restored St. Cecilia's group home after the fire. Earl was more than a contractor. He was a man with a passion for the work Pete and I were doing.

"Fire doors? Emergency exits? By when? February 2nd?" Earl sounded incredulous. He paused for a few seconds and said, "The sprinkler system might take a little longer."

The next-to-last item on our to-do list was to buy furniture—enough to equip this enormous building. A few abandoned tables in the dining room were useable. But we needed beds, mattresses, and dressers as well as desks and chairs. Pete compiled the inventory.

"How much will it cost?" I asked.

"Sixty thousand dollars," he said. "That's if we go to garage sales. If we buy this stuff retail, it'll cost as much as the building."

We hit up three Ann Arbor banks for $30,000 in loans—$10,000 from each bank—putting our own homes up for collateral. We had the good fortune of preceding the current state of technology, and by applying with all three institutions on the same day, we were able to garner more proceeds than our homes could actually support. But it was for a good cause.

Between meetings with bureaucrats, contractors, and job-seekers, Pete and I hit several garage sales and second-hand stores in the Detroit area and transported our bargain purchases back to the convent in borrowed trucks.

Pete and I began to interview job-seekers in earnest. We initially hired six of our former colleagues from Boysville (now renamed

Holy Cross Children's Services) one of whom is still with us—Nolan Moore. He ultimately went on to earn a master's degree in social work and is now the director of training for our Wolverine Human Services' (WHS) southern region. Shortly thereafter, several additional people from Boysville came to join our new venture. They were willing to take a risk, but they also were loyal to me and my philosophy about working with adolescents who had become law violators; and they were caught up in the excitement of launching a new program.

I knew that I would need a good accountant. I had talked with Dudley Spade, who at that time was the chief financial officer for Boysville and who later went on to serve as a state representative and the chair of the Sub-Committee on Social Services Appropriations. I sought his advice on hiring an accountant although I secretly had hoped that he might be willing to accept the challenge of helping us start a new program. I was not able to match his salary nor was it feasible for him to make a move at that time. (Hell, I wasn't able to meet my *own* previous salary.) However, he suggested that I submit an advertisement to a couple of trade magazines which I did.

One of the first respondents was a young twenty-three-year-old recent graduate of Arizona State University who had just moved to the area to seek employment (he was living with his sister at the time). He was a handsome man with an intelligent face, and black curly hair. He was a bit chunky and stood about five-foot-seven. During his first interview, I peppered him with stories of the great Bo Schembechler and U of M. I took note of his keen observation of the maize walls and blue baseboards that would become a hallmark of all of our facilities. For his second interview, this young punk had the audacity to come to the interview wearing a sweatshirt that proclaimed in bold letters: "Arizona State Bowls Over Bo!" As some of you may recall, Arizona State had defeated Michigan in the Rose Bowl a month earlier. John Cooper was then-coach of Arizona State and, as a result of his having defeated Michigan, he was hired by Ohio State as the head coach of its football team. Michigan went on to defeat Ohio State nine times out of the next ten confrontations. In spite of the young man's audacity, Pete and I were pleased with the interview we had had with Robert Blumenfeld. He promised that if hired he would begin that very night to explore the accounting requirements for non-profit organizations.

Pete and I were impressed with his intelligence and energy, and we admired his courage to wear that sweatshirt for an interview with two rabid Wolverine fans. I wanted to offer him a position on the spot, but we also had two other candidates lined up and we felt obligated to go through with those interviews. Besides, one of those interviewees might have been a person with more experience. After completing the other two interviews, Pete and I decided that we should sleep on it and make our final decision the following day. However, somehow or other, neither Pete nor I could find Blumenfeld's application. Apparently, we had mistakenly thrown his application out along with the others. I was in a panic as I really wanted to hire this guy. Less than fifteen minutes later, Bob Blumenfeld called me because he wanted to share with me what he had learned about non-profit organizations through research in the library. I immediately offered him the position and explained that I wanted to talk with him about a compensation package and invited him to come to my office as soon as he could. He was there in less than thirty minutes and this time with a different shirt. So began a great friendship that has continued to this day. Bobby "B" has moved on to become the chief financial officer of the Orchards Children's Services. After working in the for-profit sector for a while, he realized that he really was committed to the non-profit child welfare field.

Pioneer Human Services had gone from a dream to a reality. That name had derived from my days on the wagon train. But ultimately I wanted to recognize all that the great University of Michigan had afforded me in the way of education and upward mobility. My wife Judy promoted the idea. "You're always bringing in athletes from the University of Michigan as role models. And you've incorporated them into your board," she said. "How about the name *Wolverine*?—*Wolverine Human Services*," she said. "Make the

They Will Be Victors

'W' an upside down 'M' and use the same type-style and colors—maize and blue—as the University of Michigan name and colors."

"That's it!" I exclaimed. "*Wolverine Human Services!*" The decision was made and within the year the transition would be completed.

"We need a motto to go with it," I said.

Without skipping a beat she said, "I have an idea for that, too—*Helping Children To Be Victors.*"

But where our first facility was concerned, I was sure of the name I wanted. I had thought about it for years. During my own personal struggles, when Tony Sablowski had died, and each time I saw a young person in need of guidance and support the same name came to my mind. For years I had been wearing a medal of St. Jude, the patron saint of desperate situations. The name "St. Jude's Home for Boys" had a special meaning for me. It was a concept that was close and personal and spoke to what we were about to embark on. We ourselves were now in a desperate situation, and we were about to become responsible for boys who had suffered neglect, abandonment, and abuse, and who, no doubt, recognized the desperation of their own circumstances. I recall invoking the prayer attributed to St. Jude on almost a nightly basis during this period, and I believe God answered my prayers. St. Jude's Home for Boys would be the name of our facility!

I drove back to the former convent and nailed a sign on the dining room wall listing my seven principles: *Reality, Responsibility, Respect, Communication, Negotiation, Education, Love*. The rapping of the hammer was the most beautiful of symphonies to my ears that night.

It was close to midnight when I got home. Judy, who was pregnant with our second child, was reading in bed. I checked on Zack our two-year-old, and I found him fast asleep. Before I turned out the light I turned to Judy and said softly, but with assurance, "We're ready!"

The day we opened—February 2, 1987—was just about the happiest day of my life. Not only had we accomplished the implausible—if not impossible—task of converting a nunnery into a home for delinquent boys, but we'd met all of our deadlines and gotten all of our approvals—including the fire marshal's occupancy permit—in the nick of time. A brand new sign in the front yard proclaimed our name in bright maize and blue letters:

ST. JUDE'S HOME FOR BOYS
"HELPING CHILDREN TO BE VICTORS"

The name couldn't have been more fitting. The morning we opened, a police van pulled up and delivered our first nine charges. I was discouraged to see them shackled in handcuffs, reflecting on the shame I had felt in similar circumstances. Their crimes had consisted of everything from drug sales to armed robbery and attempted murder. Moved out of the Wayne County Youth Home, a short-term detention facility in Detroit, these were the kids society deemed hopeless.

Still, they were kids. "First, the handcuffs have gotta go," I told the police as they ushered the boys into the building. "This is a home, not a prison."

Pete, who did intake the first day, saw to it that each boy got cleaned up and assigned to a room. At noon he ushered them into the cafeteria.

"This is Willie," he said, introducing me to a fourteen-year-old African-American youth.

"Hello, Willie," I said. "I'm Robert Wollack. Welcome to St. Jude's."

Willie refused to look up or speak. Later I learned that he had been abandoned after his father was killed and his mother, a junkie, went to jail.

A few days later I encountered Willie again. This time he looked me in the face and shook my hand.

"How are you doing, Willie?" I asked.

"I'm doing good," he said.

"How are things going so far?"

"It's alright I guess—better than being at the Youth Home." And he smiled.

It was a start, but only a start. Meanwhile ten more boys arrived, bringing us to nineteen—our limit until the sprinkler system got put in. One of them DeShawn had already been thrown out of two other treatment group homes. "Resists authority," his chart said, and "frequently bullies other kids."

Jimmy's problem was just the opposite: kids bullied him. "He's not going to school," his distraught mother said, "because he says the kids make fun of him. That's on the good days. On the bad days they beat him up."

Either way, Jimmy would come home crying. After a while he refused to go to school at all.

"You know, Pete," I said, "some of these kids will make it, and others just won't. The odds are totally stacked against them. But we won't let that stop us from doing what we can for them."

"Let's pray they don't wind up in prison," Pete said.

Paul Seal, a burly tall, black kid from Detroit, found his way out of the ghetto the only way he could: through a football scholarship at the University of Michigan. After graduating from Pershing High School, he starred four years at tight end for the Wolverines and was co-captain during his senior year. He played in the NFL for nine years—half with the New Orleans Saints and half with the San Francisco 49ers. Like other athletes who had worked with me—first at St. Cecilia's, and now at St. Jude's—Paul really cared about kids. When asked during the writing of this book why he was willing to follow me to St. Jude's, Paul explained, "I loved what I was doing, and you taught me how to handle these kids. You are one of the most down-to-earth people I have ever met. When you were at St. Cecilia, you never acted like you were too important to be with us. You ate with the boys and with the staff. You played basketball with the boys and you also held group meetings with them. You never allowed the boys to disrespect staff, and you never allowed us to disrespect the boys."

My first meeting with Seal was a memorable one. The summer after I re-opened St. Cecilia's following the fire—1981—a dark green Mercedes Benz with gold trim pulled up in front of the build-

The Launch

ing. Out of the car climbed Paul Seal who proceeded through the front door and into my office. He was an imposing figure with an easy manner and a disarming smile.

"Howard Babson sent me to see you," he said. "He told me about the good work you're doing. I'm wondering if you might have a place for me." Babson was a professor of social work at the University of Michigan.

I looked at Paul's Mercedes Benz through the window. "I don't think you can live on what I can afford to pay you," I said.

"Look, I've got some money saved up," he said. "I just wanna do what you're doing and help troubled kids get a break."

I hired Paul on the spot. I knew the salary I could pay him was a pittance compared to what he had made in the NFL, but that didn't matter.

The first kid Pete assigned to him was DeShawn who had trouble with authority. "We went at it for days, weeks, even months," Paul said later. "But I stayed with him. I took a personal interest in him because I knew he was a good kid. He just had all this anger inside of him. I had to let him get all that anger out."

Finally, there was a breakthrough. "I don't know if he just got tired of buttin' heads with me or what," Paul said, "but finally his whole attitude changed. He asked if we could talk. He said he wanted to apologize for all the bad things he'd done."

Thanks to Paul and the other staffers who came with me from St. Cecilia and other Boysville programs, we had some early success stories. But we had our setbacks too. In our second week, a youth stole the secretary's keys and drove her car into a highway median. Another kid who was out on a weekend pass—Timmitt "Big Papa" Richardson—was killed by a rival gang member over a gold chain. I along with my staff were so incensed by this tragic event, that we actually assisted the Highland Park police by obtaining evidence which helped to convict the killers. Another youth who had gone AWOL threw a chunk of concrete over a highway overpass and killed a young mother in her car. He wound up in prison—rightly so—for making really bad decisions that resulted

They Will Be Victors

in the tragic and unnecessary loss of life; I was determined all the more to help troubled youth to make RIGHT decisions.

When you see youth make bad choices, you scratch your head and ask yourself, "Is what I'm doing really making a difference?" There is a story about a boy walking on a beach, throwing starfish that have washed up on the shore back into the surf. A man comes by and suggests that his efforts are an exercise in futility. "Throwing those starfish back doesn't make a difference," he says. The boy looks at the man as he tosses another one out to sea, and says, "It does to that *one* starfish." The metaphor is as true for young people as it is for starfish. While we clearly cannot save them all, we should never use that as an excuse not to try.

With youth in care we were able to generate some much needed revenue. By September we scraped together enough funds to install the sprinkler system and admit our next group of fifteen boys. We upgraded our furniture and remodeled our kitchen. At his own expense Earl Thomas, the contractor, put a boxing ring in the room that had been the chapel—something that surely would have mortified the good sisters of the Guardian Angel Convent.

But when you think about it, chapels and boxing rings have something in common—it's where people seek affirmation. The difference is that for adolescent boys the seeking is generally more physical than spiritual. Rollo May says every human being cries out for significance. While most of us find positive ways to satisfy that need, a kid whose need for self-affirmation and self-realization is blocked will sooner or later act out his frustration through physical aggression or violence.

Thanks to Earl Thomas' unusual gift, boxing not only helped our kids channel their aggression, but it gave them a framework for playing by the rules—the same as in any other sport. They soon learned that if you break the rules, you pay a penalty—the same as in real life. Our first boxing instructor and trainer was Bill Moran who was a social worker and also a former boxer and football player with the University of Michigan. Other instructors followed, including Hilmer Kenty, former lightweight boxing world champion

(1980). Well-known Detroit boxing instructor Eddie Carr (whose son Oba was a former lightweight championship contender) also served our young men until his retirement. These men proved that boxing can help prevent violence and teach youth to control tempers by applying the rules of the sport of competitive boxing.

In January 1988 we opened our first emergency shelter. I had the news media to thank for that, because of a series of stories they ran about "lobby bodies"— neglected children and homeless youth who were in need of foster care placement but who were being kept in the foyer of the MDSS office building located on Baltimore Street in Detroit. The MDSS awarded us a contract for a twenty-bed respite care center for adolescent boys to alleviate the "lobby-body" problem. The service was reminiscent of the program I had established years before at St. Cecilia.

Pete Walsh identified the vacated Brent Hospital building, located on Detroit's west side across from the University of Detroit, as a viable site for the program. We named it simply Brent Center. Within a year we would relocate to Lenox Street on Detroit's east side and rename the program the Wolverine Shelter. It functions as a critical link in the continuum of services—an assessment center serving as a lifeline for kids who have fallen through society's safety net. Many of them have profound mental health issues and severe emotional problems which, if left unattended, would pose grave consequences down the road. One of the staff I hired to work at the Lenox Street Shelter (now renamed the Wolverine Diagnostic and Assessment Center) was another University of Michigan athlete named Ricky Davis.

Ricky joined the staff in October 1989 as a direct care staff member. He is now a residential care coordinator at the same facility. Ricky is one of our loyal, competent staff members who continues to enjoy the challenge of working with troubled youth. His original career goal upon graduating from the University of Michigan in 1984 was to play professional football and then become a school teacher. Ricky was a running back with the U-M Wolverines from 1980-1983, and then played with the St. Louis Cardinals (NFL Football Team) for four years but left after suffering a knee injury. He recalls his first interview with me in the fall of 1989. He recounted how he thought to himself that I reminded him of his football coach, "Bo" Schembechler. "Mr. Wollack was energetic, enthusiastic, and vibrant about working with youth. I knew this was a man I wanted to work for."

We launched three more programs before the year was out. The first of these was Victors' Center, a residential treatment center at the former St. Ambrose Convent on Detroit's east side. We leased the property from the Archdiocese of Detroit for the purpose of converting it into a residential program for young teen-age boys. This presented us with some unique and unexpected challenges. Some of the local residents were very worried about having "bad kids" in their neighborhood. Consequently, the Detroit Zoning Board of Appeals scheduled a public hearing to enable the two sides to make their presentations before making a final decision. The meeting was held on a wintery morning in mid-January 1988. *The Beehive* (St. Ambrose RC Church newsletter) reported on the meeting. The attorney for nearby property owners warned about possible loss of property values. It also reported that, in response, Pete Walsh successfully conveyed that the program would operate safely and would not compromise their neighborhood. The Detroit Zoning Appeals Board approved our request for a zoning status change.

A second program, Supervised Independent Living, was designed to teach older adolescents how to manage living on their own. This was our first non-residential program, and it served as a community reintegration endpoint in our continuum of care.

Our third program was the Pioneer Work and Learn Center. It was our first venture into a non-urban setting, and it was a challenge I had been longing to pursue. I believed in the VisionQuest model, but without the violence that was being perpetrated by their staff. The zoning controversy that we had overcome at St. Ambrose would prove invaluable in the battle that we would face in our efforts to establish our own brand of wilderness adventure training for troubled youth.

CHAPTER 17

WAR AND PEACE

AS BABIES BORN IN the post-1967 riot era came of age, Detroit faced severe economic and social challenges. White flight and rising unemployment, drug abuse, and violent crime contributed to Detroit's downward spiral. Despite all that the region has to offer, Detroit's image as a center of urban decay persists even to this day.

With the advent of the crack cocaine epidemic in the mid- to late 1980s the city had more young criminals than it could handle. Juvenile courts couldn't keep up with their caseloads. Kids at the Wayne County Youth Home were forced to sleep on the floor. In an evaluation report in February 1991, Professor Rosemary Sarri commented on the escalation of juvenile delinquency, especially among urban minority males residing in neighborhoods with high rates of social disorganization and crime.

> *Whether the growth of juvenile crime is founded in reality or not, the media as well as policy and research literature depict a difficult and nearly hopeless situation for poverty-stricken young people and their families. This*

pattern of increasing institutionalization was particularly evident in Michigan where the proportion of youth committed to the state from Wayne County for delinquency shifted from 54% in the mid-1980s to 80% in 1989.[8]

Several violent events in the community precipitated a public outcry for more aggressive responses to juvenile crime. During the last week of December 1986 *The Detroit News* ran a four-part series of articles entitled, "Kids Kill, Kids Die." The articles focused on the level of violence being perpetrated by juveniles. The only thing experts "agree on is that the juvenile justice system is failing. . . . And no one person or group can change it alone," the paper stated. The final article concludes with this announcement: "Earlier this month, the state Legislature approved a $9 million plan to add 180 beds to the state's 1,569-bed treatment system."[9] That was a threshold day. The following day Governor Blanchard was inaugurated for his second four-year term of office and his appointee to head the Department of Social Services, C. Patrick Babcock, assumed his new responsibilities.

Front-page headlines of Detroit newspapers throughout 1987 continued to highlight teen involvement in violent crime. For example: "17-year-old charged in boy's murder."[10] "Youth charged in brick death."[11] "14-year-old convicted in homicide."[12] "Detroit has a level of violence that has no equal among other U.S. cities."[13] Eager for a solution, Detroit Mayor Coleman Young proposed sending juvenile offenders to work camps in the state's Upper Peninsula for rehabilitation and job training. But the MDSS took a more practical view: "A career in forestry," a MDSS study concluded, "cannot be considered viable for inner city youth who are going to be living in downtown Detroit."

Eventually the mayor and Governor James Blanchard struck a compromise: expand Michigan's residential facilities to accommodate a potential several hundred juvenile offenders from across the state, but build the facilities closer to Detroit where most of the offenders were coming from. It was up to C. Patrick Babcock to put the plan into operation. During 1987 he had an official Request for

_____ War and Peace

Proposal (RFP) developed and released to invite qualified organizations to submit their ideas for a "Work and Learn Camp" for one hundred youth. The hope was to offer thirteen-to-seventeen-year-old boys an Outward Bound-type alternative to detention. The program was to combine education and social treatment modalities that used both group and individual counseling with a wilderness-based experiential component. The residential component of the program was to be for a six-month period which would be followed by six more months of community–based counseling and guidance. In addition, the residential component was designed to develop among the boys a sense of teamwork and improved self-esteem through participation in high adventure experiences that included vigorous activities, back-packing treks, and obstacle courses. These strenuous activities were designed to require the boys to function as a team in order to complete the various physical challenges and to perform problem-solving tasks as a team. These activities served to enhance feelings of trust among the group members. This "work-and-learn" approach to juvenile rehabilitation would be a first for the State of Michigan, but it was also going to generate considerable controversy.

No sooner was the plan announced by MDSS than opposition groups started forming in communities that were named as possible sites for the camp, including a possible site in Oakland County. "We don't want teen predators coming into our backyards and preying on our children," was the common outcry. Bowing to the pressure, public officials in three lower-Michigan counties put the kibosh on the state doing any such thing in their jurisdictions.

I called my friend and mentor, Jim Minder. "Jim," I said, "Why don't we submit a joint proposal? We'll run the camp together."

Thanks to Jerry Meter, a member of my board, we had found a potential site outside Kingston, a small town in Tuscola County in the Michigan Thumb. This location was within the one-hundred mile radius of Detroit mandated by the issued RFP. But as the political winds changed, so did the word from Lansing. The Michigan Department of Social Services withdrew its one-hundred bed proposal and replaced it with a new RFP for only fifty youth. A proposal for a *fifty*-person camp? It didn't pay for Minder and me to team up on a camp half the size of the one we had planned, so instead of submitting a proposal together we agreed to each submit one on our own. For the first time since I did my student placement with him, we were competing with each other for a state contract.

It was during our first annual Sportsmen's Banquet which was held on March 24, 1988 that Mr. Babcock announced that we were to be awarded the contract to operate the state's first Work and Learn Camp. That was an exciting event. "Bo" Schembechler, Michigan's head football coach, gave a speech with the theme of "Giving Forward." The title of his speech meant that by investing in the rehabilitation of young people we would reap dividends in the future as these young people became productive citizens of our society.

The question may come mind as to why Mr. Babcock selected Wolverine Human Services when it had only been in operation for such a short time. Well, he didn't—not at first. But in an interview undertaken in connection with this narrative, Babcock shared the following recollection:

"The pressure from the Governor clearly escalated in a matter of three or four days. He wanted us to develop a new concept of residential care that would include meaningful work experiences, outdoor adventure, and educational components. I don't recall that many of the established providers came forward to develop a proposal. Wolverine Human Services was not our first choice, and that was a mistake. The person we first found was untested and was looking for a financial advantage. By the time we went to Bob Wollack, we had learned a lot from the previous process. Wollack was a risk taker and clearly understood troubled boys—his own experiences as a youth gave him that edge. I suspect (without putting words in his mouth) that Bob saw himself in those kids—he was looking out for the kids. . . . I had been to St. Jude's several times. I observed on one occasion that as we walked into a room, a youth who was very upset required more than one staff member to control the situation. It was one of those circumstances where you, as the agency administrator, couldn't have had a full understanding of what had happened just ahead of your entry into the room. It could have been the result of a youth acting out, or a staff member having handled a situation inappropriately; but it was the kind of issue where you walk into the room (and you have a high state official with you) and you would just as soon get out of there right away. Bob did not react like that. Bob Wollack is one of the few, in fact he is the only child welfare agency director that I have had this experience with. Instead, he took time to talk with the youth and then talked with the staff individually and he sorted it all out. I have always been impressed with that action—he took time to talk to each of the people involved. Bob put together a credible and exciting proposal in response to our RFP and we awarded him the contract."

While Lansing had made its decision, the community proposed for our program site—Kingston, Michigan—still needed a little convincing. The experience made me wonder what it must have been like for a black person living in Selma, Alabama, in the early '60s. A town of four hundred inhabitants, Kingston sat in the heart of Michigan Militia country. It was a stone's throw away from where Terry Nichols, Timothy McVeigh's accomplice in the Oklahoma City bombing, grew up. I never saw hooded white robes or a burning cross in town, but I didn't have to go very far to get a feel for the place.

The camp we hoped to use was located a mile south of town and occupied a sixty-acre site surrounded by pike and bass-filled ponds. The cabins were typical of what one might find at a summer camp: screen doors that didn't latch, cracked window panes, sticks of sunlight poking through rustic walls. But the basketball courts, playing fields, and swimming pool made it a perfect setting for what we had in mind.

The camp's owner, who was a district court judge from Royal Oak, a Detroit suburb, was sympathetic to our cause. The Honorable Keith Leenhouts had seen what happened to young offenders after they were tried and convicted in his courtroom. They'd pay a fine or go to jail and two or three years later they would find themselves back in his courtroom. The system was a revolving door, and the kids who entered were no better off when they got out.

The judge had purchased the camp to give his young remandants an alternative to jail. But he soon discovered he couldn't manage a youth camp and an overloaded court docket at the same time, so leasing the camp to us was the next best thing because of our common mission. The only difference was, he had purchased the camp to use in the summer and we intended to use it year around. That meant we had to get a special use zoning permit. "Oh, but that would take months, even years," we were warned. "Besides, you don't want to deal with the chairman of the Koylton Township Zoning Board."

I couldn't wait and neither could DSS. My attorney Sam McCargo came up with a solution. "Look, we have the camp permit that was issued to the owner," he said. "Let's go with that. It'll buy us time till we straighten things out with the zoning board."

Meanwhile, word got out that a "penal colony" was coming to town. "We don't want inmates in our backyard," one resident protested to the *Tuscola County Advertiser*. "Why do we have to take outcasts from the big city?" cried another. Petitions circulated and yard signs began popping up with the acronym *RAID (Residents Against Institutions for Delinquents)* displayed in bold letters. Obviously the opposition was organized.

But we had work to do in preparation for our first arrivals—staff to hire, cabins to paint, and grounds to spruce up. The pool leaked a quarter of its capacity every day, but with fall approaching that could wait. Most crucial, however, was the need to hire staff, including a director for the program. I again looked to former colleagues with whom I had worked at Boysville. I had heard that Mike Jones, who had been the director of Boysville's northern region, had been demoted by Brother Francis, CEO of Boysville. Rather than accept a demotion, Mike resigned. I hunted him down. Pete and I interviewed him and asked if he was interested in being the director. He agreed to the terms we offered and became the

War and Peace

director of the Pioneer Work and Learn Camp. He brought with him other Boysville staff, including Bill Haines, Jim Furbish, Matt Mitchell, and several others. All but a few are still with Wolverine Human Services.

The first campers arrived the first day of October 1988. Orlando, sixteen, was a Hispanic kid from Detroit whose father had deserted him and whose mother sold crack from an ice cream truck. Then there was Pren who was hardly your typical intake case. An ethnic Albanian, Pren arrived at the camp in a three-car caravan—all shiny black Cadillacs filled with men in dark suits. His grandfather climbed out of the lead car and motioned his grandson out of the second car. "I heard about your camp," he told Matt Mitchell, our intake coordinator. "This is my grandson. He's having some problems, and this is what I want you to do with him." Leaving instructions, the grandfather rejoined the caravan and sped off. Matt never asked Pren what his grandfather did for a living. "I am not sure I wanted to know," he said.

In spite of the yard signs, petitions, and letters to the *Tuscola County Advertiser*, the camp carried on without interference. Over the next three months more and more kids arrived from Detroit and elsewhere, which meant more and more jobs for local residents and more and more business for local merchants. By December not only were we at full capacity with fifty kids, but we had become the second largest employer in Tuscola County. I began to think the longer we stayed and the more townspeople saw how we helped the local economy, the more the resistance to our presence would taper off.

But two events happened that proved me wrong. The first incident occurred during Christmas break. Three of Matt Mitchell's young charges (including two African-Americans) had finished the first three months at the top of their class. For a reward Matt decided to treat them to lunch in town. He and the three boys climbed into the Pioneer Work and Learn Center van and headed to Suzy Q's, a mom-and-pop restaurant in town. When they entered and sat down, all the other customers in the restaurant—as if by some prearranged signal—got up and walked out.

The second incident happened at one o'clock in the morning when our van, which was parked by our office in downtown Kingston, mysteriously caught on fire. It was like St. Cecilia all over again, but this time it was worse. This wasn't the act of a disgruntled employee; this was a hate crime. It was reminiscent of Selma in the '60s.

Even so, it was one thing for private citizens to act out their prejudices; it was another thing for public officials to do it. I had been warned about the chairman of the Koylton Township Zoning Board. However, I was not prepared for the vitriolic outburst made by a shotgun-toting local citizen who called our kids "biological garbage" on the six o'clock news. Nothing had prepared me for that level of unapologetic hate cloaked in the guise of protecting property values. I didn't know what would happen next. And I didn't know how much the outside world would be tuning in until I read the following article:

Detroit Free Press
June 12, 1990
RULING IMPERILS STRUGGLING DSS CAMP PROGRAM

A controversial state plan to reform juvenile delinquents by sending them to rural "work and learn" camps faces a struggle to survive after an unfavorable court ruling....Last week, Tuscola County Circuit Judge Patrick Joslyn ruled that the operators of the Pioneer Work and Learn Camp near Kingston violated local zoning ordinances when they converted it into a detention facility from a summer recreational camp. The ruling gives Koylton Township the authority to seek an order to close the camp. An attorney for the township zoning board said the board will ask the judge to order "immediate termination of the project."

On June 13, the day after the story came out, Judge Joslyn ordered the Pioneer Work and Learn Camp to "cease and desist." Rejecting our argument that Kingston residents were turning in favor of the camp, the Court of Appeals affirmed Joslyn's ruling on the grounds we had violated the township's zoning ordinance. Under the encouragement of our attorney, Sam McCargo, we decided to appeal to the Michigan Supreme Court.

Meanwhile, Bill Haines and Jim Leggett the camp's co-directors, and Clinton House, a local attorney I hired to advise them, sought a zoning variance from the Koylton Township Zoning Board. Not surprisingly, Chairman Mayer ignored their requests for a public hearing. Frustrated by his unresponsiveness, Haines, Leggett, and House went over his head to the Koylton Township Board of Trustees. A reporter from the *Saginaw News* covered the meeting:

> KINGSTON—A fight to keep open the Pioneer Work and Learn Center here is back in the hands of the Koylton Township Zoning Board. The Township Board of Trustees voted Monday to order the zoning panel to host a public hearing on whether to grant the juvenile detention facility a special use permit....The only way the zoning panel would consider the issue is if the township board forced it to do so, said Zoning Board Chairman Russell Mayer, a staunch opponent of the camp.

The Koylton Township Board of Trustees gave the two opposing parties six months to work out a good faith arrangement which would allow the camp to stay. Ignoring the board's directive, Anthony Sykora, a Sandusky lawyer hired to represent the zoning board, secured an August 30 date on Judge Joslyn's docket to enforce his cease and desist order. He also demanded that we pay the zoning board $76,888 to cover legal expenses incurred in their effort to kick us out of Kingston.

On August 30, Judge Joslyn made his ruling: Vacate in ten days and pay the court a fine of $100 a day from the date the Michigan Supreme Court denied our appeal (which in fact they already had on August 5). "You're here for a day of accounting and you've got it," Joslyn said. His order gave me until midnight, September 9, to close the camp. If I didn't comply, I'd be hauled back into his court for contempt.

The only problem was how to pick up and leave on ten days' notice with fifty juveniles who had nowhere else to go, not to mention all those Kingston residents who counted on the camp for their livelihood. It would take months to comply with the judge's order. The Koylton Township Board of Trustees, which met in special session after Judge Joslyn entered his order, took a more realistic view:

> *Tuscola County Advertiser*
> *September 4, 1991*
> KOYLTON TOWNSHIP CAMP DOESN'T PULL STAKES
> *Koylton Township officials passed directives...insuring that no Township official will seek a contempt charge against Pioneer Work and Learn Center after Joslyn's 10-day period has expired. . . At a special township meeting Tuesday night...it was agreed to take no further action against the camp without prior written approval of the township board, and, specifically directed the zoning board to take no action to enforce the court order to cease and desist.*

At least the Koylton Township Board of Trustees was willing to be reasonable. But their "take no further action" mandate didn't stop Mayer, the zoning board chairman, and Sykora, the zoning board lawyer from going back to Judge Joslyn. On September 25, the judge issued the following summons:

> *It is ordered that Pioneer Human Services, Inc. and its Executive Director, Robert Wollack....shall appear before this court on the 4th day of October, 1991, to show cause why he should not be held in contempt of court.*

Thanks to the Koylston Township Board of Trustees, which had already granted me a six-month reprieve to work out an agreement with the zoning board, the judge withdrew the contempt citation. But he wasn't in the mood to grant the six months. "It's going to be half that," he said. "If you don't vacate by January 4, 1992—three months from today—I'll see you back in this courtroom on contempt."

Then he added: "Bring *War and Peace* with you, because you'll have plenty of time to read it."

War and Peace

There was still the unresolved matter of the zoning board hearing. Not until Judge Joslyn entered his final order did Russell Mayer finally call a public hearing. But by then the issue was moot. Bill Haines, co-director of the Pioneer Work and Learn Camp, had already found us a site twenty miles west of Kingston in the town of Vassar, whose four thousand inhabitants were eager for an economic boost.

The hearing at Kingston High School drew a sea of supporters. "I'm proud to have them as neighbors," testified a woman from South Kingston Road, referring to the fifty boys at Pioneer Camp. "We don't have children like that in our own community who show respect for elderly people." A neighbor on Phillips Road declared, "If you do good for someone else, good will come back to you." Another neighbor Carl Silvernail thundered, "I'm a Christian! To refuse service to these people would be contrary to everything I believe. The day of judgment will come."

With a heavy heart I listened to their pleas, but it was too late. I even felt guilty about my own attitude toward the town. Maybe it wasn't like Selma after all. Can you judge the whole town on the basis of a few people who happen to be in positions of power? But what happens when those few people prevail? That *isn't* how democracy is supposed to work. A few days after Christmas I returned to the camp for one last inspection. Matt Mitchell greeted me in one of the cabins, a boy at his side holding a slip of paper. "This is Jim, he's sixteen," he said. "He wrote a poem that he wants to show you." Jim handed it to me and I began to read:

> One special day I sat and waited...
> I thought my gift would come.
> Please come. Please come.
>   The phone rang..."Jim, is that you?"
> "Yes, Dad... Are you coming?"
> "Sorry...not today," he replied.
> I hung up the phone and cried....
>   I still thought my gift would come.
> Please come. Please come.

I handed the poem back to Jim, trying to think of what to say. "You're not going to desert me too, are you?" he asked.

"Don't worry," I replied, putting my hand on his shoulder. "Wherever we go, you'll go too."

> *Detroit Free Press—January 4, 1992*
> YOUTH CAMP CLOSES UP OVER ZONING
> *Exhausted by a three-year legal battle over zoning, the state's first work-and-learn camp for delinquent youths closed Friday outside Kingston....Fifty teenagers at the Pioneer Work and Learn Center were moved to temporary quarters in neighboring Dayton Township to fulfill a court order to vacate the original site by today. Robert Wollack, executive director of Wolverine Human Services, which operates the camp, said the move was unfortunate, "but we have to do what we're doing to keep our program alive and well....The opposition was a small conglomeration of people," he said. "A majority supported us. And racial discrimination was a factor with those that didn't."*

Russell Mayer, the Koylton Zoning Board chairman, called the discrimination charge "baloney."

"Come, we'll take you" was the message from Vassar. Meanwhile, the Koylton Township Board of Trustees by a 4-to-1 vote finally granted us the zoning permit. But the effective date—January 22, 1992—came eighteen days after Judge Joslyn said we had to get out. Albeit, we were able to tough it out for three years which gave us time to develop and refine our program; three years is what our attorney Sam McCargo had committed himself to achieving for us, and he had accomplished just that through his various motions and appeals.

The Koylton Township supervisor who opposed the camp was forced out of office in a recall election. As for Russell Mayer, the Koylton Township Zoning Board chairman, it wasn't a recall election that cost him his job. It was a violation of a Koylton Township zoning law that forbade him from putting a septic field in his backyard.

More than simple irony, I saw this turn of events as poetic justice.

CHAPTER 18

THE GENTLE GIANT

THANKS TO BILL HAINES, my point-man in Vassar, we already had a site picked out on the Cass River—a lush eighty-four-acre pine forest interspersed with fields of sand. And thanks to Earl Thomas and other benefactors, we managed to scrape together enough funds to purchase the land and open Camp One in February of 1992. In the dead of winter, Matt Mitchell had strung out a wilderness trek with his young charges from two weeks to four weeks to comply with Judge Joslyn's evacuation order. When they returned, all fifty kids plus staff had been safely transferred to the new Vassar camp.

In Detroit meanwhile, Pete had acquired another boarded-up convent, church, and adjoining property. St. Philip Neri Convent and Church were located Detroit's east side. The area surrounding the church and convent was a deteriorating neighborhood of vacant lots strewn with garbage and parts of abandoned cars half hidden in the tall weeds. Many houses were abandoned, some of which showed the dark stains and shadows of charred sides from a previous fire. Businesses were boarded-up and side-streets were lined with the detritus of people who had given up hope. I believed we could make a difference in this neighborhood. The convent was converted to an emergency shelter which has since evolved into a diagnostic-assessment center with a licensed capacity of thirty-six children. When the facility was first opened, we moved the children into it from the Brent Center located on Detroit's west side. We then terminated our lease for the old Brent site as it was no longer needed.

St. Philip Neri Church was turned into a combination soup-kitchen and community center. Charles Dukes was partially instrumental in helping us to focus on community development. He was an exceptionally gifted community organizer and I quickly came to value his abilities. He is still a member of the Detroit Police Reserve. He played an important role for Wolverine Human Services and continues to be a consultant for us on city government relations. Charlie became an effective liaison for Wolverine with the City Council and various city governmental offices over the years as Wolverine expanded its operations. He played an important role by increasing my awareness and understanding of city government and persons to contact and work with. Another community activist who was associated with me for a few years as an educator was Dr. John Telford. He helped manage and coordinate the educational programs for our residents in the Detroit facilities. His familiarity with the Detroit Public School system enabled him to effectively improve our educational programs.

The Community Center is a one-hundred percent charity operation of Wolverine Human Services. No city government grants were received during the tenure of Detroit mayor Kwame Kilpatrick; however, the current mayor, Dave Bing, has reestablished the Neighborhood Opportunity Program, and we are expecting a small grant to help with our $300,000 annual budget. I consider this Center to be a powerful and important social work activity. The Community Center provides after-school recreational and tutorial programs for neighborhood children. It provides a place for various neighborhood meetings; it provides classes for children, youth, and adults. The Center also operates a soup-kitchen that feeds thousands of persons and families throughout the year. Over the years we have been able to make improvements to the physical plant. More recently we added a fenced-in playground with state-of-the-art equipment. The Center has become a beacon of light in an otherwise blighted neighborhood.

In 1992, *Crain's Detroit Business* Magazine named Wolverine Human Services one of the top twenty-five non-profit organizations in the Greater Detroit area. A mere five years after our founding, we were serving more than three hundred different young people a year at our five facilities with a success rate of 97 percent. That meant more than ninety-seven kids out of a hundred, once they had successfully finished the Wolverine program, had either found jobs or gone back to school within a year or—at minimum—had not become repeat offenders.

One of the people responsible for that success was Clarence Fischer, my father-in-law. He had earned a master's degree in social work from the University of Nebraska and had worked as a social worker while in the military from which he had retired as an Army lieutenant. He then began his career with Lutheran Child and Family Services in Detroit, and he became the director of the agency's Detroit operations during which time the agency's foster care program expanded considerably. He was later reassigned to the agency's Bay City office and was displeased with the change in his responsibilities. He retired at age sixty after thirty-three years of professional social work. But Clarence still had a desire to serve youth and his unique experience in launching, growing, and managing community-based programs filled an important gap for our service continuum. He came to work for me in April 1990. I hired him and put him in charge of our new community services division, which included the foster care program, Families First (an intensive family intervention program for families referred to us from the state's Child Protective Services program), and Supervised Independent Living program for older adolescents who were living semi-independently and involved in either school, work, or both. This division became a rapidly growing program for us. Clarence's long tenure in the child welfare field was a strong asset to the growth of Wolverine Human Services.

Clarence's invitation to join Wolverine stemmed from my firm belief in hiring social workers—professionals educated and experienced in a complex body of knowledge incorporating various social treatment modalities, an understanding of human development and behavior, and good counseling skills. My efforts at engaging athletes in helping kids similarly derived from their unique skill set—an ability to channel the aggression into purposeful and constructive activities. Sports help youth to understand the importance of playing by the rules. Athletics teaches structure and self-discipline. Youth learn the importance of teamwork and leadership. People who achieve success in sports can often provide superb role models for boys, who for the most part, have not had a caring father figure in their lives.

Nobody knew this better than John Vitale. A product of Detroit's tough east side, he found his niche early in life. He became a football star at De La Salle Collegiate High School where he caught the eye of Michigan football coach Bo Schembechler. He went on to become a four-year starter for the Wolverines, first at guard and then at center. By his senior year he was a first-team All-American and team captain. In the 1989 Rose Bowl he led his team to a 22-14 win over the University of Southern California.

John loved few things more than his mother's spaghetti and his affirming relationship with Coach Schembechler. Players didn't dare to call the god-like Schembechler anything but "Coach." Except for John. "Hey, Chief," he'd say, suiting up for practice, "you gonna work us today?"

"I'm gonna kick your ass," Schembechler would respond.

"Good, I'm ready."

After graduating from the University of Michigan in 1989, he tried out for the Houston Oilers, but a back injury cut short his dream of playing in the NFL. The following year he went to work for the Special Olympics in Washington, D.C., but he yearned for

The Gentle Giant

Detroit—specifically the east side where he had grown up—and a year later he was back—June 1991. That's when I first met him.

"Bob Chmiel sent me to see you," John said. Chmiel had been his line coach at U-M and was a member of my board at that time. John continued, "I grew up in this neighborhood, and I want to work with kids. Do you have an opening?"

For a moment I wondered if Paul Seal had been his job interview coach. John's timing was perfect, and so was his fit for the job. I hired him on-the-spot as a residential care coordinator at St. Jude's, a job that allowed him to play part-time for the Detroit Drive, a team in the newly-formed Arena Football League. I came to think of him as the Gentle Giant.

Before long his work at St. Jude's drew the attention of a *Detroit News* sports reporter, Bob Malinowski, who compared him to basketball superstar Charles Barkley. "Barkley," he wrote, is "a bald-headed, loud-mouthed purveyor of controversy and contradiction. He demands to be heard. John Vitale is...a purveyor of simple logic and complex dreams. He strains to be heard." The reporter continued:

> *Different people, different methods, similar message. Barkley delivers it to your home daily through his latest sneaker commercial: "I am not paid to be a role model....I am paid to wreak havoc on the basketball court....Parents should be role models....Just because I can dunk a basketball doesn't mean I should raise your kids." Barkley may have a larger stage but Vitale...may have a larger role. Both have the same goal — to tighten the grip on America's parents. Barkley does it loudly. Vitale does it quietly and constantly...."We want to put athletes on these high pedestals when it's the parents who need to take charge. The parent has to be the person a kid looks up to."*[14]

Even as a U-M football standout, John Vitale never affected as many lives as he did working with the kids at St. Jude's. Vitale was fond of saying that for him sports was a short-term goal, "but growing up is a long-term goal." Of all the curiosities I've confronted in my career, perhaps the most confounding is the most fundamental.

They Will Be Victors

How is it that the services that Wolverine provides even come to be needed? How is it that parents come to ignore, neglect, exploit, and viciously abuse their own children? To John's way of thinking, the only thing he could do was to try and fill the void that is too often left by misguided parents and all-too-often absent fathers.

It was during the springtime of 1994, I was at the Community Center when John Vitale approached me.

"Can I have a word with you, Chief?" he said. He called me Chief, just like he did Coach Bo Schembechler.

"What's up, John?" I said.

"Well, I'm not sure. I'm having some problems with my feet."

"What kind of problems?"

"They tingle and then I feel dizzy—like I'm going to faint—I don't have my balance and I don't feel my feet."

"Have you seen a doctor?" I asked.

"No, but I have an appointment at St. John's Hospital in a few weeks," he said.

After he got the results, John gave over to see me. "Chief," he said, "I have something to tell you."

"What?" I asked. I was pouring over a map of the Vassar site and I was preoccupied with our latest expansion plans.

"I went to the doctor."

"So?" I said my eyes still fixed on the map.

"He told me I have something called *ependymoma*."

I looked up from the map. "He said you have what?"

"Ependymoma." He pulled a piece of paper from his pocket on which was written in his doctor's handwriting: "E-p-e-n-d-y-m-o-m-a. It's a growth on my spinal cord—like a tumor," John said.

Now John had my full attention. "What kind of tumor? Does that mean you—?" I didn't want to say the word.

"No, it doesn't mean I have cancer," he said. "But, he wants to do some more tests." John was twenty-nine.

Another two weeks passed, and John was back in my office. "Chief," he said, "I just got the news."

I looked up from my desk – now he had my full attention pretty much every time he entered the room. I waited for him to continue.

The Gentle Giant

"It isn't good," he said. "The tumor—it's malignant and they want to take it out. And then I might have to undergo radiation treatment. They don't know for sure yet."

I found John's use of the word *they* disconnected—*they* want, *they* might, *they* don't know—as if he was talking about something wholly unrelated to himself.

"Chief," he continued, "they told me I'll need some time off."

"You take all the time you need, big fella. Let me know if there is anything you need and we'll take care of it, John."

A few weeks later the Gentle Giant greeted me from his bed at Bon Secours Hospital. "Hi'ya Chief," in his trademark gravely voice, his face breaking into a smile.

Before I could ask him about his operation he said, "Remember what you told me about needing a wife to look after me?" He motioned to an attractive young woman adjusting the crank at the foot of his bed. "This is Lynn—Lynn Abdelnour," he said. "We're not married yet, but we're going to be."

Taking Lynn's hand I said, "I hope you know what you're getting into." It was an attempt at dry humor.

"Oh, I do," she replied cheerfully. "We've been going together for two years."

John's operation was not totally successful. A second operation would be required to remove the rest of the tumor from his spinal column. And the doctor said that he would have to go through a series of radiation treatments to get rid of vagrant cancer cells.

A few months later John was strong enough to come back to work, but he looked wan and pale and it was apparent that even a Gentle Giant was susceptible to the ravages of cancer.

"Well, Chief, you gonna work me today?" he said on his first day back.

We both laughed.

"I'm gonna kick your ass," I said, "but not today. Maybe tomorrow."

CHAPTER 19

A NEW VENTURE—
GATOR HUMAN SERVICES

I ORIGINALLY BECAME INTERESTED IN Florida early in 1992 while researching requests for proposals related to juvenile justice programs. Newspaper headlines across the country were reporting on the increased involvement of youth in serious crimes, and I thought there might be an opportunity for us to expand into another state. Florida's child welfare/juvenile justice programs were receiving a considerable degree of negative publicity because of reports of mismanagement. Findings confirming these allegations ultimately led to the Florida Department of Health & Rehabilitative Services (HRS) being placed under a court monitor for its child welfare and juvenile justice programs. I thought this might be a worthy challenge and I decided to launch a new venture to create high quality programs for youth in the state of Florida. With a population that was about 50 percent greater than Michigan's, I saw the state as having potential for expanding our approach to rehabilitating troubled youth. It was good for business, but more importantly it was good for kids.

There were two Requests for Proposal that came our attention. Both proposals were for the "management and operation" of existing facilities and programs. Florida, unlike Michigan, owned the facilities where youth were housed, but outsourced the management, operations, and programming of the facilities. Both facilities were in the Okeechobee area. One proposal was to manage and operate a fifty-bed facility referred to as a camp; the second proposal was for the "Florida School for Boys," which was a two-hundred fifty-bed juvenile correctional facility for males fourteen to eighteen years of age who had committed "life or first degree felonies or [had committed] second and third degree felonies with at least two prior felony commitments involving violence against persons or property. . . ." The second Request for Proposal stated that the "primary goal of the Training School Program is to provide care, custody and control of the youth by providing programs and services that will improve the youth's attitude and behavior and reduce further involvement of the youth in delinquent behaviors."

In preparation for submitting a proposal, I had Mike Jones (one of my senior executives specifically charged with compiling responses to other RFPs) fly to Florida and inspect the camp facility to get an idea of what the program was like. Mike made an appointment to tour the facility without explaining what his purpose was. Mike reported that the treatment approach was simply custodial. He observed little rapport between staff and youth. Staff used a heavy-handed approach to resolving conflicts. He further observed that youth were out-of-control while he was there. He observed several fights and staff were constantly having to use physical restraint in an effort to exert control. We felt confident that we could do much better; we were just hoping to have an opportunity to put into practice what we had already successfully developed at our Pioneer Work and Learn Center.

It is always more of a challenge to change an existing culture than it is to create a new social treatment milieu. Nevertheless, I be-

A New Venture–Gator Human Services

gan to dream of taking my experience and the Wolverine treatment philosophy to the Sunshine State. The prospect of turning around an existing program stirred my thinking and I began to formulate a methodical, well-crafted strategy for implementing service delivery in the Florida delinquency market.

I knew we would need a good attorney to enable us to form a corporation in the state of Florida and to guide us through the labyrinth of Florida's state government. I had my aide, Jeff Ferguson, call the Florida Bar Association and ask for the names of three leading administrative lawyers in the state. He identified three qualified candidates, and he set up a phone conference with the first name on the list, Mark Levine. I connected with Levine and I inquired as to his experience in handling administrative issues involving state government. He named a number of prominent client-organizations, including the Florida Teachers Association, and the successes he had had with them. During the course of our conversation, it became readily apparent that he had a busy and important clientele whose interests coincided in many regards with ours. I only had one more criterion to be satisfied. I got right to the chase and asked him what his political party affiliation was. I wanted a Democrat who was well connected with the political power structure of the state because Democrat Lawton Chiles was then the Governor of Florida and fellow Democrat Bob Graham was an influential U.S. Senator.

Governor Chiles' nickname was "Walkin' Lawton" which he earned in 1970 when he ran for a seat in the United States Senate. To gain state-wide recognition, he hiked 1,003 miles over a period of ninety-one days from Pensacola to Key West, a feat that contributed to an easy win in November 1970. Levine responded that he was a Democrat and it also became apparent during our phone conversation that he was actively involved in the state's Democratic Party. I was impressed with him and we agreed to terms. A check for $2,000 was immediately sent as a retainer fee. Mark Levine was instrumental in filing the necessary papers to create Gator Human Services, Inc. using the same slogan we had for Wolverine Human Services: "Helping Children to Be Victors."

They Will Be Victors

Mike Jones and I submitted the two proposals in the spring of 1992; each proposal exceeded three-hundred pages in length. These were a very different type of proposal than any we had previously written because they were for existing programs. We submitted these proposals under the name of Wolverine Human Services. However, the cover letters included the following sentence: "I must point out that we are in the process of forming a non-profit Florida corporation {501 (c) (3)} and will have this process completed prior to the effective date of the contract." We met the deadlines and waited for the results.

The Eckerd Family Foundation was our primary competitor and was at that time the manager and operator of the large Florida School for Boys. In June I received a telephone call from Maria Dawson, the chairperson of the Bid Review Committee. She informed us that we had won the bid to operate the Okeechobee Youth Camp by a margin of two-hundred fifty points. Our approach to rehabilitation, which employed the point system that I had developed at the Pioneer Work and Learn Center in Michigan, was in sharp contrast to the corrections model which was being used at the Okeechobee Boys Camp. The good news was diminished, however, when Ms. Dawson informed us that despite the fact that we had prevailed in the bid process for the Boys Training School, the Eckerd Family Foundation had filed an appeal. We had won the bid by a narrow differential of twenty-seven points.

The appeal was presented to an administrative law judge who ruled against us and awarded the management contract for the Florida School for Boys to the Eckerd Family Foundation. Mark represented us well, and presented our arguments with professional competency and a strong personal commitment to our purpose. Nevertheless, the administrative law judge ruled against us; he had determined that continuity of care and continuance of management of this large facility was of greater importance than strict adherence to the narrow margin of difference the bid reviewers had calculated. Consequently, the contract was awarded to Eckerd.

A New Venture–Gator Human Services

We went on to win additional bids and ended up managing and operating seven moderate-sized facilities throughout the state located near the following cities: Okeechobee, Panama City, Jacksonville, Jasper, West Palm Beach, Jupiter, and Homestead. At the peak of programming our operating budget exceeded $5 million. Many of the facilities had been badly neglected and required extensive cleaning and some renovations. I recall one facility where the mold in the bathrooms was so thick that it had to be scraped off. I was sickened by the realization that until we raised the bar and set a standard of dignity and respect for the young people we were dedicated to serving, many of them had been living in what could be reasonably characterized as squalor.

I knew I needed a few strong, experienced staff from my Michigan programs to train and model the point/level system. The staff I was to inherit from the previous contractor were not college educated and expectations for the operation of the program had been very low. John Vitale and his brother Anthony along with a couple of other Michigan staff became our leaders in the camp program at Okeechobee. No one was going to challenge the Gentle Giant and soon the program took on a new spirit. Even the appearance of the buildings and grounds was drastically improved. All of this served to emphasize to the residents that they were valued. It did not take long for attitudes to change on the part of staff and boys alike.

I developed some lasting friendships and associations as a result of our Florida venture. Dan Wilson became the Chief Executive Officer of Gator Human Services, and performed admirably under difficult and challenging circumstances. I had become acquainted with Dan when we were graduate students at the University of Michigan. He earned his master's degree in social work one year after I did.

I cannot thank Mark Levine enough for getting me involved in Florida's Democratic Party. I recall meeting with Mark Levine at his law office located in Tallahassee, the state's capital. I remember observing that his office was nicely appointed without being ostentatious. It was located in a small office building in a neighborhood of quintessentially southern homes with magnificently manicured yards. He had both sports and political memorabilia in his office—reminiscent of my office in Michigan—and a check in the amount of $749,000 that was framed and hung on his wall. While some people might interpret this as arrogance, I saw it as appropriate pride and self-confidence. A man of average height, in his early 40's with wavy black hair and his trademark pipe, Mark had a friendly manner, enhanced by his soft southern accent that belied a keen intellect. Bob Blumenfeld was with me and we were invited to Mark's home for dinner; his wife was a gourmet cook and served us a sumptuous southern-style dinner. Mark was later instrumental in obtaining an invitation for Judy and me to attend a White House Christmas Party in December of 1993 where we personally met President and Mrs. Clinton. Mark also introduced me to Barney Bishop, a lobbyist par excellence. Between Mark and Barney, I learned a lot about the world of lobbying and how one can influence public policy formulation. I was also able to put into practice some of the lessons I had learned from Jon Smalley, our Michigan lobbyist.

I became a founding member of the Juvenile Justice Association a Florida-based juvenile justice advocacy organization. It was one of the ways I had found to help shape public policy debates. I had the privilege of meeting Governor Lawton Chiles on several occasions. However, my efforts and that of the association failed to bring needed improvement in the state's juvenile correctional programs at that time.

The state of Florida refused to increase its per diem rates making it impossible to operate quality rehabilitative programs; consequently, we withdrew from competing anymore. I was not willing to operate residential programs that were nothing more than basic custodial programs.

I first met John Dupont during our Florida experience. He is native of Florida and has proved to be an invaluable advisor and trusted friend to me over the years. He is knowledgeable about the juvenile corrections scene and understands how to convert program purpose into building design. While John is neither an architect

A New Venture–Gator Human Services

nor an engineer, his knowledge about the designing and construction of juvenile detention facilities with a view toward functionality has proved to be invaluable. Early in his career he worked in a juvenile detention facility in Florida and developed an uncanny understanding of the relationship between program purpose and building design. When I needed to build a facility to fulfill the contract requirements of the bid we had won in Michigan for a secure facility for delinquent youth, I called on John and he was instrumental in introducing me to the Wolgast Construction Company. John has become an important collaborator with us on various construction projects including the Wolverine Secure Treatment Center and Vassar House.

In all, Florida served as both a training ground and a proving ground. We promoted improved services in the state simply by creating competition in a system that had become complacent and, in many respects, ineffective. I honed my political skill, fostered growth, and guided the development in key organizational leadership positions. I also demonstrated the efficacy of programming models that I had developed over the years. Youth who resided in Gator's programs had more meaningful experiences and came away better equipped to confront their personal challenges than young men who were served by other institutions at that time. Despite my decision to sell our stake in Florida programming, our time there was well spent and many kids in that state benefited from Gator Human Services. I also learned the value of lobbying, which I was soon to use with greater intensity in Michigan.

CHAPTER 20

MEETING NEW CHALLENGES

ON NOVEMBER 12, 1992, the *Detroit Free Press* described how abused and neglected children in Wayne County were caught in the middle of a dispute between county and state governments over which should pay for their care. Under the headline, KIDS LEFT IN LURCH, I read the following article in disbelief:

> The county does not believe it has any further obligation to the children. The county's decision to cut off payments was based on an Oct. 23 ruling (by Chief Circuit Judge Richard Kaufman) that said nothing in state law required a county to care for wards of the state. The state insists it does not have any more money—leaving foster parents, child-care agencies and about 1,100 already-troubled children in the lurch.

I always get a little uncomfortable when I read stories like this because I question whether it's me that's out of touch, or only the people who can't relate and do not choose to even try to understand. I want to shout, "What is wrong with you?" These kids already face barriers most of us can barely comprehend—victims of abuse and neglect—only to become unwitting pawns in a political pissing-match between two governmental entities. I've always wondered how these kids' parents could do the things they have done, but it is even more troubling when I contemplate how our society got to where it is, when it comes to caring for them. I wonder when it happened that a pervasive anti-tax sentiment came to trump the Judeo-Christian ethic that defines civilization by how we treat the least among us.

Tax dollars or not, I managed to secure sufficient funds to open Camp Two at Vassar in February of 1993. Our master plan called for adding five cabins, plus a pond, pavilions, and playing fields, trails, a campground, and a community lodge—all for the tidy sum of $1.2 million.

To raise the money I had to do my own share of role-playing. Although I was trained as a social worker, I knew I had to wear more than my social worker hat to succeed in this business. So I traded in my former duds—cowboy hat and boots—for a tie and sport coat off the rack and became a professional beggar. Judge Kaufman's ruling convinced me that public dollars alone weren't going to do the job. Private contributions would be needed just as much; as a result my role as a fund-raiser began—my wife Judith had super ideas for accomplishing that.

Despite our money problems, Wolverine Human Services continued to grow. Chronic, persistent overcrowding at the Wayne County Youth Home and other detention facilities across the state hastened the expansion of our Work-and-Learn Center. By the time we opened Camp Three in February of 1996, the number of kids at our Vassar campus had increased from fifty to one hundred sixty-eight.

In hindsight this expansion was neither remarkable nor entirely unpredictable. Southeast Michigan—and Detroit in particular—had all of the usual problems of a large urban center, compounded by the gradual decline of the auto industry on which the entire region relied. The crack epidemic was exacerbated by massive lay-offs

Meeting New Challenges

leading to acute poverty, crime, broken homes, and broken kids. What was unique to Wolverine in all of this was that we had become a preferred provider of services to troubled youth.

Although juvenile delinquent facilities across the state were bursting at the seams, it took the 1993 murder of a female social worker at the state-run high security Green Oak Center of the W. J. Maxey Boys Training School to put the issue in the public spotlight. Dr. Gerald Miller, director of MDSS, convinced Governor John Engler that non-profit agencies provided low-cost, effective services and should assume an expanded role for the operation of high security programs for juvenile delinquents. The investigation into the homicide at Green Oak Center resulted in serious and troubling findings: "Almost all of the female and many of the male staff interviewed, reported that Green Oak Center was a work environment that was hostile to women. . . . sexual comments were made to female staff by male staff in the presence of residents. . . . Overall, many staff male and female, felt that women were not safe at Green Oak Center."[15]

In the spring of 1995 Dr. Miller gave the green-light to develop a formal Request for Proposal (RFP) for a high security residential program for seriously troubled male youth. Harold Gazan called on Joe Jerome of the Services Contracts Division of MDSS to draft the RFP. The letters conveying the RFP went out to various qualified private, non-profit agencies that autumn.

In September of 1995 I received a letter that was to signal the next major phase of our expansion. It said:

> *The Michigan Department of Social Services is issuing Requests for Proposals (RFP's) for the delivery of residential treatment services for male, delinquent State wards in a high security facility, 24 hours a day, 365 days a year....Youths shall be 14 through 17 years of age at the time of initial placement....The Department will be contracting with a provider for 60 high security beds.... The (center) must be located within a 100-mile radius of downtown Detroit.*

The letter was signed by Harold S. Gazan, Deputy Director for Child and Family Services.

"We've got work to do," I told Pete Walsh. "Think we can get a proposal together by January?"

A high security facility operated by a non-profit agency like Wolverine would be another first for Michigan, just as our work-and-learn camp had been. In 1996 the State's Auditor General released to the public a *Performance Audit Report for the W. J. Maxey Training School* which determined that within five years of release, 64 percent of the youth from the Maxey Training School had been convicted of a felony. Also, it was rumored that frequent truancies from Green Oak Center had been a matter of concern to various Juvenile Court Judges. I knew we could do much better than what the state was doing at the Maxey Training School; and I was just hoping that we would be given an opportunity to prove that we could.

I pulled together a team of my top staff that included Bob Blumenfeld, my chief financial officer, Mike Jones, vice president for programs, Pete Walsh, vice president for human resources and facilities, and John Dupont, who was a consultant of mine based in Florida. John was an expert on building institutions for juvenile delinquents. The team was charged with developing the very best proposal that we could design. I was interested in finding property in the Saginaw area with a view toward locating near our established complex in Vassar. John Dupont came up from Florida and began to look for a contractor and property in the Saginaw area that might have potential as a construction site. He connected with the Wolgast Construction Company which already owned vacant property in Buena Vista Township. Our proposal was written and it included an excellent potential site. We submitted our proposal and hoped for the best. On May 23, 1996, the governor's office issued this press release:

> *Governor John Engler today announced the awarding of a bid to Wolverine Human Services of Detroit to build a high security residential treatment facility for delinquent youth in Saginaw County's Buena Vista Township....The*

> *facility will house youth who are committed to the state for treatment by the local courts . . . . It is also expected to generate 60-80 jobs.*

We broke ground in December 1996 and opened the Wolverine Secure Treatment Center nine months later on September 2, 1997. It was the first privately-run high security facility for youth in the State of Michigan and it provided a welcome economic boost for Saginaw County. Most importantly, it gave worst-case juvenile offenders an alternative to jail—and a better than even shot at turning their lives around. It is important to note that the unique design concept for the secure treatment center was the brain child of John Dupont.

When asked about the planning and construction of this facility, John remembered that he was given the mission "to design a facility with superior quality physical characteristics that would provide staff and residents a safe and secure environment. My basic concepts such as line-of-sight and optimal behavior control were achieved by the separation of residents into small, individual treatment groups. In addition to security the goal was to provide the best recreational, educational, and living experience possible for the residents that would serve their multiple needs over a long-term period. The design incorporated a large, environmentally-controlled central mall area that not only allowed for simultaneous recreation activities but gave an open environment that relieved the sense of confinement during Michigan's long winter season when outdoor recreation would be restricted. The dormitory areas surrounded the central mall and were designed to house groups of ten youth each."

Managing a secure treatment facility for delinquent youth is an ongoing challenge that requires commitment to the practice of Wolverine's seven principles on the part of management and staff. Vigilance is also required to ensure that youth are not undermining the institution's culture, reverting to gang loyalties, or succumbing to violence. The influence of peer culture is a powerful means of teaching positive values.

Opening a new institution, particularly a secure facility, is a special challenge because there are no youth already residing in the facility who have been through the program and in whom there has been an inculcation of positive culture that reinforces the Wolverine principles and basic positive values that undergird our social treatment programs. Both staff and youth are new to the facility. Therefore, we realized the importance of receiving only one group of ten boys at a time and allowing a period of time to go by before accepting another group of ten boys. This carefully planned procedure turned out to be fortuitous in a way that I had not anticipated.

The first group of ten youth who were received were some of the toughest in the juvenile justice system. That is why the committing judge had ordered that they be placed in a highly secure facility. Of course, the youth were determined to demonstrate their power, and we were equally determined to exercise our authority. The first group of ten youth had been in the facility only a few days when I went to the facility on a weekend. I wanted to talk with this first group of boys and be able to look them in the eye and explain the basic framework of our program. I was accompanied to the facility by my long-time friend, Stanley Farrow, who had traveled from New York City to join us on a salmon fishing trip that we had planned for later that weekend. I was also accompanied by John Dupont, who had helped to design the facility and was interested in seeing it in operation. The three of us entered the wing and I had the ten boys gather in the day room. They were seated in a semicircle. I was sharing with them the seven principles and explaining the purpose of Wolverine Human Services and this new program.

Suddenly a large, muscular youth stood-up and yelled, "What makes you the boss here?" Another youth yelled, "Fuck you!" Almost as if on signal, all of the youth sprang out of their chairs and began to move toward us. Stanley, John, and I formed a triangle—expecting to be rushed. I relied on my years of experience and firmly talked them down. I made them aware that their choices would have serious consequences for good or ill depending upon what they did in the next few minutes. The atmosphere was tense. The

Meeting New Challenges

staff person on the outside of the wing momentarily panicked and was unable to unlock the door and enter to assist us. There was considerable confusion and a lot of profanity. The boys were obviously testing our resolve and their limits. My heart was pounding, my adrenaline was flowing, and the hairs on the back of my neck were standing up. Eventually, we prevailed and order was restored. I was able to talk them down using a loud terse voice.

"Think about what you are doing! Are you ready to spend the rest of your life in an adult penitentiary?" This was immediately followed by, "This is your second chance—don't fuck it up!"

An incident that could have ended in violence came to a positive conclusion.

Later, on my return from the successful salmon fishing trip, I met with the same youth; we explored the incident together and I encouraged each of them to write a letter of apology for their lack of respect to my friends. Each of them followed through.

Out of this same group emerged some leaders who were willing to help share the Wolverine values and culture when the next group of boys was received. The process of taking leaders from one wing and placing them in a wing with several new boys was instituted. Ultimately, a culture was established as the youth began to understand the rules that governed the program, but we had experienced a close call, one of many throughout my career.

The incident became a meaningful illustration for staff training. It emphasized the need for ongoing vigilance and for staff to backup other staff when tension among the residents is detected.

The completed facility was awarded the *Outstanding Achievement Award for Building Design and Construction* in 1998 by The Engineering Society of Detroit making John Dupont and the Wolgast Construction Corporation team very proud. Of course, I was also very proud.

A high security facility like ours wasn't the only thing the governor had in mind. He also wanted to have the private sector develop a military-style academy that would instruct young offenders in the art of self-discipline. And Wolverine had a unique advantage in pursuing this opportunity. It was an approach to juvenile rehabilitation that my father-in-law Clarence Fischer, an ex-Army lieutenant and psychiatric social worker, had successfully employed at an Army prison in California. He would be the natural choice to run a program like that at Vassar. Thus another contract and another first for Michigan and another first for Wolverine Human Services.

No sooner had we put the shovel into the ground to begin preparing the site than my wife, Judy, received a phone call from her mother. It was Sunday, December 7, 1997. Clarence and his wife, Shirley, were just leaving from church—St. Martin's Lutheran in Birch Run—when he suffered a stroke. Four days later, at St. Mary's Hospital in Saginaw, he died.

Clarence who was sixty-eight had touched more lives than I ever hoped to. In 1970 the Detroit chapter of the National Association of Social Workers had named him social worker of the year. In 1988 the Michigan Association of Children's Alliances, a professional training group, had honored him as administrator of the year. Ed Overstreet, my former boss at Boysville, called him "the grand old man of child welfare." But one of the people he touched most was my eleven-year-old son, Zack—Clarence's grandson—who wrote:

We are all here for a purpose.
We only have each day to use once.
We can make that day...productive
Or we can waste the time....

So it was fitting that we name the facility the Clarence Fischer Leadership Academy in honor of Clarence, even though he never had a chance to see it, much less run it. His contributions to the field, to the project, and to countless young lives—would be indelibly recognized through the academy that bears his name.

When the academy opened on August 30, 1998, the *Detroit Free Press* was there to cover it:

> *Two and a half years after Gov. John Engler called for juvenile boot camps to deal more sternly with young offenders, a military-style academy opened Sunday in Tuscola County. The First Lt. Clarence Fischer Leadership*

> Academy will try to impress delinquent boys ages 14-16 with the benefits of a strict regimen, physical training, marching in formation and military discipline. About two dozen youths have been sent to the facility from all over southeastern Michigan....Eventually the complex will handle 60 cadets.

The Fischer Academy brought the total capacity of our Detroit, Saginaw, and Vassar sites to over six hundred juveniles. Wolverine was now the second largest non-profit child welfare organization in the state, and word from the Michigan Department of Social Services was that we had the highest rehabilitation rate.

While the time leading up to the opening of the program was bittersweet, the days following its inception were nothing less than joyous. A few days after we opened the academy, John Vitale came into my office at St. Jude's. He looked stronger than he had in months—more like the Gentle Giant he had been before he got sick—and his crew cut was growing back.

"Chief," he said, "I have an announcement to make. Lynn and I are getting married in September."

I sprang up from my desk and gave him a hug. "That's terrific, John. Congratulations!"

After I let go of him he said, "I have something else to tell you." And he added, almost as if it were an afterthought: "The doctor says my cancer is in remission."

John Vitale assured me he was well enough to handle returning to his position of being in charge of the community center (the former St. Phillip Neri Church) on the east side of Detroit. John, who had a degree in sports management, assumed his administrative responsibilities for the center with typical gusto, and continued to do what he did best—interact one-on-one with the neighborhood kids. Their problems became his problems, and the more he let them sound off the more they attached themselves to him.

The Gentle Giant was also the Pied Piper of the neighborhood where the community center was located. One of his charges, a seventeen-year-old named Lamont, had been a drug addict since

fourteen. Thanks to John's efforts Lamont was able to get off drugs and he became a crusader to get dealers and addicts off the street:
The people out there are nothing but losers [he wrote].
Some of them are nothing but users.
They think they're bad 'cause they're wearing a rope.
But they're hurting people by selling them dope....
You're doing nothing but hurting yourself.
You're not hurting the dealers.
You're hurting yourself.

Lamont's poem may not have qualified as Pulitzer material, but it did take second place at an annual conference of the Michigan Association of Children's Alliances. More importantly, in writing his thoughts, Lamont was giving something back from what he had learned at Wolverine. And he made what John had given him real and enduring.

In 1996 I was awarded the Social Worker of the Year Award by the Michigan Chapter of the National Association of Social Workers. It was their way of recognizing my hard work and innovative approach to working with troubled youth. I could not have anticipated receiving such a special honor twenty years before, when I first decided to pursue my dream of becoming a social worker. It was then that I realized it was my turn to start giving back.

In May 1997 Judy and I established *The Robert Wollack & Family Endowed Scholarship* at Eastern Michigan University in appreciation of my undergraduate professor and adviser, Don Loppnow. In 1999, Wolverine Human Services established the *Wolverine Human Services Scholarship* at Eastern Michigan University to benefit undergraduate and graduate social work students. In the year 2000 we established *The Robert Wollack & Family Endowed Scholarship* at the University of Michigan School of Social Work. These scholarships afforded me the opportunity to help others contending with adversity to pursue a graduate education in social work. It felt incredibly fulfilling to provide these gifts.

Eastern Michigan University had meant a lot to me as a student and I was now also able to give back by serving as an adjunct instruc-

Meeting New Challenges

tor for the university for fifteen years (1984-1999). I generally taught the following courses: Introduction to Social Work, and Substance Abuse Problems and Services. Another course I taught was one which I personally conceived and developed, and it was the one that I enjoyed teaching the most. It was called Social Work Practice with Legal Offenders. I discussed the course concept with Dr. Loppnow who encouraged me to write the syllabus and teach the course. I believed that the issues and content covered by this course were salient to students who were particularly interested in doing social work in the inner-city. It soon became the largest class in the social work department with more than forty students consistently enrolled.

I was honored by Eastern Michigan University in a most unusual way in 2006. I can best describe it by quoting from the Eastern Michigan University Newsletter entitled *EMU* dated, Fall 2006: "Our campus recently took a step that was long overdue—bestowing a bachelor's degree on Robert E. Wollack. . . . Wollack took classes at EMU from 1973 to 1976. EMU's current provost, Don Loppnow, was a former professor and describes Wollack as a superlative student who not only earned outstanding grades but enriched every class with his wealth of life experience. Today, Wollack is a field supervisor for EMU social work students."

A great honor was given to me when I was invited to deliver the commencement address at The University of Michigan School of Social Work on April 29, 2000. It had been thirty years since my arrest in Brooklyn and nearly twenty-seven years since my release from the Federal Correctional Institution at Milan. Now I was fifteen miles up the road from that prison and facing three-hundred new graduates of the number one School of Social Work in America (according to *US News & World Report*). The symbolism, the irony, the validation, the rarefied company that I now kept all converged in my mind as exhilaration and nervousness. I clutched the podium and began to speak:

"I am proud and extremely honored to be the commencement speaker for the graduating class of 2000," I said. "I've delivered many speeches, but this one is by far the most significant....

They Will Be Victors

"Life is a series of goals—short-term and long-term—but you must have vision, drive and be relentless in pursuit of your goals in spite of the many barriers you will face...," and I sounded off on the issues I cared most about:

On poverty: "It's a disgrace that children make up twenty-six percent of the nation's population but thirty-nine percent of the poor. According to Duncan Lindsey, 'When we examine how a society cares for its children, we are peering into the heart of a nation.' Obviously our hearts are not very big. . . . Poverty is the major causative variable that leads to family dysfunction, lack of education, child abuse and neglect, and finally to delinquency."

On criminal justice: "There are over two million people in U.S. prisons—a rate six to ten times that of most industrialized nations.... However, ninety-five percent of the people that go to prison will come out, and they will need your help. They need a second chance." On the challenge facing social workers: "We need to fight hard to maintain our place in delinquency services and regain our place in adult corrections the way it was in the '60s and '70s." I thought of how I had been helped by Ramsey Clark's prison reforms and how the philosophy of rehabilitation had vanished from our prisons during the Reagan years. "We have to give hope to the seven million people being filtered through our criminal justice system."

On juvenile rehabilitation: "It's a constant battle to win the game. My agency has had a much greater success rate than failure.... We at Wolverine have seen aimless, parentless, abused, neglected and delinquent kids change and go on to college or learn skilled trades and technical services...."

"My goal will always be helping children to be victors," I continued, shifting the focus to my own work with kids. "I want to share with you seven principles that have helped me develop my agency, train my staff, and have allowed me to touch the lives of thousands of children."[16] And I listed them as I do for our staff:

1. REALITY — Don't let your clients dwell on the past and don't do it yourself. It is a fruitless journey. Stick with the here and the now and the future.

2. RESPONSIBILITY— *You have a responsibility to do the very best you can do....Work hard and diligently. Be leaders with resolve and determination. And don't forget your family and community.*

3. RESPECT — *Show respect for your clients, supervisors, colleagues, and people in general. Everyone wants to be respected, but it must be earned through your hard work, and care and respect for your fellow man!*

4. COMMUNICATION — *Effective communication allows you to influence people's lives. Use this skill wisely for it is the essence of being a great social worker and therapist – social work practice depends upon an effective communication process.*

5. NEGOTIATION — *Negotiate with your clients; help them establish short-term goals. Listen and advise. Be willing to give and take with your clients and with your colleagues. Be humble and kind, but when necessary be tough.*

6. EDUCATION — *We should not only use all the brains we have, but all that we can borrow. You can't steal second base with your foot on first. Take an educated lead...take a calculated risk!*

7. LOVE — *If you master the above six principles, you will love yourself. Not in a narcissistic way, but in a way that brings a sense of accomplishment, self-realization, and self-actualization. Then you will be able to truly share that love with your clients, as well as your family and friends. For as Dr. William Glasser asserted, "you have become worthwhile to yourself and to others.'*

I concluded with the following: "When I was younger and stronger, I ran against the winds of apathy and cynicism. Now I am older and wiser and I am still running against the winds. My weapons are empathy, altruism, and the will to win—to be victorious in the game of helping people.... Go out there and be winners!"

As my voice trailed off, one or two graduates in the front row stood up and applauded and the others followed suit. I felt a rush of pride and embarrassment; I hadn't expected a standing ovation. The University's Provost and the Dean of the School of Social Work both complemented me on my speech. It meant a lot to me to be recognized by the University that had done so much for me, and that I truly loved.

CHAPTER 21

THE CONTINUING CHALLENGE FOR SOCIAL JUSTICE

IT WAS SEPTEMBER 1988—almost two years since Pete and I had made our first trip to the headquarters of the Michigan Department of Social Services to find out whether we would be licensed to develop our own residential programs for troubled youth. Once again I was driving to Lansing, where I would face another crucial meeting. This time the appointment was with State Senator Robert Geake (Republican from western Wayne County). Pat Babcock, the Director of the Department of Social Services, had strongly suggested that I meet with Senator Geake and provide him with my perspective on the Pioneer Work and Learn Camp. Babcock had encouraged me to do some lobbying. He believed that legislators should have a well-rounded perspective on where the state's money was going and how it was being used, and he said that I was the best one to give them a perspective from the non-governmental side.

I was tense and unsure of myself. The idea of lobbying was foreign to me, and not generally accepted in the nonprofit mindset. I kept thinking, "How can I lobby effectively on my own behalf without sounding self-serving? What should I say?" I was apprehensive about this first meeting with the senator, whom I knew to be an important member of the state's legislature. He was the Chairman of the Appropriations Sub-committee for Social Services. As I noted in Chapter 17, 1988 had been a challenging year for us. We were trying to find a suitable location for the Pioneer Work and Learn Center. We had won the contract bid, but local community attitudes were less than welcoming. Consequently, it was important that this key legislator understand who we were and what we were proposing. I needed to explain to him the philosophy of social treatment for delinquent youth. Little did I realize how important lobbying would become in the years ahead. It would become my single most effective strategy for bringing our story to the attention of key legislators. There was no substitute for that face-to-face meeting during which important facts were shared, false impressions and perceptions were mitigated, and opinions were swayed.

This was the beginning of what would become a major part of my responsibility as the chief executive officer of Wolverine Human Services. My advocacy extended beyond the boundaries of Wolverine Human Services as an organization. I promoted social policies that positively impacted children, youth, and families and I directly addressed issues of poverty, racism, and injustice. I actively supported candidates and elected officials regardless of their political affiliation, to the extent their positions advanced the cause of child welfare and juvenile justice.

This first meeting with Senator Geake went well. Though the details of the conversation have faded, I recall it as more than just a polite hearing. The senator was receptive and I felt sure that I made a positive impression on him. Geake represented the western district of Wayne County which would someday include my home residence. He had a Ph. D. in psychology and had more than

The Continuing Challenge for Social Justice

a passing interest in the mission of Wolverine Human Services. And the meeting would prove to be fortuitous with regard to my development as an advocate in ways neither I nor the senator could have foreseen. At that time he had on his staff a very bright, energetic young man—Jon Smalley—whose athletic build, reddish hair, winsome smile, and air of self-confidence instantly inspired trust. Within three years from the date of my meeting with the senator, Smalley would join one of the most respected lobbying firms in Michigan, eventually rising to become a partner at Muchmore Harrington Smalley and Associates. Jon has become an extremely good friend and trusted advisor to me, and he serves tirelessly as the lobbyist for both Wolverine Human Services and the Association of Accredited Child and Family Agencies. Jon, along with Pat Harrington, taught me the importance of lobbying as a means of ensuring that the Wolverine story was being heard accurately rather than being represented to legislators through the jaundiced voices of others who usually had their own agendas.

As Wolverine began to expand its operations, it became increasingly important for government and legislative officials to know the facts about our organization. We wanted to get the word out regarding our achievements which we believed were extraordinary, and we had objective evaluation findings to support our position. Wolverine continued to experience a high rate of success as determined in 1991 by the Institute for Social Research (ISR) of the University of Michigan.

> *Ninety-one percent of the youth who enter PWLC successfully complete the program and graduate to be placed elsewhere.*[17]
>
> *First, an effective program was established at costs below the average residential program for juvenile delinquents in the state of Michigan. Second, dedicated and responsible staff were secured, trained and performed their tasks in an effective and caring manner. . . . Third, it provided for youth an explicit reinforcement of pro-social behavior, modeling and problem-solving alternatives to*

> *pro-criminal thinking and behavior. . . . Fourth, the quality of interpersonal relationships at the camp were warm and supportive, although staff also maintained discipline and control.*[18]
>
> *The results. . . . reveal that compared with youth who completed the 24 month Intensive Probation Programs, those from Pioneer had far lower recidivism rates. Only 22% of the former had "no charge" during the study period [meaning 78% had been charged with a criminal offense], while 60% of those from Pioneer had no subsequent charge in the 18-month period of observation . . . . 53% of those from the juvenile correctional institution had subsequent criminal charges versus 34% of those from Pioneer.*[19]

Profoundly and tragically, I need to inform the reader that the kind of research to which I made reference above is no longer possible because public funding levels have been decimated under the weight of the anti-tax sentiment which has prevailed since the early 1980s. MDHS no longer tracks meaningful data nor does the state have the necessary appropriated funds to conduct research projects such as the ones that were conducted in previous decades. Consequently, there no longer exists the capability to objectively evaluate the effectiveness of various juvenile justice programs or initiatives in the state of Michigan.

One of the ways we ensured that our voice was being heard was by forming a professional association whose members were private, non-profit child welfare agencies. In May 1994, I was instrumental in organizing the Association of Accredited Child and Family Agencies (AACFA). The original agency members included Spectrum Human Services (which was headed by my friend and former mentor Jim Minder), Methodist Children's Home Society (John Schmidt was the long-time executive director), Orchards Children's Services (then headed by the late Jerry Levin), Children's Center (led for decades by Ted Lewis), the Federation of Youth Services, and several other child welfare agencies. All of these agencies operated in the

The Continuing Challenge for Social Justice

greater Detroit metropolitan area. Collectively, the member agencies had served more than eleven thousand clients during the previous year. The oldest agency in the group was the Methodist Children's Home, founded in 1921. Wolverine Human Services had been in operation for six years. The association has now grown to become a respected advocacy group in Michigan. All agencies seeking membership must be accredited by a nationally recognized body in child welfare or a related field. This ensures that member agencies will be in compliance with the highest professional standards in excess of state licensing requirements. The association is also committed to best practices. I was the first president of the association, and we forged a partnership with Muchmore Harrington Smalley and Associates. Smalley and his associates have done and continue to do an excellent job of representing the interests of the association by bringing before policy makers the often superior performance records and increased cost efficiencies that are achieved by the non-profit, non-governmental sector.

Objective findings by auditing organizations have frequently documented that the cost of care at public institutions for comparable programs is often more than double the rate of care at non-governmental facilities. Our only recourse in the interest of communicating information about our commitment and successes was, therefore, to become skilled practitioners in the art of lobbying.

The issue however is not governmental versus non-governmental enterprises, but competitiion on a level playing field as opposed to a monopoly as stated by Osborne and Gaebler in their landmark book entitled, *Reinventing Government: How the Entrepreneurial Spirit is Transforming the Public Sector*. The following quotation brilliantly explains this important principle:

> *Those who support privatization in all cases because they dislike government are as misguided as those who oppose it in all cases because they dislike business. The truth is that the ownership of a good or service—whether public or private—is far less important than the dynamics of the market or institution that produces it . . . . The determining*

> *factors have to do with the incentives that drive those within the system. Are they motivated to excel? Are they accountable for their results? Are they free from overly restrictive rules and regulations? Is authority decentralized enough to permit adequate flexibility? Do rewards reflect the quality of their performance? Questions like these are the important ones—not whether the activity is public or private.*[20]

I observed meaningful distinctions in the quality of services provided to clients solely based on whether they were being served by governmental or non-governmental agencies. The inconsistent application and interpretation of licensing statutes and rules in public versus private institutions exacerbates the problem. For example: non-governmental child care agency would be placed on a moratorium if a serious violation of a licensing regulation was documented, but at the same time publicly run programs often emerge unscathed even for violations of a similar or more egregious nature. The Association of Accredited Child and Family Agencies advocated strongly for equal enforcement of licensing requirements.

One of our earliest lobbying successes occurred in September 1994 with the approval of the Wayne County Department of Health & Community Services for our member agencies to be providers of Wrap-around-services to juvenile court wards. Wrap-around-services referred to a social treatment strategy which enabled the juvenile court to contract for a variety of intensive social work or clinical treatment services, special education services, or other remedial services to be provided on an as needed basis in an effort to avoid institutionalization. It was primarily aimed at those delinquent youth who had "serious emotional disturbances." Our association used increased leverage with policy-makers to shape policies that impacted children and youth. Our entrepreneurial spirit and status as private enterprises enabled us to respond more quickly and flexibly to critical issues that impacted our operations and our clients.

In 1996 we vigorously opposed the criminalization of offenders under the age of fifteen when the governor pushed the state

The Continuing Challenge for Social Justice

legislature into enacting a series of bills which lowered the age at which a child could be tried in a criminal court. Incomprehensibly, an eight- or nine-year-old child could be tried as an adult in court for serious offenses. In fact some very young boys were convicted under the new statute.

We also lobbied against the prison for youthful offenders. In spite of our efforts it became a reality. However, as Bergmann says in his book, "The so-called punk prison was a correctional facility designed to detain minors sentenced as adults until they turned twenty, at which point they would be transferred to a regular adult correctional facility. The pet project of former Governor Engler, the punk prison was meant to house an anticipated wave of young 'superpredators.'"[21] After continued dialogue with newly elected Governor Jennifer Granholm, the punk prison was ultimately shuttered in 2005.

We advocated for increased resources to reduce the inequities that existed between state and privately operated child welfare programs. As a result, the legislature approved a rate increase of 1.5 percent for all private child welfare agencies. We also succeeded in having legislation enacted that required the state to place children or youth with Michigan non-profit child welfare agencies before placing them in out-of-state agencies.

One of the key elements to my success has been my effectiveness in lobbying state and local officials to support initiatives related to improving services to Michigan's children and families. The notion of lobbying sometimes elicits negative connotations in the mind of the public. But lobbying is advocacy, and advocacy is not only legitimate but obligatory. Part of our responsibility is to give voice to the voiceless. Meeting with decision makers and policy makers, both formally and informally, enables those voices to be heard. Lobbying is a means of breaking down misconceptions, promoting effective services, and educating legislators.

I believe that people make choices and are accountable for those choices whether good or bad. However, I also believe that poverty is a causal factor of juvenile delinquency. The observations of one of my heroes, Ramsey Clark, are as true today as they were when he stated them in his 1970 book entitled: *Crime in America*.

> Most crime in America is born in environments saturated in poverty and its consequences: illness, ignorance, idleness, ugly surroundings, hopelessness. Crime incubates in places where thousands have no jobs, and those who do, have the poorest jobs; where houses are old, dirty, dangerous; where people have no rights.[22]
>
> The children who will become criminals live mostly in the slums. Their older brothers and sisters are dropouts—unemployed. Their mother comes around some, but grandmother raises them, more or less. Father, they never knew. . . . They live in a place where violence is common, where a few, finding power in no other way, achieve it with a gun. . . . It will never be easy to help a child while the filth, disease, ignorance, poverty and vice of the slums permeate his existence.[23]

Poverty and deteriorated urban centers continue to breed hopelessness. "Detroit is now one of the poorest big cities in the country. One in three people there is living in poverty, and the mean income is several thousand dollars below the national average."[24] The lack of a solid property tax base coupled with the flight of industry and business to the Detroit suburbs and the resultant impact of urban decay has been most sharply observed in the deterioration of public education in Detroit. A February 2009 Brookings Institution report found that the Detroit Public School system was the worst overall major urban school district in the entire nation. A June 2007 report published by *Education Week* found that Detroit had the lowest graduation rate of any large school district in the 2003-04 school year—24.9 percent.

Further evidence that Detroit is a decaying urban center is the percentage of its children and youth who end up in out-of-home placements. The city of Detroit has less than 10 percent of the state's population; yet about 50 percent of children in foster care and about

The Continuing Challenge for Social Justice

40 percent of the youth who are committed to institutions for delinquent youth are from Detroit. This is a condition that should not be allowed to continue. Luke Bergmann, an anthropologist, lived in Detroit and wrote a book which is based on his experiences and documented observations. The book's title—*Getting Ghost*—comes from a term used by the youth of Detroit's inner city and refers to their involvement in the drug trade. He made this observation regarding the youth of Detroit's inner urban centers:

> *Among the young people locked up in downtown Detroit with whom I spent time, the most important social institution – the locus for their sense of identity, politics, and promise in the world – was the street drug trade. As they would describe it in the detention facility, drug dealing governed the seasonal cycles of their lives and taught them about the nature and power of the state, capitalism, and family. It shaped their senses for the shifting distinction between childhood and adulthood, the length of a natural life, and a timely death.*[25]

America needs a type of *Marshall Plan* that is aimed at our large urban centers. The *Marshall Plan* (officially the European Recovery Program) was the primary means by which the United States effectively helped to achieve the reconstruction of war-torn Europe following World War II. The United States contributed thirteen billion dollars which was spent to create a strong foundation for the countries of Western Europe and to repel the influence of communism. If we could spend billions to rebuild a war-torn continent, we should be able to spend generous sums to eradicate urban decay, improve inner-city schools, make health care accessible to everyone, and bring hope to the millions of children who remain caught in the web of poverty.

It is interesting to reread what George Marshall declared in a speech that he presented at Harvard University on June 5, 1947 in which he outlined the essential elements of the European Recovery Program: "Our policy is directed not against any country or doctrine, but against hunger, poverty, desperation and chaos."[26] I believe we need an Urban Recovery Plan that would be directed against hunger, poverty, ineffective education, deteriorating infrastructures, inadequate housing, and lack of access to quality health care.

Another area of concern for which I continue to be a strong advocate has to do with juvenile justice legislation. In 1996 Michigan enacted a number of changes to the criminal code which resulted in many inappropriate prosecutions of youth as adult offenders. In a June 2009 National Prison Rape Elimination Commission Report, the observation was made, "Nearly one out of every five youth surveyed (19.7 percent) reported at least one nonconsensual sexual contact during the preceding 12 months… Youth were just as likely to report abuse by staff as they were to report nonconsensual sexual encounters with their peers in the facility." A number of government financed studies have shown that minors prosecuted as adults commit more crimes and are more likely to become career criminals than youth who are processed through juvenile courts and receive rehabilitative services in a non-correctional facility designed especially for them. Unmistakably, there are young people who commit serious, violent crimes who deserve severe punishment and need to be incarcerated in accordance with the Michigan criminal code. But Michigan Department of Corrections data would suggest that there are too many youth who have committed non-violent crimes (property offenses) and have been adjudicated as adult criminals simply because the county where they lived lacked the financial resources to provide adequate community based care or to commit the youth to a juvenile justice rehabilitative residential program. Michigan Department of Corrections data would also suggest that there have been youth who have committed non-violent crimes who have been inappropriately prosecuted as adults and who would have benefited from receiving rehabilitative services in the juvenile justice system. The data also suggests that there is a significant disparity of criminalization of youthful offenders based on geographical location and ethnicity.

Ramsey Clark rightly called prisons "factories of crime." To send youthful offenders to correctional institutions where over-

The Continuing Challenge for Social Justice

crowding and personal violence are commonplace is to further condition or perhaps even direct those youth to a life of crime.

Lastly, we must reexamine policies that lead to the incarceration of a youth who has committed a serious violent crime to life imprisonment without parole. Presently, there are over three hundred prisoners within the MI Department of Corrections who have been given life sentences without any chance of parole. Michigan's law forces judges to give children as young as fourteen the maximum adult penalty. Many were convicted for aiding and abetting a crime, and they are serving a harsher sentence than the adult who was convicted of perpetrating the actual crime. One third of these juvenile lifers are serving this life-time sentence for a crime that was their first offense. Two-thirds of Michigan's juvenile lifers are African American. I am strongly advocating for the repeal of Michigan's juvenile life law. This law has drawn criticism from many organizations.

The issue is not unique to Michigan. Many states have similar laws. According to the September 25, 2009 issue of *US News & World Report*, the United States and Somalia are the only two countries in the entire world where mandatory life sentences are given to children. "Nationwide, more than 2,500 children are serving life sentences without the possibility of parole."[27]

I have not limited my advocacy for social justice to my leadership in the Association of Accredited Child and Family Agencies. On my own initiative, I have become a strong and outspoken advocate for social justice before various policy-making forums. I have held fund-raising events for candidates from both political parties who have indicated their support for improving child welfare and youth services. I personally worked for and made contributions to Dennis Archer's campaign for mayor of Detroit. I strongly believed in his leadership ability and introduced him to various groups with which I was affiliated. Dennis Archer was a highly regarded Michigan Supreme Court Justice and was named "most respected judge in Michigan" by the *Michigan Lawyers Weekly*. He won the mayoral race and served two terms from 1993 to 2001. He was later elected as president of the American Bar Association, becoming the first African American president of that organization. Because of Mr. Archer's long-time support of human services, I awarded him the Wolverine Achievement Award at our annual banquet in 2002. I also have sponsored fund raisers for several political leaders of both parties including Senator Hardiman, Speaker of the House Dillon, State Representative Dudley Spade, State Representative Jim Barcia, and State Senator Roger Kahn.

I never worked harder for a political candidate than I did in 2004 when I devoted a lot of my personal time and personally donated to the presidential campaign of U. S. Senator John Kerry. I passionately believed that President George W. Bush had gotten us into an unnecessary war in Iraq and that it was bleeding money away from juvenile justice and child welfare programs. I was determined to increase the voter turnout for the democratic candidate in Tuscola County where Vassar is located. Tuscola County has historically voted Republican even though it is a relatively poor county. I personally led the drive to establish the Tuscola Democratic Club and rented a small store-front office in Vassar from which we launched our effort to support Kerry's candidacy. We were instrumental in getting Kerry for President signs on lawns throughout the county and we mobilized various other strategies for increasing the public's awareness of Kerry for President.

I was privileged to be part of a small strategy meeting along with about fifteen other persons and with Senator Kerry in the Pontchartrain Hotel in Detroit prior to a fund-raising banquet which was held in that same hotel later that evening. I was able to personally ask him a question that had been bothering me for some time—why had he voted for the Iraq war? He explained that he had been convinced by the testimony of Secretary of State Colin Powell. It was only later that he discovered that the basis for Powell's testimony was unfounded. He made it clear that he was opposed to the war. He also indicated to me his support for affirmative action.

Our efforts were modestly successful in that the number of votes

_____ The Continuing Challenge for Social Justice

for all Democratic candidates that November had increased by ten percent from previous presidential year elections. The county still voted Republican but by the narrowest margin in recent history.

The Wolverine annual banquets have become a powerful means of bringing the work of Wolverine Human Services to the attention of business and government leaders. Beginning with our very first Annual Awards Banquet in 1988, I have sought to give recognition to college athletes and leaders from various professions who have excelled in their field of endeavor, and who have also demonstrated an enduring commitment to humanitarian causes. This has become a way of encouraging others to become involved in humanitarian causes.

I established the Wayne Anderson Champion Award in 1996 to honor Wayne Anderson, an outstanding social worker, child welfare advocate, and an administrator within the Office of Child and Youth Services whose life had been cut short by a heart attack. This award recognizes an outstanding client from the agency who has overcome challenging obstacles in his life and has demonstrated exceptional personal growth while in Wolverine's care. The award reflects our commitment to recognizing the successes of our clients and our continuing efforts to reach and support future generations.

Among some of the outstanding athletes who have been recognized as award recipients are Steve Palmateer (1989) of Eastern Michigan University (EMU), Desmond Howard (1992) of the University of Michigan (U-M), Brian Pruitt (1995) of Central Michigan University, Charlie Batch (1998) of EMU who went on to play in the NFL, Anthony Kiner (2004) of Western Michigan University, and Brian Griese (1997 & 1998) of U-M who went on to enjoy an outstanding eleven-year career with several NFL teams. One of the memorable acts of compassion that I recall Brian doing was taking a severely physically disabled high school senior girl to her senior prom. He lifted her from her wheelchair and literally held her as they danced across the ballroom floor. Brian also volunteered at the Mott Children's hospital and at a special day camp for physically challenged children. The various athletes we honored were recognized as much for their off-the-field compassionate activities as for their prowess in the field of sports.

I have also recognized various other leaders for their contributions to the cause of children and troubled youth. Among the people so honored were the late Coach "Bo" Schembechler (1990), C. Patrick Babcock (1990), State Senators Dr. Robert Geake (1994), John Kelly (1991), Joe Gougeon (1996), Jon Cisky (1997), Jim Barcia (2008), Bill Hardiman (2008), and Dr. Roger Kahn (2008), as well as many State Representatives, including Hubert Price (1998) and Dudley Spade (2008). In addition I recognized the achievements of the late Edward McNamara (1994), who for 15 years was the County Executive of Wayne County, Lt. Governor Richard Posthumus (1999), U-M Head Football Coach Lloyd Carr (2002), and Ismael Ahmed, founder and long-time president of the Arab Community Center for Economic Development and current director of the Michigan Department of Human Services. (For a complete list of the various award winners see Appendix B.)

There is still much work to do in the area of social justice advocacy and legal reform. It is my hope that there will be many young people who will see the need and take up the challenge, so that our youth—our next generation—may have that *second chance* and build a better society for themselves, their neighbors, and their communities.

CHAPTER 22

GIVING FORWARD

IT WAS A MONDAY IN THE YEAR 2000 at St. Jude's when John Vitale poked his head into my office. "How did it go at commencement, Chief?" he asked, referring to my recent commencement address that I had given at the University of Michigan School of Social Work.

"Okay," I replied without looking up. I was reading about Wayne County's plans to close a day treatment center for juvenile offenders—the same kind of thing I had decried in my speech a few days before.

"I don't want to disturb you, Chief," John said, approaching my desk, "but I think I'm going to need some time off again."

I looked up at the Gentle Giant. I hadn't seen him since the last staff meeting. If he had lost weight, I didn't notice it then but I sure noticed it now and his face was sallow and pale.

"I went back for a follow-up visit," he said. "I thought it was going to be routine, but the doctor said he wants to do more tests. And he wants me to lie low till he finds out what's going on."

Ultimately, the news would not be good. John's cancer had come back and spread to his brain. "That sucks," was his reaction when the doctor told him. But as *Detroit Free Press* sports columnist Mitch

Albom recalled, "Those were the first and only negative words anyone heard him say."

Judy and I were out of state on a much needed break when we got the terrible news. I knew how aggressive cancer could be once it metastasized to the brain; we immediately caught a plane back to Detroit. John passed away as our plane touched down, and we were not able to see him alive again. He died on Sunday, July 9, 2000, at Bon Secours Hospital. His funeral, at St. Jude's Church near his home, drew hundreds of friends and co-workers, boys from Wolverine, former teammates, and, of course, his old coach, Bo Schembechler.

"When he called me Chief," Bo said, "it was out of respect, and I knew it."

"John was never outworked—never," Bo continued. "Nobody prepared harder or played harder than he did. And what you like as a coach is a player that will pay the price to prepare."

I thought of the time when Bo Schembechler was the keynote speaker at our first anniversary banquet March 24, 1988. He talked about "giving forward"—helping young people and discovering the benefits it paid. As a coach he had helped a generation of young people learn discipline and compassion by his example. Now he was talking about a former player of his who once showed up on the football field with a U-M winged helmet shaved onto the side of his head, but who off the field was as unassuming as anybody could be; a young man who after having an NFL career stolen from him because of a nasty back injury, dedicated himself to helping disadvantaged and abused kids; a young man who, at age thirty-four, died before his time.

In the eight years I had worked with him, John was a perfect example of Bo's idea of giving forward. So it was fitting that we should name the Community Center where he had made such an impact *The John S. Vitale Community Center*. But, it also saddened me to know that he was not here with us to witness our love and appreciation for all he had brought to us and to the kids whose lives he touched.

CHAPTER 23

IN ANOTHER TIME

EVER SINCE COMING TO Michigan I had kept in touch with Stan Farrow, my old Brooklyn buddy and classmate at the Food and Maritime Trades School and fellow meat-cutter at the 14th Street Market in lower Manhattan. Stan had traded in his meat cleaver for a pair of scissors, taking up hairstyling and then finding himself a wife. For years I tried to talk him into coming to Vassar and starting a culinary arts training program for the kids. It wasn't until after his divorce, and the demise of his Manhattan hair salon following the horror of 9/11, that he finally made the move from the Big Apple to the home of the sugar beet: Vassar with a population of 4,000.

For a Brooklyn-born Jew, relocating to Vassar is likely the very definition of culture shock. But the move couldn't have made me happier. And Stan came prepared. He had saved all the manuals from his meat cutting days. ("You just never know when you're going to need stuff," he said.) When Stan arrived in 2002 he began the design and implementation of Wolverine's meat cutting and culinary arts training program for youth. It wasn't long before this foray into social entrepreneurship was paying for itself in three significant ways. We reduced food costs by over 15 percent; Stanley was training boys in the art of meat cutting, providing them with genuine job-readiness skills; and Wolverine was again proven to be an innovator.

There are few programs like it, and I'm convinced Stanley engineered the best meat-cutting training center for troubled youth in the country. He worked with the architect to design a state of the art culinary arts kitchen as a part of the new addition at the Wolverine Secure Treatment Center. In addition to the teaching kitchen, Stan incorporated a small classroom which can also double as a café. We now have a bona fide job-readiness training program in culinary arts that is a part of the secure treatment center. The program is neither mandated nor formally funded by MDHS. We incurred the cost of this enhancement because of our commitment to make troubled youth *victors*.

In June of 2008 and I was traveling up to Vassar to witness yet another expansion of our programming. A billboard popped into view as I headed up Interstate 75 from Detroit to Saginaw. It displayed the Peace Corps logo and the words, *Never have to start sentences with "I should've...."* I wondered how many times I had started sentences with "*I should've....*" or "*I shouldn't have…*" It is the paradox of my career path: if someone had warned me against that before I went to prison, would my life be any different today? And if so, can I be certain it would be for the better?

Three-and-a-half decades later I'm heading to another secure facility, although it is far different from the one I experienced as a prisoner. Officially, I named it the Wolverine Secure Treatment Center—unofficially, *The Blue Roof Inn* because its bright blue roof stands out prominently from the highway as one passes the building. I cannot help but allow my mind to wander back to humble beginnings of the organization I founded some twenty years ago. And preceding that, I can say assuredly that my commitment to rehabilitating delinquent kids began while I was incarcerated at the Milan Federal Correctional Institution.

As I continued north on I-75, I thought of the people who had helped me reach this moment—people like Mark Glesener and Charles Wolfson, two University of Michigan social workers who were not only my therapists in prison, but who became my role models. It was they who made me believe that I could make a difference in people's lives after I served my time. They inspired me to take up a career in social work.

I thought of Ramsey Clark who, when he was the U. S. Attorney General and ran our federal prison system, stressed rehabilitation over punishment. Even though Ramsay Clark was no longer Attorney General when I was incarcerated, his philosophy still prevailed into the early '70s. If there is anything about my incarceration I'm thankful for, it's that I was in prison during that era, and not today when the prevailing attitude toward people like me has returned to "Let's lock 'em up and throw away the key!" In today's penal system, I would never have come into contact with people like Professor Wolfson and Mark Glesener in a meaningful way.

I thought of Jim Minder, my first social work mentor at Boysville of Michigan, the one-time legendary "Gentleman Bandit" of Detroit who later founded his own organization to help delinquent kids. Urbane and sophisticated, he eventually became the Chairman of the Board of Smith & Wesson, though his tenure was prematurely cut short when his history of bank robberies, ironically perpetrated with the company's own product, came to light. Talk about rehabilitation! I thought of Petey, my very good friend whom I met while at Milan Prison; and Bill Tilton who helped make it possible for us to launch Wolverine on a shoestring and the blessings of St. Jude himself. And I thought of Harold Gazan, the tough but fair-minded deputy director of MDSS, who in spite of my checkered past had the courage to look beyond my file and to see the person I really was.

As I approached my destination, I contemplated who I was and who I had become. To some small-minded, spiteful people I would never rise above the status of an ex-con. But to those who have walked in shoes like mine, mistakes are not indelible and redemption is attainable. Carol Moseley Braun said, "Defining myself, as opposed to being defined by others, is one of the most difficult challenges I face."[28] I refuse to participate in exercises that define people by past mistakes.

I am Robert E. Wollack, the founder and CEO of Wolverine Human Services, Inc., a non-profit agency begun in 1986 with the sole purpose of offering troubled young people a second chance. Our far superior success rate (as high as ninety percent in one study) and business-oriented approach to accountability and positive outcomes is the reason we have grown from serving fourteen troubled boys in a once-abandoned convent on Detroit's east side to operating nine residential treatment centers, a foster care and community case management division, and a community center with services stretching from Detroit to Saginaw and across to Michigan's "thumb."

I pulled off the Interstate at Exit 151 and turned left. Just ahead stood The Blue Roof Inn. I turned into the parking lot and looked at the brand new wing with its signature roof, and I felt a rush of satisfaction mixed with nostalgia. Today we are welcoming ten new youth, adding to the eighty already being cared for in this large and uniquely designed complex.

A security guard let me in the door, and I passed through a metal detector. In the lobby, staff members greeted me with words like, "Hi'ya, R.E.," "How ya doin', Chief?" We formed an entourage and proceeded through the building, across the gymnasium and into the living quarters of the new wing where I met the ten newcomers. Their group leader had already taught them basic greeting skills. "Hello, I'm Robert Wollack," I said, taking the hand of the first boy in line.

"Hello, I'm Carlos, age fourteen," he said," looking down.

"Look me in the eye and repeat your name," I told him.

"Carlos, age fourteen," he repeated struggling to look up.

Still clutching his hand, I looked into his eyes and saw a mirror image of myself—Robert Wollack fifty years ago, a troubled kid from the streets of Brooklyn, a petty thief, gang member, and future felon. And I think the same thought every time I greet a new kid in this place: "Maybe I can help him or maybe I can't, but at least I'm giving him a second chance."

The new wing of the Wolverine Secure Treatment Center has added classrooms, a computer lab, the culinary arts kitchen and simulated café that Stanley had designed, and a life-skills preparation classroom. This latter room is designed and furnished like a small apartment. Life-skills classrooms have also been developed and successfully used in Vassar House and on the Vassar campus. Equipped with a washer and dryer, small fully-appointed kitchen, and a small furnished sitting room, the Life-skills Preparation Classroom actively prepares youth for living in the real world. They are taught basic household maintenance skills, including budgeting, meal planning and preparation, shopping, laundry, and other aspects of living independently that many of the youth we serve have never experienced. Each new concept—the wilderness experience, the horticulture program, the meat-cutting work-study, and now a life-skills laboratory—is another expression of our faith made real. Ultimately, I can't change how people define me. But I take great pride in helping to create all the opportunities Wolverine presents for young people willing to embrace their strengths and to work to overcome their challenges. To be a part of this is to witness something wonderful, and yet humbling.

In the next few years we opened several more facilities — a new gymnasium and community activity center at the Vassar Campus, and the Wolverine Center for Addiction, Recovery Education (W-CARE) drug treatment program, which we operate in collaboration with Growth Works, Inc. Early in 2006 we established the Harold Gazan Center for the Treatment of Drug and Alcohol Addiction, a residential facility located on the Vassar Campus that is designed to treat drug-dependent male youth. I wanted to honor Harold for his 45 years of dedicated social work service on behalf of vulnerable children and troubled youth. Since his retirement from the State of Michigan in 1996, he has become a mentor and a close friend to me and to the agency. He along with Bob Blumenfeld have modestly provided invaluable assistance in compiling this memoir.

During 2006 on a beautiful crisp, clear autumn day I named two other cabins in Camp One on the Vassar Campus after two men who have been long-time supporters of Wolverine Human Services. They were important financial backers during 1991-2 when we were developing the Vassar Campus. Without their financial support, we could not have constructed the buildings that comprise Camp One. Both of these gentlemen have been strong donors to Wolverine as well. The cabins are named to honor Earl Thomas, a retired contractor and builder, and George Mosher, a retired patent attorney.

By February 2007 our twentieth anniversary, Wolverine Human Services had served over twenty thousand different children and youth and now had eight residential programs with a capacity to serve seven hundred youth.

One autumn evening I joined Stan Farrow and a few friends at the Wolverine Guest House. The sun was sinking below the horizon and the oak and maple leaves were starting to make their fall descent. It had been a long day, and I felt very tired. Although I was only 64, I was forced to walk with a cane, the residual effect of complications from hip replacement surgery that had not been totally successful. Stan was out on the patio grilling steaks, so I hobbled out and offered to give him a hand. "No, No, go sit down," Stan said. I stood there and watched him work with the steaks, and I thought back to those days when we worked together at the Fourteenth Street Market in Manhattan more than 45 years ago. Now we were here in Vassar, Michigan; two old friends reunited in a common cause. We started out as kids in Brooklyn, learning a trade and trying to better ourselves. We are still learning, but now we are about something much more. We are working together in a positive way to give kids a chance that they might otherwise not have.

CHAPTER 24

VASSAR HOUSE

WHEN BO SCHEMBECHLER ORIGINALLY spoke of "giving forward," I had no idea what that would eventually mean for Wolverine Human Services. Ever since Ed Overstreet, my former boss at Boysville, had put me in charge of Cabrini Center in Detroit, I had vowed never again to try to run a girls' home. I wanted nothing to do with troubled girls. But then, Growth Works, Inc., the agency with whom we collaborated on the development of Wolverine's W-CARE drug treatment program for drug-dependent boys, approached me and said, "We need help."

Based in Plymouth, Michigan, Growth Works had been in business since 1971 providing drug treatment and juvenile justice services for youth and families in western Wayne County. "We know of your reputation and work with male teens," Dale Yagiela, the executive director, said. "We don't have a good residential treatment program in Michigan for female teens. Can you help us?"

On October 10, 2008—a radiant and unseasonably warm morning in Vassar, Michigan—I stood at the podium outside the brand new, beautifully constructed Vassar House. My son Craig the chaplain for Wolverine Human Services, delivered the invocation. Then

I introduced my wife Judy who was then the executive vice president and in late 2009 assumed the position of chief executive officer of Wolverine. This expansion of Wolverine into operating a residential program for troubled girls would not have occurred without Judy's vision, leadership, and experience.

The gathering was the formal opening of our new 25,000 square-foot, state-of-the-art residential facility to provide a social treatment program for drug dependent or emotionally troubled twelve-to-eighteen-year-old girls. This facility was constructed at a cost of $2.9 million in less than nine months. Two hundred guests were gathered in the courtyard including state senators and representatives, the mayor of Vassar, members of the city council, the Vassar Public School Superintendent, members of the school board, Growth Works representatives, including its executive director, and Wolverine Human Services board members, donors, and friends. Behind me stood some of the key people at Wolverine—people who had stood by me almost from the beginning—Pete Walsh, Mike Jones, Matt Mitchell, Derrick McCree, and Bob Petti.

"I did not develop this program," I told the assembled crowd, somewhat embarrassed. "I didn't have anything to do with it except to sign for the bonds." My confession drew a tittered response.

So here we were—like Spanky at his club house—taking down the *No Girls Allowed* sign twenty-one years after we put up our first sign, the one that said *St. Jude's Home for Boys*. The first six girls had already arrived and another fifty-four would be arriving over the next several weeks.

Judy described meeting the first arrivals. "I went around to each girl and said, 'Hi, I'm Mrs. Wollack.' Soon I came to one young lady who said, 'I'm No-Name.' I said, 'Hi, No-Name,' and continued on to greet the other girls. The next morning I went into the living area and I saw six girls with beautiful smiling faces. I spotted No-Name and said, 'Hi, No-Name.' She smiled back and said, 'Hi, my name is Tiffany.'"

After the ceremony I joined the others for a tour of the building. I felt more like a guest than the CEO of Wolverine Human Services.

Vassar House

We visited Lynn Thompson's classroom. Her high school English class is one of many classes that are taught throughout the various residential centers that comprise our Vassar campus. The classes are taught by teachers from the Vassar Public School system. I saw a half-dozen poems posted on the wall under the title *I Am*. "I am a fun, loving person," read one by Jay Lynn, a ninth-grader. "I want to be loved," read another:

I say God loves me....
  I hope in the end he cares.
    I am a fun, loving person.

I saw another poem by a sixteen-year-old named Christina:

I cry about missing my kids....
  I hope I can change.
    I am outgoing and caring.

There was a poem by Keosha, seventeen, who's working on her GED:

I dream bigger than my head can think....
  I hope I can stay away from the street life.
    I am all things within, apart and out of me.

This 62-bed facility is beautifully designed and furnished with teen girls specifically in mind. Aesthetics and hominess have been built into the ambience. The classrooms include a Life-Skills Preparation Laboratory as well as a computer lab. Vassar House incorporates all of the quality treatment components of the standard Wolverine Human Services curriculum, such as group therapy, individual counseling, restorative justice, and drug testing. Clinical care provides a holistic approach using a personal recovery program whereby the young women can learn about the relationship between substance abuse and the traumatic experiences which they have encountered. Wolverine contracts with Growth Works, Inc., to provide the specialized therapy programs to address drug dependency issues.

With the addition of Vassar House, Wolverine Human Services now encompasses nine residential facilities and programs—each uniquely designed to meet the varied needs of troubled young people—both boys and girls!

CHAPTER 25

FROM VICTIMS TO VICTORS

SINCE WOLVERINE HUMAN SERVICES opened its first program in February 1987, the staff have helped more than twenty-five thousand troubled youth (including abused and neglected children) turn their lives around through its residential programs, foster care, Families First initiatives, supervised independent living, and its community center. I reflect on my story—sobering, humbling, paradoxical, and exhilarating. Yes, I've overcome adversity, but I am neither so naive, nor so arrogant, as to dismiss the role that fate has played in my journey. I reflect on my achievements with pride. I share a bond with all the young people touched by Wolverine and pray that in their lives they will come to know what it is to achieve, to love, and to be loved. It is only fitting that a few pages be set aside for some of them to tell their stories.

ERIC S., AGE 18

"My foster parents adopted me when I was four. They were old enough to be my grandparents. I was fourteen when I first got arrested for safe-cracking and that was just the beginning. I spent four months at the Macomb County Juvenile Justice Center. When I got out, I violated probation by smoking weed. I also skipped school a lot.

"When I got arrested the second time for breaking and entering, I was sent to Wolverine [the Secure Treatment Center]. Being there made me realize I had two choices — either I could be violent and end-up in prison, or I could do something with my life and become productive.

"A lot of people on the staff made a difference in my life—Miss Hadley, Miss White, Miss Anthony, and Miss Jordan, just to name a few. Even though I argued with them a lot, they stuck in there. Mr. Hunter too. He helped me a lot. When I was down, he helped turn me up.

"Before I went to Wolverine I didn't care about the world. I didn't think there was anything in it for me. But now I'm back in school, and I'm starting to think positive. I'm even supervising kids at the Boys & Girls' Club in Bay City. My goal is to own my own business someday. Thanks to the people at Wolverine, I'm on my way."

RYAN R., AGE 18

"I didn't like listening to my parents very much. I ended up getting into trouble and doing what I wanted to do, and trouble just came my way.

"I got put on probation for MIP—minor in possession of alcohol. But I didn't do probation like I was supposed to. I was doing marijuana and failing drug tests, so they sent me to the Clarence Fischer Leadership Academy at Wolverine. At first it was tough. They had a lot of stuff for you to do and I wasn't used to having my day full, but the structured treatment there really helped me. So did the anger management and counseling. I did a lot of reading there. I read books about troubled kids and how they turned their lives around. It got me to thinking about my future and what I could do to better myself.

"I got into the culinary arts training program with Mr. Farrow. He really helped me. So did Mr. Drake and Mr. Wynn. I did well in school and got my G.E.D. while at Wolverine. It made me feel good about myself. It made me want to go on to school. Now I'm going to Davenport University and going for a degree in business management. I want to start my own company someday.

"Being at Wolverine helped me think about the good side—what you can do with your life and how to be productive."

PHILLIP W., AGE 19

"My mother passed away when I was five months old. Then my father and I went to live with my grandmother. She passed away when I was thirteen. She basically raised me, and then I was on my own.

"At fourteen I went to the state institution [W.J. Maxey Boys Training School] for child molestation, but I refused to go along with their program. I had everything I wanted there—shanks, pills, and porno. I even had somebody smuggle in Vicodin for me. After four years they said they could no longer help me, so the judge sent me to Wolverine.

"At Wolverine the staff really cared. They treated me like a person—they were willing to take the time out of their day to help me. They treated me with more respect than at any other facility I had been in.

"I earned my G.E.D. while at Wolverine. My dream is to become a mortician. I plan to go to college and get a license as a mortician and start my own business."

ANTWON J.

Antwon was interviewed in April 2009 at Antwon's place of employment, *Crepes Café*, in a Detroit suburb where he was employed part-time as a bus-boy and waiter. He is a handsome seventeen-year-old African American with a broad winsome smile. He has a tall, muscular build. When conversing with him you are immediately drawn to his warm personality, politeness, and quiet demeanor and you are impressed with his keen mind. He is self-confident and a keen observer of others.

He explained that he was raised in Inkster, Michigan. He came from a family that included older and younger siblings; his parents were separated. "I was about twelve years old when I left my mother to go and live with my father. I did not get along with my mom's boyfriend. My mom had a drug problem and she and her boyfriend were always fighting," he explained. However, when he moved in with his dad and his older brother and sister, he began to be negatively influenced by his older siblings. Antwon shared with me that his father was a graduate of a university but that he had an alcohol abuse problem.

"I began to follow the paths of my older siblings which caused me to skip school, hang-out with friends, and party with my siblings and their friends," he explained. This led to his being willing to help his sister who wanted to get revenge on a friend. They trashed some of the girl's belongings at her home. Antwon was charged with malicious destruction of property and school truancy. He was initially placed on probation but violated his probation, which caused him to be sent to Wolverine's Vassar Campus. Antwon was assigned to the Thomas Cabin in Camp One when he was only thirteen years old.

Shortly thereafter, he became a part of the original group of boys assigned to the new Wolverine Center for Addiction Recovery Education (W-CARE) program in the cabin named in honor of Harold Gazan. He was viewed as being a youth who would be a natural leader among the new boys and would be able to communicate the positive culture that was to be established among the youth. Mr. Roy Brewer, the group leader, and Antwon developed a positive rapport with each other. Roy informed me that Antwon demonstrated self-confident leadership ability right from the very beginning. Antwon looks up to Mr. Brewer as a positive role model and they continue to maintain contact.

Antwon said that the big difference between juvenile detention and Wolverine Human Services was the staff. "I knew that the staff at Wolverine were trying to help us. The boys at JD [juvenile detention] had no hope—it was crazy. Everything was forced—staff didn't motivate you. . . . At Wolverine I just followed the program. Staff seem to know where you're coming from. They help you to make the right decisions. They didn't force you—they motivated you. . . . I began to encourage other boys to get along in the program and the importance of following the rules. It helped me to make myself a better person. I think I found myself—it [the program] built me up."

Antwon is just finishing his junior year at Southfield Regional Academic Campus. He plans to complete his high school and then enter the police academy. He is looking forward to a career in law enforcement. He works part-time—about 20 to 25 hours a week—at the *Crepes Café*.

JOMO W., AGE 23

"I grew up as one of fifteen siblings in two separate families. My father split from my mother and I went with him, but he wasn't a good role model. Even though he had all these kids to look after, he was the leader of one of Detroit's most notorious gangs.

"At sixteen I was a fugitive from justice. After four guys beat up my twin sister, I went over to their house with a baseball bat and a gun. An altercation followed and gunshots were fired on both sides. Nobody was killed, but among other things I was charged with assault to commit murder.

"When the police came to my school to arrest me, I slid out the back door. For the next month and a half I was on the run. When the police finally caught up with me, they hauled me before the judge who put me in the Wayne County Juvenile Home while I awaited trial. I faced up to twenty-six years in prison if found guilty on all the charges, but I copped a plea bargain on a felony firearm possession which gave me juvenile time till I reached twenty-one.

"That's when I came to the Clarence Fischer Leadership Academy. The first person I met was Derrick McCree who told me I had a choice—either I could spend the rest of my life in prison, or I could use Wolverine as a stepping stone and turn my life around. I knew it would be hard, but I decided to turn my life around.

"Eight months later Mr. McCree asked me if I would like to work at the retail meat distribution program at Wolverine as a full-time employee? I thought, Wow! Yes! He introduced me to Mr. Wollack who looked me dead square in the eyes and said, 'There's something about you that I believe in, and so I'm going to give you this opportunity to change your life.'

"Mr. Wollack himself taught me how to cut meat. So did Mr. Farrow—they both got right in the trenches. Even though Mr. Wollack is the CEO and has friends in high places, he can sit down and talk with you like he's a regular guy. He has a very big heart.

"Mr. Wollack inspired me to fulfill my dream, which is to 'pay forward' the help I received and to offer a helping hand to anyone who needs it, like he did to me. Now I'm in my fourth year at Delta College. My major is criminal justice, and my priorities are one hundred percent lined up. What I want to do eventually is to open my own facility for troubled youth."

Jomo has been employed at Wolverine Human Services meat processing center for nine years and has proven to be a conscientious and trustworthy manager and an excellent role model for other young men who participate in the program.

JACOB & JOSEPH BONAS, AGE 15

In a lengthy article in the *Detroit Free Press* (September 10, 2009) twins Jacob and Joseph Bonas were featured. The boys (now 15) had grown up in a very rough neighborhood in Detroit and were "the meanest, toughest kids who had ever walked into a gym," said Emanuel Steward of the Kronk Gym. The twins were in trouble at school and had come to the attention of the police by the time they were eleven.

Their parents were refugees from the communist regime in Romania, but their dad is now serving time in a federal prison (out of state) for "conspiring to deliver and distribute" drugs. I was reminded of my own conviction and time in prison.

The twins were arrested in connection with a robbery in Detroit and were sent to the Wolverine Secure Treatment Center in February 2007. We worked with them for sixteen and fourteen months respectively. They benefited from the typical program activities. We also enabled them to continue their training in our formal boxing program. Both boys are back with their mother, who moved her boys to Sumpter Township. And both are under the tutelage of "Sugar" Hill, boxing coach from the new Kronk Gym, with dreams of becoming professional boxers. I like to think that we had a part in stimulating a change of attitude in these two young men who now have a definite, positive goal for their lives.

THESE ARE A FEW OF THE many youths who have become victors. They were able to overcome their previous pattern of failures and develop a sense of self-worth. Through their accomplishments they achieved self-affirmation.

The youth who come to Wolverine Human Services are unique individuals with differing potentials, but they also have similar backgrounds; they have generally lacked consistent parenting and positive, nurturing experiences in their early years. They have often grown-up without a father or a consistent positive adult male influence in their lives. Often they have had a parent or a sibling who has spent time in jail or is currently in prison. They have encountered many moves from one living arrangement to another or from one school to another. Their lives have been characterized by confusion, abusive adults, poverty, and social rejection, often resulting in little motivation to live organized, disciplined lives and to pursue education. They have great difficulty in postponing gratification or planning for the long-range. Instead they often abuse alcohol and drugs.

These are the youth Wolverine Human Services seeks to reach and to redirect their lives. These are the youth to whom we dedicate our activities, our social therapy skills, and our resources that they might become inspired to pursue new goals, to make achievements commensurate to their abilities, and to become worthwhile to themselves and to society. These are the ones who have had an opportunity to become *victors*.

EPILOGUE

I AM THANKFUL FOR THE opportunities I have been afforded, for the friendships and loves I have known, and for the many lives that I have touched and that have touched mine. But I am still haunted, even in my proudest moments and my deepest reflections of the good I have done, by the winding and often dark path that I took to arrive at my destination. I remain puzzled by the paradox that I am sure I share with many who will read this book, "Would I be who I am today were it not for these acts that leave the sting of humiliation and the bitterness of regret?" It is a question without an answer, and in large part the source of my drive and passion. In my quest to help others, I know that I also am seeking my own salvation.

I maintain a deep abiding belief in the presence of providential forces at work in my life preparing me for a future which I could not possibly have imagined. It isn't our misdeeds that define us, but what we learn from them and do with them that define who we are. From a place of humiliation and disgrace, I would come to know good, kind, intelligent, and caring people who would guide my life, and, in so doing, would bless me with the opportunity to influence the lives of thousands of youth whose stories were not significantly different from my own.

Epilogue

I am especially grateful for my wife Judith, and my life-long friends Bill Tilton and Pete Walsh, and I recognize with appreciation Professor Wolfson, Mark Glesener, Professor John Tropman, and Harold Gazan, my mentors and supporters. Although the stigma of prison will follow me to my grave, it ironically may have been the seminal event which led me toward a life of helping others. In fact, I have never seen a kid that I felt I couldn't help.

I would like to leave you with this final reflection. Striking my breast with my hand as when I was an altar boy so many years ago: *"quia peccai nimis cogitatione verbo, et opera; mea culpa, mea culpa, mea maxima culpa."*—I have sinned exceedingly in thought, word and deed through my fault, through my fault, through my most grievous fault. I pray for myself and for those who have been part of my life—through good times and bad—and for all those whose choices take them to places they would rather not have visited, but whose salvation lies in what they are learning, and what they will ultimately do with their lives.

ENDNOTES

1. Niederhoffer, Arthur. *Behind the Blue Shield*, p 65.
2. Goddard, Donald. *Easy Money: The High-Rolling, Superflying, Drug-Powered World of the Spanish and Black "Mafias,"* p 124.
3. Niederhoffer, Arthur. *Behind the Blue Shield*, p. 61.
4. Goddard, *Easy Money: The High-Rolling, Superflying, Drug-Powered World of the Spanish and Black "Mafias,"* p 124.
5. Kamisar, Yale. "Criminals, Cops and the Constitution," *The Nation*. November 9, 1964, p 322.
6. Glasser, William. *Reality Therapy: A New Approach to Psychiatry*, p 47.
7. Wollack, Robert. *Group Work and Its Applicability to the Adolescent Client: A Review of Four Approaches*, p 17.
8. Sarri, Rosemary, et al. *New Directions: An Evaluation of Pioneer Work and Learn Center of Wolverine Human Services*. February 1991, p 137.
9. *The Detroit News*, December 31, 1986, p 4.
10. *The Detroit News*, July 22, 1987, p 1.
11. *The Detroit News*, August 23, 1987, p 1.
12. *The Detroit News*, August 28, 1987, p 1.
13. *The Detroit News*, April 26, 1987, p 1.
14. *The Detroit News*, May 19, 1993, p 1F.
15. *Administrative Review Team Final Report*, Michigan Department of Social Services, July 30, 1993, p 13.

Endnotes

16. For additional information regarding The Seven Principles, see my self-published booklet entitled: *The Wolverine Philosophy*.
17. Sarri, Rosemary, et al. *New Directions: An Evaluation of Pioneer Work and Learn Center of Wolverine Human Services,* February 1991, p 24.
18. *Ibid.*, p 144.
19. Rollin, James and Rosemary Sarri. *A Follow-up Report on Recidivism by Youth on Pioneer Work and Learn Center*, September 1991, p 13.
20. Osborne, David and Ted Gaebler. *Reinventing Government: How the Entrepreneurial Spirit Is Transforming the Public Sector from Schoolhouse to Statehouse, City Hall to the Pentagon.* p 46-47.
21. Bergmann, Luke. *Getting Ghost: Two Young Lives and the Struggle for the Soul of an American City*, p 303.
22. Clark, Ramsey. *Crime in America.* p 57.
23. *Ibid.*, p 242-243.
24. Bergmann, Luke. *Getting Ghost.* p 39.
25. *Ibid.*, p 13.
26. McCullough, David. *Truman*, p 563.
27. *US News & World Report*, September 25, 2009, p 6.
28. *The New Republic*, November 15, 1993.

SELECTED BIBLIOGRAPHY

Aichhorn, August. *Wayward Youth.* New York: Viking Press, 1953.

Bergmann, Luke. *Getting Ghost: Two Young Lives and the Struggle for the Soul of an American City.* New York: The New Press, 2008.

Clark, Ramsey. *Crime in America.* New York: Simon and Schuster, 1970.

Currie, Elliott. *Crime and Punishment in America: Why the Solutions to America's Most Stubborn Social Crisis Have Not Worked and What Will.* New York: Henry Holt and Company, Inc., 1998.

Gambrill, Eileen D. *Behavior Modification: Handbook of Assessment, Intervention, and Evaluation.* San Francisco, CA: Jossey-Bass Publishers, 1977.

Glasser, William. *Reality Therapy: A New Approach to Psychiatry.* New York: Harper & Row, 1965.

Glesener, Mark. *The Utilization of the Ex-offender as a Para-professional in Group Therapy.* Unpublished Manuscript, 1972.

Goddard, Donald. *Easy Money: The High-Rolling, Superflying, Drug-Powered World of the Spanish and Black "Mafias."* New York: Farrar, Straus and Giroux, 1978.

Selected Bibliography

Hawkins, David R. *Power vs. Force: The Hidden Determinants of Human Behavior.* Carlsbad, CA: Hay House, Inc., 2002

Kamisar, Yale. "Criminals, Cops and the Constitution," *The Nation.* November 9, 1964, pp 322-326.

Kennedy, Edward M. *True Compass: A Memoir.* New York: Twelve — Hatchett Book Group, 2009.

Kennedy, John F. (Edited by Allan Nevins) *The Burden and the Glory: The Hopes and Purposes of President Kennedy's Second and Third Years in Office as Revealed in His Public Statements and Addresses.* New York: Harper & Row Publishers, 1964.

Lardner, James and Thomas Reppetto. *NYPD: A City and Its Police.* New York: Henry Holt and Company, 2000.

MacKenzie, Doris L., and Eugene E. Hebert. *Correctional Boot Camps: A Tough Intermediate Sanction.* Washington, DC: U. S. Department of Justice, National Institute of Justice, 1996.

Maslow, Abraham H. *Motivation and Personality.* New York: Harper & Row, 1954.

May, Rollo. *Man's Search for Himself.* New York: W. W. Norton & Company, First Paper Back Edition, 2009 (Originally published in 1953).

May, Rollo. *The Discovery of Being: Writings in Existential Psychology.* New York: W. W. Norton & Company, 1983.

May, Rollo. *Power and Innocence: A Search for the Sources of Violence.* New York: W. W. Norton & Company, First Paperback Edition, 1998 (Originally published in 1972).

McCoy, Alfred. *The Politics of Heroin in Southeast Asia.* New York: Harper & Row, 1972.

McCullough, David. *Truman.* New York: Simon & Schuster, 1992.

Niederhoffer, Arthur. *Behind the Blue Shield: Police in Urban Society.* Garden City, NY: Doubleday & Company, Inc., 1967.

Selected Bibliography

Oates, Stephen B. *Let the Trumpet Sound: The Life of Martin Luther King, Jr.* New York: Harper & Row Publishers, 1982.

O'Donohue, William T. and Kyle E. Ferguson. *The Psychology of B. F. Skinner.* Newbury Park, CA: Sage Publications, 2001.

Ohlin, Lloyd E. and Frank J. Remington, Editors. *Discretion in Criminal Justice: The Tension Between Individualization and Uniformity.* Albany, NY: State University of New York Press, 1993.

Osborne, David and Ted Gaebler. *Reinventing Government: How the Entrepreneurial Spirit Is Transforming the Public Sector from Schoolhouse to Statehouse, City Hall to the Pentagon.* Reading, MA: Addison-Wesley Publishing Company, Inc., 1992.

Rollin, James and Rosemary Sarri. *A Follow-up Report on Recidivism by Youth from Pioneer Work and Learn Center.* Ann Arbor, MI: The University of Michigan, Institute for Social Research, September, 1991.

Rollin, James and Rosemary Sarri. *New Directions for Youth: A Follow-up Report on Pioneer Work and Learn Center of Wolverine Human Services.* Ann Arbor, MI: The University of Michigan, Institute for Social Research, February, 1992.

Sarri, Rosemary and James Rollin. *Preliminary Findings from Program Evaluation: Wolverine Human Services – Pioneer Work and Learn Camp.* Ann Arbor, MI: The University of Michigan, Institute for Social Research, February, 1990.

Sarri, Rosemary, et al. *New Directions: An Evaluation of Pioneer Work and Learn Center of Wolverine Human Services.* Ann Arbor, MI: The University of Michigan, Institute for Social Research, February, 1991.

Sarri, Rosemary, et al. *Report on the Evaluation of the Substance Abuse Education and Prevention Program at Wolverine Center, Detroit, Michigan, October 1, 1990 – September 30, 1991.* Ann Arbor, MI: The University of Michigan, Institute for Social Research, undated (presumed to be early 1992).

Selected Bibliography

Sarri, Rosemary, James Rollin, Deborah Stephens, and Charles Wolfson. *Youth-Community Reintegration and Delinquency Outcomes: An Evaluation Report.* Unpublished Manuscript, September 1995.

Scott, Elizabeth S. and Laurence Steinberg. *Rethinking Juvenile Justice.* Cambridge, MA: Harvard University Press, 2008.

Skinner, B. F. *About Behaviorism.* New York: Vintage, 1976.

Skinner, B. F. *Science and Human Behavior.* New York: Free Press, 1965.

Skinner, B. F. *The Behavior of Organisms.* New York: Appelton, 1938.

Stein, Herman D. and Richard A. Cloward. *Social Perspectives on Behavior: A Reader in Social Science for Social Work and Related Professions.* Glencoe, IL: The Free Press, Publishers, 1958.

Vorrath, Harry H. & Larry K. Brendtro. *Positive Peer Culture – Second Edition.* New Brunswick, NJ: Aldine Transaction Publishers, 1985.

Wollack, Robert E. and James Peter Walsh. *Narcotic Rehabilitation – Treatment with the Closed Milieu: Milan Federal Correctional Institution. Milan, Michigan.* Unpublished Manuscript, 1975.

Wollack, Robert E. *Group Work and Its Applicability to the Adolescent Client: A Review of Four Approaches.* Unpublished Paper, 1977

Wollack, Robert E. *Police Power: The Law of Search and Seizure and the Exclusionary Rule.* Unpublished Paper, 1977.

APPENDIX A
WOLVERINE HUMAN SERVICES TODAY

F OUNDED BY ROBERT WOLLACK IN 1987, Wolverine Human Services (WHS) is a social services agency providing rehabilitative services to adolescents suffering from the social injustices of abuse and neglect, and who have become enmeshed in drug dependency or delinquent activity. This is the major focus of WHS. In addition, WHS provides safety, sustenance, nurturing, and therapeutic intervention to abused and neglected children through its foster care and community services programs.

Our mission is to offer the most appropriate setting and most effective social treatment services possible to children, youth, and their families. Our approach is eclectic and is founded on the premise of unconditional care. Wolverine's continuum of services and effective network of referral sources provides a responsive and cost-effective system.

Wolverine has become the fastest growing private, non-profit juvenile justice/child welfare agency in the state of Michigan and operates nine residential facilities along with several other programs. These are each described in the order of their initiation:

Appendix A

- **St. Jude's Home for Boys** is where the story of Wolverine Human Services began. This forty-bed facility was opened on February 2, 1987, on Detroit's east side, and serves boys ages twelve to seventeen. Group, individual and family counseling is provided. Educational services are provided through local charter schools of the Detroit Public School system or on-site for youth with special needs. A consulting clinical psychologist and a consulting psychiatrist are available on an as needed basis.
- **Wolverine Diagnostic, Assessment, and Treatment Center** is located at 2629 Lenox Street on Detroit's east side. This facility was opened in January 1988, and consists of two different programs. The Diagnostic and Assessment Center is licensed to serve twenty-two boys six to eighteen years of age who are in need of short-term emergency residential care. The main goal of the facility is to provide emergency, short-term placements for boys who have had to be removed suddenly from a very abusive situation or have been abandoned. The boys are given a complete diagnostic assessment (health, emotional, behavioral) for the purpose of developing an appropriate comprehensive treatment plan. The facility also has a licensed fourteen-bed program that is dedicated to working with twelve to seventeen-year old boys who are cognitively impaired and may need counseling revolving around sexually acting-out behaviors. Each youth has his own sleeping room. Educational services are provided on-site through a local charter school.
- **Victors Center** was opened in September 1988 and is licensed to serve forty-two cognitively impaired boys between the ages of twelve to seventeen. This program provides low security residential care with specialized programming to youth who have been abused or neglected. Victors Center also provides group and family counseling. Education is provided through local charter schools. On-site education is an option for youth who are unable to perform in a community-based school because of their disability or special needs.

Appendix A

- **Pioneer Work and Learn Center** was the first program to be established on the Vassar Campus in 1992. As the Vassar Campus grew, the Pioneer Work and Learn Center became known as Camp One. The Pioneer Work and Learn Center was initially launched in September 1988 near Kingston, Michigan and was later moved to Vassar. The Vassar Campus comprises Camp One plus two other camp programs. Each camp has a distinctive program and each is licensed separately. An explanation of these programs which were previously known as Camp Two and Camp Three follows.
- **Wolverine Growth and Recovery Center (WGRC)** is a residential program that is licensed to serve one hundred boys between the ages of twelve through seventeen. This was formerly known as Camp Two. WGRC is a unique program developed to provide specialized treatment services. It includes Addiction Recovery for youth who are experiencing severe addiction problems. Wolverine contracts with Growth Works, Inc., located in Plymouth, Michigan. This organization is a leader in the field of addiction recovery, and is responsible for providing cognitive/behavioral therapeutic treatment services to the youth in WGRC. Youth in this program receive intensive services for a short period of time. Residential care does not exceed three months and is geared to addiction recovery. Counseling continues post residential care. WGRC also has a program that is geared for adolescent males who have had offenses that involved offending sexual behavior. This program is a three-part integrated program that includes six to nine months of residential care, followed by three to six months of intensive outpatient treatment, followed by an additional six months of general aftercare supervision. The social treatment services for these youth are provided by contract with Ennis and Associates, Inc., a leader in the field of treating youth who have had problems with offending sexual behaviors.

Appendix A

- **Wolverine Adventure, Vocational and Educational Center (WAVE)** is also known as Camp Three. This program is licensed to serve eighty-seven youth and provides youth with a general social treatment approach that makes use of an eclectic combination of social treatment modalities. Outdoor adventure activities are a part of this program.
- **Community Based Services Office (CBS)** is the division within Wolverine Human Services that has responsibility for the foster home program and supervised independent living services. This division was initiated in 1990 under the direction of Clarence Fischer with twelve foster families and approximately twenty foster children. The program has grown rapidly over the years. Presently, Wolverine's foster care program serves more than two hundred foster children, who are being provided nurturing care by the more than seventy-five foster parents who have been recruited, licensed, trained, and are being supervised. Foster children may range in age from infancy through eighteen years. Wolverine also works with a number of older adolescents who are a part of the Supervised Independent Living program. These are youth who are living on their own, attending school, or are involved in full-time employment. Wolverine staff provide intensive supervision during this important transition from foster care to full independence. This has been a very successful endeavor on the part of the agency.
- **The Wolverine Community Center and Soup Kitchen** was opened in 1991. This program was established as a prevention program for children and youth who live in this economically depressed neighborhood on Detroit's east side. The Community Center is operated solely from donations and contributions, many of which come from agency administrators and staff as a way of giving back to the community. In the year 2000, the Community Center was rededicated as the **John S. Vitale Community Center** in honor of its director who died of cancer while still a young man. The Com-

munity Center on Detroit's east side provides after-school activities and tutoring opportunities for neighborhood children and youth; it supervises recreational activities, and provides informal counseling to the kids in the neighborhood. The Community Center provides hot meals for at-risk children following school Monday through Friday. On Tuesdays, Wednesdays, and Thursdays, a soup-kitchen is operated in the Center's lower level during the noon-time for at risk individuals and families who live in the neighborhood.

- **The Wolverine Secure Treatment Center (WSTC)** was opened in Buena Vista Township outside Saginaw, Michigan in September 1997. This secure facility originally housed eighty adolescent males. In June 2008, an addition to the center was opened which added twenty more beds. Presently, this facility serves one hundred male youth who have been committed to WSTC by a judge who has mandated placement in a maximum security facility. The facility has its own dental care station which has all of the equipment required to provide routine dental services. There is also a health service center and physician's examination room that is equipped to handle routine health care services. The facility has a 30,000 square foot indoor multipurpose recreation area that contains two full-sized basketball courts. Outdoors there is a softball field, a soccer field, basketball courts, and an area designated for a vegetable garden. The entire institution, including the outdoor recreational areas and gardens, is enclosed by a sixteen-foot-high-perimeter fence and surveillance cameras. The master control security center is located in the front of the facility and is equipped with audio and video monitors that are used to maintain visual and audio control of all doors and of youth movement throughout the facility and the parking and outdoor recreation areas. Staff do not carry keys; entering and exiting various sections of the complex is totally controlled from the Master Control

Appendix A

Security Center. The social treatment program uses an eclectic approach combined with point/level system, group counseling, and individual counseling for certain designated youth. Professional counseling is provided by a clinical psychologist or a psychiatrist who are on contract with WHS. There is a specialized program for sex offenders. WSTC also has an excellent education program; the teachers are a part of the Buena Vista Public Schools. The facility has several classrooms, a computer laboratory, and job-skills readiness programs that are provided in concert with the local community college. The new addition to the building includes a vocational and community living preparedness classroom, a state-of-the-art culinary arts kitchen, and a computer technology educational center. This remarkable facility is located on ten acres of land immediately northwest of the I-75 and M-81 intersection. It is visible from the freeway and is immediately recognizable because of its distinctive blue roof (see Chapter 22).

- In August 1998, the **Clarence Fischer Center** was opened and named in memory of Lt. Clarence Fischer, a long-time, dedicated social worker. It was originally known as the Clarence Fischer Leadership Academy. It is a part of the Vassar Campus and houses up to seventy-eight adolescent males. CFC provides a quasi-military leadership program designed to instill self-discipline, education, and physical fitness in a highly structured program. The CFC program is a treatment-based military high school program and not a boot camp. It boasts a 97 percent completion rate since its inception in 1998. CFC intentionally **does not use** any type of denigrating communication; it seeks to build up self-confidence and self-esteem. Youth referred to this program must be thirteen through seventeen years of age and have been adjudicated for delinquent offenses, but are not in need of a secure program. Youth must be capable of engaging in rigorous physical activity.

- **Vassar House** is Wolverine's newest residential program and the first to serve girls, which opened in September 2008. It is a sixty-two-bed residential treatment center for twelve-to-eighteen-year-old girls who have developed drug dependencies often accompanied by additional emotional and social problems that have resulted in poor social adjustment and educational achievement. The program uses intensive treatment approaches and makes use of group and individual counseling. Vassar House incorporates all of the quality treatment components of the standard Wolverine Human Services curriculum, as well as didactic lectures, group therapy, individual counseling, restorative justice, and drug testing. Clinical care will provide a holistic approach, using a personal recovery program whereby these young women can learn about the relationship between substance abuse and traumatic experiences which they have encountered. Wolverine contracts with Growth Works, Inc., to provide the specialized therapy programs to address drug dependency issues. Growth Works is a leader in this field of treatment.
- **The Vassar Campus** is comprised of several distinct programs each of which has already been described and comprises approximately one-hundred thirty-five acres of land. The Vassar complex includes athletic fields, an overnight camping area, and a ropes and obstacle course. The property is adjacent to the Cass River and is located on the eastern edge of the City of Vassar. **The Vassar Campus includes several Job-Skills Readiness Programs**. These include:
    1. *The Meat cutting and meats packaging program*. Wolverine has its own Meat Cutting Science and Distribution Center. A select number of boys are engaged in a professionally taught trades program where they learn the various aspects of meat cutting, packaging, storage, and distribution. Meats are prepared for Wolverine's use in its various facilities. In addition, meats are sold to the general public. The youth

Appendix A

receive a certificate upon the satisfactory completion of the program. Many youth have been able to obtain employment in the food services field as a result of completing this course of study which includes many hours of practice.
2. *Culinary Arts*. This program teaches youth the basic skills of cooking, menu planning, and food storage for health safety.
3. *Horticulture*. Wolverine has several greenhouses on the Vassar Campus and large gardens which are used to grow flowers which are planted throughout the campus to beautify the grounds. Youth learn the art of landscaping, lawn and garden maintenance.
4. *Building Trades and Woodworking*. The boys are exposed to basic building trades skills which include the safe use and storage of tools. Youth are also involved in wood working projects—making furniture that is used in Wolverine's facilities.
5. *Janitorial Services*. The youth are engaged in janitorial and basic facility maintenance tasks. These are more than just a "work assignment." The assigned tasks and the instructions the youth receive are designed to be job-skills readiness experiences for the youth for the purpose of enhancing their employability upon release from residential care.

The **Vassar Campus** includes a **Pioneer Adventure Program Center** that can be accessed by youth from any of the residential programs, including Wolverine's facilities located in the Detroit area (e.g. St. Jude's or Victors Center). The purpose of the Pioneer Adventure Program is to encourage youth to accept difficult challenges, to learn the importance of team work, and to build self-confidence. The program meets the standards of the Association for Challenge Course Technology and is fully accredited through the Association for Experiential Educators. The Pioneer Adventure Program includes back-packing treks in wilderness areas (Michigan's Upper Peninsula), canoeing, distance hiking, cross-country skiing, learning to achieve the challenge courses which include two high-rope courses, wall-climbing, and related obstacles that challenge a person physically, and requires team participation to achieve. Specialized activities and programming can be geared to the needs of specific groups.

All of these unique opportunities which are provided on the Vassar Campus contribute to making Wolverine Human Services Residential Programs outstanding and effective in helping troubled youth to become victors.

APPENDIX B
AWARD HONOREES

BEGINNING WITH MY FIRST Awards Banquet in March of 1988, I wanted to recognize three categories of people: college athletes who were exceptional in their accomplishments in sports and were also involved in community/humanitarian activities; government, community, and business leaders who had made exceptional contributions toward promoting juvenile justice and child welfare initiatives; and finally clients of Wolverine Human Services who have had to overcome many obstacles in order to achieve significant gains in their personal lives. These annual banquets have become a highlight and have served to give recognition to the many people who have either contributed to Wolverine Human Services directly or to the well-being of children and youth in general. These banquets have also been a means of spreading the story of Wolverine Human Services. What follows is a brief explanation of the various awards and a listing of honorees by the year of presentation.

THE MID-AMERICA CONFERENCE HUMANITARIAN AWARD

The Mid-America Conference (MAC) is a National Athletic Association (NCAA) Division I college athletic conference with a membership base in the Great Lakes region that stretches from

Appendix B

Buffalo, New York across to Illinois. This recognition was given annually from 1988 to 2006 to honor an athlete from a MAC University who had excelled in academics, athletics, and community involvement. This award was changed after 2006 to the Tony Sablowski Award (see the Tony Sablowski Award).

1988	Bob Stebbins, Central Michigan University
1989	Steve Palmateer, Eastern Michigan University
1990	Mark Hopkins, Central Michigan University
1991	Gordie Johnstone, Eastern Michigan University
1992	Jeff Bender, Central Michigan University
1993	Jason Wilkie, Central Michigan University
1994	Richard Palmer, Eastern Michigan University
1995	Brian Pruitt, Central Michigan University
1996	James Lowe, Eastern Michigan University
1997	Cris Parmele, Eastern Michigan University
1998	Charlie Batch, Eastern Michigan University
1999	Marvin Rushing, Central Michigan University
2000	Jason Meyer, Central Michigan University
2001	Walter Church, Eastern Michigan University
2002	Matthew Brayton, Eastern Michigan University
2003	Kyle Croskey, Central Michigan University
	Carlos Smith, Western Michigan University
2004	Anthony Kiner, Western Michigan University
2005	Kevin Harrison, Eastern Michigan University
2006	Matthew Scott Bohnet, Eastern Michigan University

THE TONY SABLOWSKI AWARD

The Tony Sablowski award is presented annually to a university athlete who has demonstrated the same strength, will, courage, and caring for others that was exemplified by Tony Sablowski. I first met Tony when I began my career as a social worker at Vaughn House, a group home for troubled boys. Tony was an effervescent, fiery redheaded boy who won the friendship of the University of Michigan athletes who often volunteered at the group home. Tony blossomed

Appendix B

under the care of Huron Residential Services in Ann Arbor. He earned straight A's and was actively involved in athletics at his junior high school. In 1979, after being the most productive member of his group home, Tony won a bus trip to Disney World. The bus was involved in a tragic accident and Tony was killed (see Chapter 10). Tony's spirit and energy live on this Wolverine award. Initially, this award was presented to a University of Michigan athlete. However, effective with the year 2008, the award was given and continues to be given to a MAC athlete who has also demonstrated a commitment to community service.

1988	Jamie Morris, University of Michigan
1989	Mark Messner, University of Michigan
	John Miller, Michigan State University
1990	Bobby Abrams, University of Michigan
	Travis Davis, Michigan State University
1991	John Milligan, University of Michigan
1992	Desmond Howard, University of Michigan
1993	Tony McGee, University of Michigan
1994	Sylvester "Buster" Stanley, University of Michigan
1995	Todd Collins, University of Michigan
1996	Tshimanga Biakabatuka, University of Michigan
1997	Brian Griese, University of Michigan
	Jarrett Irons, University of Michigan
1998	Brian Griese, University of Michigan
1999	John Jansen, University of Michigan
2000	Rob Renes, University of Michigan
2001	Anthony Thomas, University of Michigan
2002	Kurt Anderson, University of Michigan
2003	Victor Hobson, University of Michigan
2004	Dave Pearson, University of Michigan
	Chris Perry, University of Michigan
2008	Thomas "Red" Keith, Central Michigan University
2009	Brian Brunner, Central Michigan University

Appendix B

THE JOHN S. VITALE AWARD

This award is presented to a University of Michigan athlete who demonstrates commitment and loyalty to children and the community as John Vitale did. John was an offensive lineman and team captain in his senior year at the University of Michigan; he was a consensus All-American center in his senior year. John was often referred to as a "gentle giant" for his strength on the field and his gentleness off the field (see Chapters 18 and 21). He joined Wolverine Human Services in 1991 as a Residential Care Coordinator. John put as much passion into his work at Wolverine as he did on the football field. At Wolverine, John's duties ranged from Treatment Director to setting up new programs in Florida, and finally to becoming Director of the Community Center. It was not long after becoming Director that John was diagnosed with spinal cord cancer. He fought the disease for six years and always remained as committed to the youth at the community center as he had been before his diagnosis. Each day John did his best to help the children, acting as a father figure for numerous children who came from single parent families. In 2000 at the young age of thirty-four John passed away. This award was established in 2005.

2005	Braylon Edwards	2007	Jake Long
	Kevin Dudley	2008	Bettie Wade
2006	Pierre Woods	2009	Darryl Mitchell

THE ACHIEVEMENT AWARD.

The Achievement Award is presented to civic, government, and business leaders who have exemplified an enduring commitment to improving services in the areas of child welfare or juvenile justice.

1989	Annette Abrams	1996	State Senator Joel Gougeon
	Reggie McKenzie		Herb Deromedi
1990	C. Patrick Babcock		Professor Rosemary Sarri
	Glenn "Bo" Schembechler		Harold S. Gazan
1991	Jack Harbaugh	1997	State Senator John Cisky
	State Senator John Kelly		Dr. Isaiah McKinnon

_____ Appendix B

Year	Recipients	Year	Recipients
1992	Tirrel Burton Dennis Archer Ron Warhurst	1998	State Rep. Hubert Price, Jr.
1993	Maryann Mahaffey Lem Barney Lt. Governor Richard Posthumus	1999	John Urbancheck
1994	State Senator Robert Geake County Commissioner Ed McNamara Jerry Hanlon	2000	Mike Debord Joseph Dulin
		2001	Jack Kresnak Fred Jackson
1995	State Senator Jack Welborn Judge Willie G. Lipscomb, Jr.	2002	Dennis Archer
2002	Lloyd Carr	2006	Steve Morrison
2003	Hansen Clarke Robert Ficano Jim Herrmann		Kim Berrington State Senator Roger Kahn Jon Smalley
2004	Randy Awrey State Senator Jim Barcia	2007	No Awards Presented
		2008	State Rep. Dudley Spade
2005	State Senator Bill Hardiman Terry Malone Judge Greg Mathis	2009	Professor John Tropman

THE CHILD ADVOCACY AWARD

I established this award in 2008 to give recognition to governmental, civic, and business leaders who have publicly advocated for improved public policies impacting children and youth.

- 2008 State Senator Jim Barcia
  - State Senator Bill Hardiman
  - State Senator Roger Kahn, MD
  - State Representative Terry Brown
  - State Representative George Cushingberry, Jr.
  - State Representative Dudley Spade
- 2009 Ismael Ahmed
  - Stanley M. Stewart

Appendix B _____

THE VICTORS AWARD*

This award is given annually to a client of Wolverine Human Services who experiences the most growth and maturation through participation in social treatment, school, sports or recreational programs while a client of Wolverine.

1988	Melvin H.	1999	Ines H.
1989	Jamal T.	2000	Charles C.
1990	Demetrius J.	2001	Timothy D.
1991	Wyatt V.	2002	Andre M.
1992	River P.	2003	Ladon N.
1993	Robert H.	2004	Kevin L.
1994	Larry B.	2005	Temika A.
1995	Kwan B.	2006	Marti Jo W.
1996	Preciliano M.	2007	No Record
1997	No Record	2008	Ronald M.
1998	Sadie H.	2009	Margie B.

THE WILLIAM L. TILTON SCHOLARSHIP*

Bill Tilton has been a special friend to me (see Chapter 5) and an agency investor and benefactor who has made it possible for many Wolverine clients to achieve their dreams. It is in Bill Tilton's name that an annual scholarship is given to a Wolverine Human Services client who has shown remarkable progress in personal and academic pursuits.

1988	Richard C.	1995	Charles F.	2002	Nathan G.
1989	Otis H.	1996	Carlos A.	2003	Jomo W.
1990	Eric R.	1997	No Record	2004	Maurice W.
1991	Kewan F.	1998	Aaron V.	2005	Donald A.
1992	James B.	1999	Tiffany W.	2006	Timothy F.
1993	William V.	2000	Darryl B.	2007	No Record
1994	George S.	2001	Zachary F.	2008	Nina H.
2009	James M.				

_____ Appendix B

THE WAYNE ANDERSON CHAMPION AWARD*

This award was established in 1993 to honor Wayne Anderson, who was a social worker who had worked for the Michigan Department of Social Services for a number of years. At the time of his sudden death, he was responsible for the foster care program (foster homes and residential services) for the state. He was a highly respected social worker and a well-liked and admired person. He always handled his responsibilities with compassion, energy, and integrity. He was a genuine champion of children with special needs. This award is presented annually to a client of Wolverine Human Services who has faced additional struggles to overcome serious challenges and obstacles in his or her life. In spite of these challenges, the client has been able to demonstrate exceptional personal growth and has achieved personal and program goals.

Year	Recipient	Year	Recipient
1993	Melvin L.	2002	Demetrius H.
1994	Ray T.	2003	Dennis B.
1995	Andrew C.	2004	Antione J.
1996	Jacobi J.	2005	Joshua S.
1997	No Record	2006	Anthony B.
1998	Sharmayne	2007	No Record
1999	Daniel V.	2008	Marshall S.
2000	Dalila F.	2009	Nira M.
2001	Torries L.		

*Last names were not published to protect the confidentiality of minors

APPENDIX C
HOW YOU CAN HELP

If you have been inspired by Robert Wollack's story and the mission of Wolverine Human Services, and you desire to support their efforts to rehabilitate abused or neglected children, and drug dependent or troubled youth by giving them a second chance, you can make a tax-deductible contribution to

Friends of Wolverine Human Services Foundation
81 Enterprise Drive
Vassar, Michigan 48768

The Friends of Wolverine Human Services Foundation has been recognized as a tax exempt organization under section 501 (c) (3) of the Internal Revenue Code.

If you desire more information about Wolverine Human Services programs, please call 313-824-4400, or visit us on the web at: www.wolverinehs.org.

Thank you for helping us to provide troubled youth and neglected children a *second chance by turning victims into victors*.

ABOUT THE AUTHOR

Robert E. Wollack, Jr., was born on May 27, 1944—just shortly before the Normandy Invasion by the Allied Forces. He was the eldest in a family which ultimately comprised eight children in all. Bob was raised in the notoriously tough Bedford-Stuyvesant area of Brooklyn, New York. He graduated from the Food & Maritime Trades School in New York City and his buddy Stanley Farrow entered the meat-cutting business together. He later became a member of the New York City Police Department. He became a highly decorated member of the Tactical Patrol Force, but he also became a cocaine user which led to his downfall and disgrace. He was convicted and sent to the Federal Correctional Institution in Milan, Michigan.

After his release from prison, he attended Eastern Michigan University where he excelled in his academic studies while he concurrently managed a group home for troubled boys. He was admitted to the University of Michigan School of Social Work before having completed his bachelor's degree. He was an excellent student and graduated with a Master's Degree in Social Work in April 1978. He held various positions as a social worker, treatment director, and administrator for various non-profit social service agencies between 1978 and 1986. In 1986-7 he founded Wolverine Human

About the Author

Services, Inc., which has become one of the largest social service area providing residential care to troubled youth in the Midwest.

During his distinguished career, Mr. Wollack has been an adjunct professor at Eastern Michigan University; he has also been a conference speaker, seminar leader, and a consummate advocate for social justice by serving on various boards and committees. His book narrates the story of the transformation of his life from a convicted felon to a successful social worker and founder of a dynamic juvenile justice agency. Bob has also been the recipient of many awards in recognition of his outstanding contributions to juvenile justice and child welfare.

Mr. Wollack has four adult sons and four grandchildren. He resides with his wife Judith in Novi, Michigan.

INDEX

A

Abdelnour, Lynn 167
Ahmed, Ismael 204
Albom, Mitch 206
Alcindor, Lew (Kareem Abdul Jabbar) 9
Ali, Muhammad 96
Anderson, Wayne 133, 203
Arbeznik, John "Flame" 98, 99, 101, 102
Archer, Dennis 201

B

Babcock, Patrick C. 150, 152, 191, 204
Babson, Howard 145
Barcia, Jim 202, 204
Barkley, Charles 165
Batch, Charlie 203
Bergmann, Luke 197, 199
Bing, Dave 11, 162
Bishop, Barney 174
Blanchard, Gov. James 150
Blumenfeld, Robert x, 141, 174, 180, 211
Blumenfeld, Ira 24
Bonavena, Oscar 96
Boylan, Brother Francis 121, 131, 132, 154
Braun, Carol Moseley 210
Brendtro, Larry 74
Brennan, Vince ix
Brewer, Roy 220
Bush, President George W. 202
Bynum, Elvin Lee (big El) xiii, xiv, 14, 23, 24, 25, 26, 27, 28, 29, 31, 49, 51-55

C

"C," Joey 23, 28, 49, 51-55
Carmichael, Stokely 19
Carr, Eddie 147
Carr, Coach Lloyd 204
Carter, Anthony 99
Cavicchoili, James ix
Chiles, Lawton 171, 174
Chmiel, Gov., Bob 165
Cisky, Jon 204
Clark, Ramsey 59, 71, 117, 198, 201, 209
Clay, Lynn 114
Clinton, Bill 174
Clinton, Hilary 174
Cooper, John 140
Costellano, Paul 14, 21
Costellano, Peter 14
Costello, Frank 5, 59, 96, 106
Crutchfield, Leslie xviii
Cuffs, Georgie 53

D

Daly, Marty ix
Davis, Ricky 147
Davis, Russell 99
Davis, Tim 98, 99
Dawson, Maria 172
Day, Mike 99
Deming, Edwards xviii
Dillinger, John 40
Downing, Walt 99
Dufek, Bill ix, 98, 99, 107, 137
Dufek, Don 96-99, 138
Dukes, Charles 162
Dupont, John 174, 175, 180-183

255

Index

E
Edelstein, David N. (Judge) 31, 33-37, 39
Edwards, Stanley 99
Ellis, Bob ix, 138
Ellsberg, Daniel 61
Engler, Gov. John 179, 184, 197

F
Farrow, Stanley 12, 26, 29, 31, 33-35, 119, 182, 207, 208, 212, 222
Feldman, Bob 20
Ferguson, Jeff 171
Finnegan, Monsignor Thomas 114, 119
Fischer, Clarence ix, 119, 163, 164, 184, 236, 238
Fischer, Judy 118, 119
Fitzgerald, David 128
Ford, Henry 110
Frankl, Victor 56
Frazier, Joe 96
Furbish, Jim 155

G
Gambino, Carlo 21
Gandhi 95
Garelick, Sanford 20, 21
Gazen, Harold x, 84, 123, 125, 127-130, 132, 179, 180, 209, 211, 220, 226
Glasser, William M.D. 65, 77, 85, 92, 93, 99, 103, 107, 189
Geake, Senator Robert 191, 192, 204
Glesener, Mark 60, 70-72, 80, 96, 209, 226
Gougeon, Joe 204
Graham, Bob 171
Granholm, Gov. Jennifer 197
Grant, Heather xviii
Green, Cornelius 96

Griese, Brian 203
Griffin, Archie 96
Griffin, Ray 96

H
Haines, Bill 155, 157, 159, 161
Hanold, George 24, 26, 27, 31-34
Hardiman, Senator Bill 202, 204
Harrington, Pat 193
Harrison, Cindy 128
Hill, "Sugar" 223
Hitler, Adolf 59
Holloway, Bob 99
Holmes, Howard ix, 138
Howard, Desmond 203
Huckleby, Harlan 99

J
Jerome, Joe 120, 124, 127, 133, 179
Johnson, Pete 96
Jones, Mike 154, 170, 172, 180, 214
Joslyn, Judge Patrick 156, 157, 159, 160

K
Kahn, Dr. Roger 202, 204
Kamisar, Yale 57
Kaufman, Judge Richard 177, 178
Kelly, George "Machine Gun" 40
Kelly, John 204
Kennedy, John 95
Kennedy, Robert 95
Kerry, Senator John 202
Kilpatrick, Mayor Kwame 162
Kiner, Anthony 203
King, Martin Luther 18, 19, 95
Kintz, Bruce ix, 137, 138
Kirk, Dr. Grayson 20

L
Lawrence, Al 116
Leach, Rick ix, 96, 97, 99, 138
Leenhouts, Keith 153

Index

Leggett, Jim 157
Levine, Mark 171, 173, 174, 194
Lewis, Ted 195
Libs, Jim ix, 138
Lindsey, John 20, 31
Loppnow, Prof. Don x, 72, 75, 79, 186, 187
Lytle, Rob 98, 99

M

Malinowski, Bob 165
Manuel, Ward ix
Marble, George 50-52
Marshall, George 199
Matthews, Frank 23
May, Rollo 56, 63, 146
Mayday, Carol 116
Mayer, Russell 158-160
Mayfield, Richard 23, 24, 26, 32-34
McCargo, Sam ix, 154, 160
McCoy, Alfred 56
McCree, Derrick 214, 221, 222
McLean, Don 49
McNamara, Edward 204
McVeigh, Timothy 153
Meter, Jerry ix, 99, 105, 138, 151
Meyers, "Captain" Jim 73
Mileta, Tim 99
Miller, Dr. Gerald 179
Minder, Jim 80-86, 96, 103, 110, 111, 122, 123, 127, 130, 131, 138, 151, 152, 194, 209
Mitchell, Matt 155, 161, 214
Montana, Joe 97
Moore, Nolan 140
Moran, Bill 146
Morton, Mo 98, 99
Mosher, George 212

N

Nichols, Terry 153
Niederhoffer, Alfred 23, 56
Nieuwsma, Milton x

O

Overstreet, Ed 110, 120-122, 127, 213
Owens, Mel 99

P

Paciorek, Karen ix
Palmateer, Steve 203
Patterson, Floyd 25
Perles, George 115
Petti, Bob 214
Powell, Colin 202
Posthumus, Gov. Richard 204
Price, Bill 125
Price, Hubert 204
Price, Meredith 124, 125
Pruitt, Brian 203
Przygodski, George 97-99

Q

Quarry, Jerry 96

R

Rayoa, John 78
Reilly, Patty 15, 79
Richardson, "Big Papa" Timmitt 145
Robinson, Jackie 96
Rogers, Felton 84, 113, 115, 120
Roosevelt, Theodore 18

S

Sablowski, Tony 87, 101-103, 113, 142
Sarri, Professor Rosemary 149
Schembechler, Coach "Bo" 96, 97, 99, 140, 148, 152, 164, 166, 204, 206, 213
Schmidt, John 194
Schwartz, Herman 48
Seal, Paul 144, 145, 165
Sigmund, Freud 92
Silvernail, Carl 159
Skinner, B.F. 85-87, 91, 99
Slaughter, Stan 74
Smalley, Jon 174, 193, 195
Spade, Dudley 140, 202, 204

Index

Sparrow, Sidney 32, 34, 37, 40
Stant, Frederick T. 33
Story, Donald 62
Styne, Dale 24-26, 28
Sullivan, Monsignor 8
Swaninger, Roger 84
Sykora, Anthony 157

T

Telford, Dr. John 162
Thomas, Earl 139, 146, 161, 212
Thomas, Edwin 86
Thompson, Lynn 215
Tilton, Bill ix, 45-48, 57, 58, 61, 72, 73, 78, 91, 96, 124, 137, 138, 209, 226
Tokalkski, Larry 98
Tropman, Prof. John x, xix, 226
Turgovoac, Mike 99

U

Updike, Charles x, xv, 28, 29, 32-34, 37, 49-53, 128

V

Valachi, Joe 40
Valdez, Juan 24
Visser, Ken 133
Vitale, Anthony 173
Vitale, John S. 164, 166, 167, 173, 185, 205, 236
Vorrath, Harry 74

W

Walgren, Jon 137
Walsh, Lorraine 118
Walsh, Pete ix, 45-47, 57, 58, 61, 73, 78, 102, 107, 109, 116-118, 120, 122, 123, 127, 129-133, 139, 141, 143-145, 147, 148, 154, 180, 191, 209, 214, 226
Wangler, John x, 99
Ward, Jimmie Jr. 102, 113, 138
Warhurst, Ron ix, 99, 13, 1387
Washington, Sam 115
Watson, Buster 25
White, Charlie 105
Wilson, Dan 173
Wilson, Michael x
Wolfson, Chuck Professor 60, 68, 70-72, 74, 80-83, 93, 96, 103, 110, 111, 130, 209, 226
Wollack, Craig Steven ix, 15, 22, 37, 57, 67, 78, 104, 105, 119, 213
Wollack, Judith ix, 141, 178, 184, 186, 206, 214, 226
Wollack, Matthew ix
Wollack, Tommy 31, 33-35
Wollack, Zachary ix

Y

Yablonky, John 72, 85
Yagiela, Dale 213
Young, Mayor Coleman 150